Get the eBook FREE!

(PDF, ePub, Kindle, and liveBook all included)

We believe that once you buy a book from us, you should be able to read it in any format we have available. To get electronic versions of this book at no additional cost to you, purchase and then register this book at the Manning website.

Go to https://www.manning.com/freebook and follow the instructions to complete your pBook registration.

That's it!
Thanks from Manning!

Praise for the previous edition

F# in Action

A REVISED EDITION OF GET PROGRAMMING WITH F#

ISAAC ABRAHAM
FOREWORDS BY PHILLIP CARTER AND TOMAS PETRICEK

MANNING
SHELTER ISLAND

For online information and ordering of this and other Manning books, please visit
www.manning.com. The publisher offers discounts on this book when ordered in quantity.
For more information, please contact

Special Sales Department
Manning Publications Co.
20 Baldwin Road
PO Box 761
Shelter Island, NY 11964
Email: orders@manning.com

Manning Publications Co.
20 Baldwin Road
PO Box 761
Shelter Island, NY 11964

Development editor:	Dustin Archibald
Technical editor:	Michael Ciccotti
Review editors:	Adriana Sabo and Dunja Nikitović
Production editor:	Kathy Rossland
Copy editor:	Alisa Larson
Proofreader:	Jason Everett
Technical proofreader:	Sudipta Mukherjee
Typesetter:	Dennis Dalinnik
Cover designer:	Marija Tudor

ISBN: 9781633439535
Printed in the United States of America

brief contents

contents

foreword

F# is what I call a "Yes, and . . ." language. In improvisational comedy, an improviser accepts what has been said ("yes") and expands on the line of thinking ("and . . ."). The F# language design and its ecosystem, toolset, and community adopt a similar philosophy to building software. F# is comfortable for developers from almost any programming background ("yes"), and it adds functional programming idioms that open up an entirely different programming ecosystem ("and . . .").

F# in Action exemplifies the "Yes, and . ." concept thoroughly. From the very beginning, the tone is clear: F# is a good fit for many different kinds of applications. You'll find no ivory towers here, demanding that you rethink everything you know about software, rewrite all your code, and permanently try to jam the purest of functional programming into every bit of your software development life. Instead, the idea that F# is a functional programming language that can bring with it a different way of writing software is rightfully presented as secondary to the productivity gained from writing succinct code in conjunction with a rich ecosystem of libraries and tools.

In this book, you'll find one, if not the most practical, approach to learning the F# language. You'll be rooted in what the F# language community often refers to as "the F# way," a set of principles and language idioms that produce succinct, robust performance, and uniform code. This last point is worth emphasizing: in modern software development, uniformity matters. When developers search for ways to solve a problem in F#, they are often greeted by similar-looking code (that uses similar features) for similar problems. This principle is foundational to *F# in Action* throughout all of its examples, whether it's the simple data transformations you learn at first or full-stack web application development toward the end.

Personally, I am delighted at how often real-world tools and libraries are featured throughout *F# in Action*. For example, plotting data using Plotly.NET not only teaches you how to use F# for data analysis work but also how to use a powerful scientific plotting framework through the lens of the language. You'll get exposed to interoperability between languages, how package management with F# and .NET works, how to use tools like F# Interactive and the multitude of IDEs for F#, testing frameworks, and more. This is the exemplification of what makes F# unique: it's not just a language to learn for the sake of learning a language; it's an enjoyable tool to be used together with a multitude of other tools.

When I first met *F# in Action* author Isaac Abraham years ago, he was concerned about practical and sometimes even boring uses of F#. This remains true today, and that mentality comes out in this book. With *F# in Action*, you'll find a ruthlessly practical approach to learning not only F# but also how to write software for all kinds of different domains effectively. So, what are you waiting for? It's time to get programming with F#!

—PHILLIP CARTER

Phillip Carter was formerly the product manager for F# Language and Tools at Microsoft and currently explores how to improve software systems using modern AI tools.

When people talk about the evolution of programming languages, they will typically talk about what language feature was added to which language version. Yet, what enables a language and its community to evolve in a new way and become successful is often not a language feature. Do not get me wrong. I appreciate all the recent language improvements that make F# more pleasant to use, like string interpolation. But what makes it worth writing a brand-new book about F# is something else.

First, there is the move from the .NET Framework to the new cross-platform and open source .NET (formerly .NET Core). F# was always ahead of the curve. It ran on the cross-platform Mono platform in the era of proprietary .NET Framework, it was open-sourced as early as 2010, and it supported third-party code editors ranging from Emacs to Atom since its early days. Getting all the F# libraries and tooling to work on the new .NET was a painful task, but we are there now. Not only did this get F# first-class cross-platform support, but the entire .NET ecosystem has also adopted ways of working that we in the F# world always, perhaps secretly, knew were the right ones.

Second, the F# community has become a fully recognized player in the F# ecosystem. Many core libraries and tools for F# have been developed and used by its enthusiastic open source community since its early days. It took a surprisingly long time for everyone to accept that this is the right way of working. Perhaps we needed the almost 10-year history of projects like FAKE, Ionide, F# Data, and Fable to show that the F# community as a whole can take responsibility for core F# components, even if individual maintainers sometimes move on. Today, community-developed libraries and tools are the basis of much of F# development. Their longevity is ensured by the community, the nonprofit F# Software Foundation, and commercial F# companies investing time into the development of those core F# components.

Third, the way of talking and thinking about F# has also changed in the last couple of years. The cross-platform nature of .NET made F# attractive to a broader audience, and functional programming is no longer an obscure academic idea but something that most programming languages support in one way or another. Sure, it is still worth talking about how to interoperate with .NET, how to best leverage functional ideas in F#, and how the language supports techniques like functional domain modeling using types. However, we can now focus on how to get things done rather than on academic or ideological debates. F# is no longer something strange but rather a broadly accepted language that anyone can become curious about, learn, and use in practice.

It is remarkable that the move to cross-platform open source .NET, acceptance of the community as a key ecosystem player, and the new thinking about F# and functional programming all culminated at the same time. But I would even dare say that F# has reached a new harmonious, stable point where it can thrive and develop. And this new stable point in the history of F# also needs a new F# book.

The book you are looking at is a perfect fit for the new harmonious era of F#. The book is pragmatic and does not try to optimize for a reader with a special kind of background. If you are a programmer interested in F#, it gives you an excellent hands-on guide for learning the language and how to best use it to solve a wide range of problems. The book embraces the new .NET ecosystem, including the command line–oriented approach to many tasks. It also embraces a wide variety of community-led tools and libraries that make F# so powerful, ranging from the Ionide plugin for Visual Studio Code and the Fantomas code formatter to the Fable F# to JavaScript compiler and the SAFE Stack for full stack F# web programming.

Writing a book for the new era of F# requires an author with an impossible combination of traits. They need to be someone who has been using F# for a long enough time to have the right expertise and ability to explain the concepts in a clear, practical way. But they also need to see F# from a new, fresh perspective that is quite different from what many of us old-timers are used to! How can we get a book that is not biased by the particular interests of its author? Isaac clearly has the necessary expertise. Saying that he has been using F# for over a decade is not a marketing slogan. I know because he came to my F# course in London in 2012! But more importantly, he has also been helping F# to enter the new era by supporting the community, both as an individual contributor through his successful consulting company and as someone who has helped us find a new way of talking about the language and its ecosystem. In other words, Isaac and this book are the perfect guides to take you to the new harmonious era of F#!

—TOMAS PETRICEK
Assistant Professor at Charles University in Prague

preface

When I wrote *Get Programming With F#* (GPWF) in the late 2010s, I wanted to create a practical, pragmatic, and easy-to-understand guide to using F# for real-world applications. While the book achieved those goals and has received positive feedback, some parts of it quickly aged due to circumstances outside of my control—in particular, due to one factor: the release of .NET Core. When I started the book, .NET Core wasn't even a real thing. It was called DNX at the time and didn't have a clearly publicized vision of where it was going or even that it would in time replace the .NET Framework. But today, .NET Core (or nowadays just called ".NET") is both the present and future of all .NET development; this presented certain challenges for GPWF:

- The book focused on the .NET Framework.
- The book focused on Windows development and tooling. F# is now a first-class cross-platform language with associated tooling.
- The book focused on C# developers since, at the time, this was where most F# developers originated from. Nowadays, I see developers coming from backgrounds such as JavaScript, Python, Scala, R, and PHP as well as those coming to programming for the first time.

Even worse, many of the libraries and frameworks that almost half of the book focused on were either rendered outdated or completely obsolete by the advent of .NET Core.

F# in Action is my answer to these challenges: a reimagined look at F# today, based not only on a more modern, cross-platform approach to F# but also updated with my recommendations on how best to learn and use F# based on working day in and day out with a team of F# developers and engagements in the community for several years now.

Writing *F# in Action* was a different kind of challenge to GPWF. I originally imagined it would be a relatively short effort to upgrade the content of GPWF to make it .NET Core ready. But as I dug into it, I realized that it would be basically a complete rewrite as it targeted a new audience with new exercises and aimed to avoid some of the pitfalls of GPWF, especially the use of specific libraries and technologies.

acknowledgments

I am grateful to all who have helped during the writing of this book. Moving to a new country and home twice in the space of a year aren't circumstances conducive to focusing on writing a book, but the support received and patience shown by the team at Manning helped me immensely.

In particular, I'd like to thank my development editor Dustin Archibald, technical proofreader Sudipta Mukherjee, and all members of the production team for their support with *F# in Action*. Many thanks also to Phillip Carter and Tomas Petricek, who authored the forewords to this book.

Special thanks go to technical editor, Michael Ciccotti, who is a senior software engineer at Divisions Maintenance Group. He has 15 years of experience building software, with experience in a wide variety of programming languages, and enjoys the clarity and simplicity of expression that F# enables.

Thank you to all the reviewers—Abraham Hosch, Andrew MacDonald, Andy Kirsch, Artur Tadrała, Bjorn Nordblom, Christian Leverenz, Dale S. Francis, Dan Sheikh, Dmitry Dorogoy, Florian Verdonck, James Liu, Jason Down, Jean-Paul Malherbe, Joel Kotarski, John Henry Galino, Jort Rodenburg, Karl van Heijster, Kent Spillner, Kevin Orr, Kristinn Stefánsson, Markus Wolff, Milan Mulji, Pasquale Zirpoli, Rani Sharim, Ryan Gregory, Satej Kumar Sahu, Stefan Turalski, Thomas Peklak, Tiklu Ganguly, and Vincent Delcoigne. Your suggestions helped make this a better book.

about this book

The overall aims of this book are very similar to *Get Programming with F#*: to provide you with the knowledge to understand the fundamentals of F#, to gain the confidence to use it in practical settings, and, lastly, to gain a smattering of knowledge of the core principles of functional programming.

Who should read this book

This book is applicable to software developers who already have some experience in software application development. It is particularly applicable to software developers with an interest in learning more about functional programming within the context of a large, mature platform and ecosystem, as well as those who simply want to level up their game when it comes to writing higher-quality applications that are succinct, robust, and performant. Although the book focuses on .NET, readers do not need to have experience using the .NET platform.

How this book is organized: A road map

This book has 16 chapters, roughly divided into two sections. The first half details F# the language itself, looking at different language features and seeing how to solve different programming and modeling challenges using them:

- Chapter 1 is an overview of the *what* and *why* behind F#.
- Chapter 2 looks at the .NET toolchain as well as working with scripts.
- Chapter 3 examines the basic principles of core F# language syntax and type inference.

- Chapter 4 shows how F# makes it easy to write applications that take advantage of essential functional programming techniques such as expressions and immutability.
- Chapter 5 illustrates how to make use of two core types in F#: tuples and records.
- Chapter 6 goes deep into looking at functions in F# and how to organize applications using modules and namespaces.
- Chapter 7 describes the different collection types commonly used in F#.
- Chapter 8 rounds off this section by covering the use of both pattern matching and discriminated unions.

The second half of the book focuses on practical applications of F# within a variety of different use cases:

- Chapter 9 shows how to build practical domain models that utilize all the different types covered in the first section of the book.
- Chapter 10 looks at techniques around working with data, such as sourcing, wrangling, validating, and visualizing.
- Chapter 11 covers interoperability scenarios for F#, both on the .NET platform (typically with C#) and on the JavaScript ecosystem.
- Chapter 12 focuses on asynchronous programming and how to handle different use cases around concurrency and parallelism within F#.
- Chapter 13 looks at web programming in F#, both server side on .NET and using transpilers that compile F# into JavaScript, and how we can write full-stack applications entirely in F#.
- Chapter 14 discusses different techniques for automated testing on F#.
- Chapter 15 is a slightly deeper dive into functional programming techniques and covers examples of how to write applications that emphasize the use of pure functions wherever possible.
- Chapter 16 is the final chapter of the book and looks at where your F# journey might go next, with ideas on applications that you can write to further your F# knowledge.

This book is intended to be read alongside a computer. I'm a firm believer in learning by doing. In the same way that you almost certainly can't simply read a book cover to cover on how to, for example, drive a car and then pass your driving test the next day, you won't learn F# just by reading this book alone. So, although the first half is designed to be read in a linear fashion, with the second half being slightly more pick and mix, I would strongly suggest that you manually type in all the examples as you go through them to maximize the chance that you will fully understand the concepts and techniques that are shown.

About the code

This book contains many examples of source code both in numbered listings and in line with normal text. In both cases, source code is formatted in a `fixed-width font like this` to separate it from ordinary text. Sometimes code is also **in bold** to highlight code that has changed from previous steps in the chapter, such as when a new feature adds to an existing line of code.

In many cases, the original source code has been reformatted; we've added line breaks and reworked indentation to accommodate the available page space in the book. In rare cases, even this was not enough, and listings include line-continuation markers (➡). Additionally, comments in the source code have often been removed from the listings when the code is described in the text. Code annotations accompany many of the listings, highlighting important concepts.

You can get executable snippets of code from the liveBook (online) version of this book at https://livebook.manning.com/book/f-sharp-in-action. The complete code for the examples in the book is available for download from the Manning website at https://www.manning.com/books/f-sharp-in-action and from GitHub at https://github.com/isaacabraham/fsharp-in-action.

liveBook discussion forum

Purchase of *F# in Action* includes free access to liveBook, Manning's online reading platform. Using liveBook's exclusive discussion features, you can attach comments to the book globally or to specific sections or paragraphs. It's a snap to make notes for yourself, ask and answer technical questions, and receive help from the author and other users. To access the forum, go to https://livebook.manning.com/book/f-sharp-in-action/discussion. You can also learn more about Manning's forums and the rules of conduct at https://livebook.manning.com/discussion.

Manning's commitment to our readers is to provide a venue where a meaningful dialogue between individual readers and between readers and the author can take place. It is not a commitment to any specific amount of participation on the part of the author, whose contribution to the forum remains voluntary (and unpaid). We suggest you try asking the author some challenging questions lest his interest stray! The forum and the archives of previous discussions will be accessible from the publisher's website as long as the book is in print.

about the author

ISAAC ABRAHAM is a .NET developer since .NET 1.0 and has an interest in cloud computing and distributed data problems. He is the founder of Compositional IT and is a Microsoft MVP. Isaac specializes in consultancy, training, and development, helping customers adopt high-quality, functional-first solutions on the .NET platform.

about the cover illustration

The figure on the cover of *F# in Action* is "Insulaire de Wateeoo," or "Wateeoo Islander," taken from a collection by Jacques Grasset de Saint-Sauveur, published in 1788. The illustration is finely drawn and colored by hand.

In those days, it was easy to identify where people lived and what their trade or station in life was just by their dress. Manning celebrates the inventiveness and initiative of the computer business with book covers based on the rich diversity of regional culture centuries ago, brought back to life by pictures from collections such as this one.

Introducing F#

This chapter covers

- Learning what F# is and isn't
- Why you should be interested in using F#
- When is a good time to use F#
- Understanding what this book will and won't teach you
- Understanding the mental model behind F#

In this chapter, I'll be taking you through the basics of F#, how it may differ from other languages you're familiar with, and why you should learn it. We'll explore some of its great features as well as its potential as a primary programming language in your toolbox. Let's get started!

1.1 What is F#?

F# is a *general-purpose programming language* that's designed to build systems that are robust, succinct, and performant across Windows, Mac, and Linux. It has a lightweight syntax, yet a powerful type system and compiler. This makes it a compelling choice for writing applications, as it enables developers to rapidly model real-world systems in a way that does what they intend.

F# is an *opinionated* language with a set of characteristics that it is optimized toward. What do I mean by this? F# encourages us to write applications using a consistent set of simple constructs such as functions, data, and types in a very low-ceremony fashion compared to many other languages that come from a more classical object-oriented background. Although some of those languages have added in some capabilities to hide some of that complexity, in F#, this has been a core part of its design from day one. As an example, here's some basic F# code that defines a function:

Defines a function with a single input argument

Performs a calculation and assigns the result to a symbol

Creates a record result and returns it to the caller

```
let addTenThenDouble theNumber =
    let answer = (theNumber + 10) * 2
    { Answer = answer; Date = System.DateTime.UtcNow }
```

F# is fully type-safe but does away with a lot of ceremony that other languages often put in place, such as type annotations and full-blown classes, leading to a way of writing code that allows you to quickly focus on directly solving the problem at hand.

Because F# runs on the modern, lightweight, cross-platform .NET runtime, it has a large, mature ecosystem of free and commercial tools and libraries, ranging from web servers to database access, cloud, data and analytical libraries, actor frameworks, and more. This means that you won't have to create entire platforms but can reuse existing battle-tested components already out there, leaving you to focus on delivering business value. You can seamlessly interoperate with C# code, creating hybrid F#/C# solutions if required, so if you're already using .NET, much of what you already know about the platform will continue to apply.

1.2   Why F#?

There are many reasons why F# might be a great fit for you. Here are a few to whet your appetite!

F# is rewarding and fun. People who use F# find it a rewarding and enjoyable language to quickly write applications in that simply lets you get stuff done, freeing you to focus on the business of writing your application while the language does its best to help you along the way and guide you to success. I've spoken with many people who said they were in a programming rut but gained a newfound enthusiasm for software development when they switched to F# because it freed them to focus on delivering business value to their customers. This also works for the hiring manager—happier developers generally lead to less turnover, lower costs, and better results.

F# is highly productive. At its core, F# is a relatively simple language with a concise and easy-to-read syntax and a relatively consistent way of problem-solving. Yet, at the same time, it's a safe language to use, with a powerful compiler and type system (more so than many popular programming languages) that can trap many classes of potential bugs as you type. It also runs on a performant, mature, popular platform (.NET) with a wide variety of time-saving packages. In my experience, people writing applications in

F# do so more quickly than in other languages because it hits a sweet spot between simplicity, safety, and power.

F# is also very flexible. You can use it in numerous scenarios, from simple scripts for data exploration and experimentation to full-blown cloud-enabled end-to-end microservices and web applications. There's a very good chance that whatever you're doing today, you can also do in F#. There's also the possibility that F# will open the door to areas that you may not have considered before. For example, if you're coming from a C# background, F# will show you how you can use .NET for more data-oriented and analytical tasks that perhaps previously you might have thought could only be done in SQL. For those of you coming from a Python background, you'll see a language whose syntax is not a million miles away from what you already know yet is statically typed and highly performant. And for those coming from a JavaScript background, you'll appreciate how some of the functional patterns that are becoming popular in that language are first-class citizens here and that F# has a static type system and syntax that gets out of your way.

Additionally, if you're interested in learning some of the fundamentals of functional programming (FP), F# is a great way to do that; it has its roots in languages such as ML and OCaml. However, it's what I would call a "light-touch" FP language: you'll appreciate how it guides you toward writing simple, error-free code without needing to know any of the math and theory people often associate with FP. Importantly, it also provides you with enough escape hatches such that if you need to break out into procedural or object-oriented programming, you can do it without much effort.

1.3 When F#?

Since F# is a general-purpose programming language, the simplest answer to when you should use F# might be "Whatever you're doing today in whatever programming language you're working in, you can probably do it in F#." Nonetheless, let's look at a few different use cases of F# to give you an idea of what's possible:

- *Console applications*—You can write basic console applications such as command-line tools in F#. It'll happily read and write from the terminal and has libraries to make animated, colorful console applications with widgets such as tables, charts, and progress bars.
- *Background workers*—F# allows you to write background services or daemons, which don't necessarily have any console inputs. Perhaps you need a process that runs on a virtual machine that reads data from a database and creates a report once a day or an application that sits in the background and monitors a folder for new files as they're created to parse and process them. No problem!
- *Desktop applications*—F# has support for desktop applications with a number of technologies, whether they're simpler database-driven applications or richer applications with sophisticated user interfaces using either Windows-specific or cross-platform libraries and frameworks.

- *Cloud services*—You can write and deploy applications designed for just about any cloud provider; whether it's a more infrastructure-focused service or one of the platform services that the bigger players such as Azure, Amazon, or Google offer, there's support for F#.
- *Mobile applications*—Through the Xamarin and upcoming MAUI projects, Microsoft offers a full suite of frameworks and tools for developing mobile applications for both Android and iOS without knowing Java, Objective-C, or Swift. Instead, applications can be written once in F# and simultaneously target both platforms.
- *Web services*—F# can write web services that are secure, reliable, highly scalable, and extremely performant through the ASP .NET Core framework. Not only are web applications a natural fit for F#'s stateless programming model, but F# also has several libraries that give a truly first-class F# experience on top of ASP .NET Core.
- *Web applications*—Want to write applications in the browser? F# has you covered here, too! Through the Fable framework, you can compile your F# directly into JavaScript and run applications in the browser directly. This is a real boon if your team is not filled with JavaScript experts and prefers the benefits that static typing brings, where you can get the best of both worlds: use popular JavaScript libraries and frameworks such as React while writing code safely in F#.
- *Data exploration and analysis*—F# has a solid data-analysis-and-scripts story, from consuming data from multiple sources to visualizing data through charts and tables.
- *Data modeling*—One of F#'s often overlooked features is its effectiveness in modeling domains. Not only does it have a type system that allows you to easily model the real world in a minimum amount of code, but it's also *readable* code—the sort that you can legitimately sit down with a nontechnical user and explore a domain, evolving a model of the real world step by step, side by side.

1.4   How will this book teach me F#?

This book is designed to teach software developers who already understand the fundamentals of software development how to develop F# applications on the .NET platform. It won't teach you everything about the F# language—it's not a reference guide—but it will teach you the core of the language in a way that will give you the confidence to start creating applications and learning how to find out more about the language and ecosystem on your own.

As part of the journey of describing F#, this book will also teach you the basics of FP. You won't need to know anything about FP before buying this book, and you won't leave it as an expert in F#. However, you will understand the core concepts and be able to apply them in the real world to build applications from simple console applications to fully featured web applications.

1.5   How does F# work?

This section tries to give you a feel for how development in F# looks and feels. It's based not only on my own experiences of the language but also on those of many others who have used it extensively. Figure 1.1 shows you how I see some of the common features of what your development experience will look like.

1.5.1   Collaborative exploration

One of the features of the F# development experience that might not be so familiar to you is that it contains a highly interactive "scripting" mode, where you can experiment with different ways of modeling code, try different ways of implementing solutions, and see how they work. Once you're happy with the result, you can quickly migrate it into a full-blown application—whether a console application or a data-driven web API running on ASP .NET Core (the standard .NET web server).

Another aspect is the collaborative element that F# brings. F#'s syntax is highly readable for nontechnical people, and combined with its type system, it is especially effective for domain modeling. This means that you can (and I have done, many times) sit alongside a customer and, starting from ground zero, try to build up a model of a real-world system and test it out with some arbitrary code. There's no need for a console test runner or full-blown database— just some code and in-memory data. It's a much more iterative process, where ideas can be tested and thrown away at low cost, and both you and the domain experts can start to build a common understanding of the system you're trying to model.

1.5.2   Type-driven development

F# is a type-safe *statically typed* programming language, which means that you formally declare the types of your system, and the compiler will enforce rules that you define about those types. F# makes it very, very easy—and therefore cheap—to create and use types, meaning that you generally can afford to be a little more specific in how you model your systems. Doing this means that your code can be used to encode more business rules and is clearer and easier to read than it might otherwise be. Doing this not only means that we can more easily support business rules about our types but also protects against accidentally mixing and matching incorrect types of data. Finally, it also helps from a readability point of view: for example, while both `City` and `Country` in an `Address` type might be strings, in F#, it wouldn't be unusual to have "wrapper" types for both, each with their own invariant rules and constraints.

So, although F# is totally happy with you not doing any of this stronger domain modeling, it also doesn't impose much of a cost on doing so and thus encourages us to "do the right thing" up front.

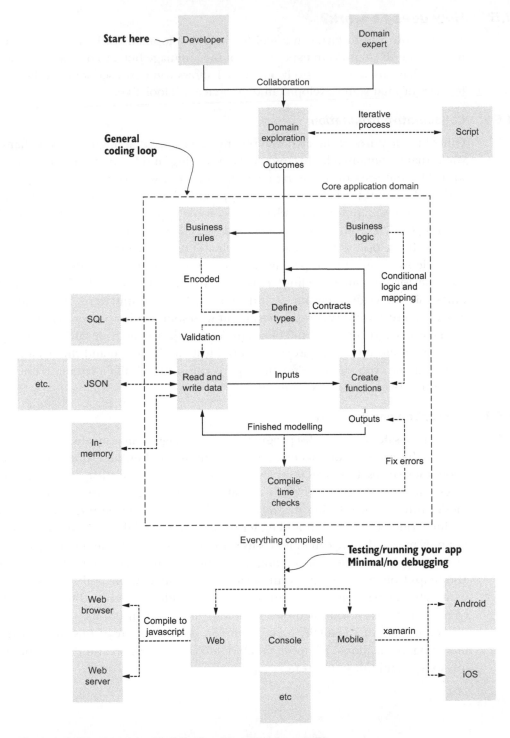

Figure 1.1   The mental model of the development process in F#

1.5.3   *Trusting the compiler*

Following from this, one of the things that F# encourages us to do is to *trust the compiler*. In many statically typed programming languages, software developers see the compiler as their enemy—something that must be somehow overcome to run your program so that you can test whether it works. In F#, this relationship changes to one where the compiler becomes your partner, giving you guidance and help to write code that does the correct thing.

Eventually, the developer trusts the compiler to prove business rules without feeling the need to run the application at all. While F#'s type system isn't all-powerful, it has enough smart features so that you can often code for several hours at a time, modeling your systems, writing functions, mapping types from one shape to another, and following the trail of breadcrumbs that the compiler gives you to follow to get your code working correctly without ever once running your application. Generally, once your code compiles, the first time you run it after the coding session, you'll find it works. So, you and your team will typically spend, as a proportion of your entire development flow, more time actually coding and less time "trying things out" in the app end to end.

I know that this sounds unlikely, unbelievable even, but it's true. This is based not only on my own experiences but also on working with and speaking to lots of different F# teams and solo developers. They all say the same thing: F# makes them more confident developers because it helps them do the right thing.

1.5.4   *An opinionated language*

F# is an opinionated language, and it optimizes for a specific way of writing applications safely that leads to fewer bugs and quicker time to market. The language makes it easy to do the right thing the first time and, conversely, makes you pay a cost for doing the wrong thing.

For example, imagine you're writing a system that needs to export a report in either Excel, PDF, or web formats. In F#, the compiler will give you a warning or error if you forget to handle any of those cases; if you add a fourth report module in the future, the compiler will again instantly show you every place you'll need to change your code to handle the new report.

This kind of approach is shown throughout the language, meaning that you'll have much more confidence when your code compiles that it actually works as you expect it to.

1.5.5   *Data and functions*

Although F# is different from the majority of popular mainstream languages out there, it's not hard to learn. It eliminates many concepts that you would need to know in the object-oriented world, such as inheritance and polymorphism. It replaces those with a simple idea: you have data that represents the state of your application and functions that act on that data. Each function knows how to transform some data of one type into another type, and you compose those transformations into *pipelines*. You repeat this pattern throughout your application until the very end of the request, at which point you'll, for example, write out a file or return some JSON data to the caller of your web service.

For example, you might have a validation function that can handle a customer purchase request, another function that can convert that request into an invoice, and another one that can email the invoice to the customer. In fact, this simplicity makes it a great choice for non-software developers, including (but not only) data analysts.

1.5.6   *Separation of business logic and external systems*

Another thing you'll notice with F# is that because of the features of the language, it encourages (but doesn't force you) to maintain a separation between your domain logic and external dependencies such as databases or web services.

Doing this has many benefits. To start, your code will generally be more easily testable. If you want to create some unit tests for a specific portion of code, you'll find that it's more likely to already support testing or, if not, be easier to refactor out to do so. This also feeds into the exploratory scripting phase that I mentioned at the start of this section: using scripts is something that you might well carry on into the main development cycle of your application as a way to quickly call parts of the codebase in an ad hoc fashion. This is especially useful for parts of the system that are more difficult to reach within your main application. People commonly use console test rigs or even unit testing libraries for this, but an interactive script is normally a much more effective and efficient tool.

1.5.7   *Varied targets*

F# has a flexible and varied set of target devices and platforms that it can compile into. .NET itself supports Mac, Linux, and Windows platforms, as well as all the major cloud vendors, and can develop desktop app software or backend services. Alternatively, you can write web applications with F# that either focus on backend data-oriented web services using ASP .NET Core, or you can target the browser using the Fable project, which compiles F# directly into JavaScript, or Xamarin/MAUI, which compiles into iOS or Android.

Regarding data access, a plethora of libraries are available to you, including those built into .NET, C# packages that you can seamlessly use in F#, or bespoke F# wrappers, designed to give the highest fidelity F# experience. So you'll have ready-made access to SQL and JSON libraries, cloud platforms such as Microsoft Azure or Amazon Web Services (AWS), and much more.

In some ways, F# gets the best of both worlds: you have a feature set that many other languages (including C#) have been playing catch-up to for a few years now, but at the same time, you'll have access to a popular, mature, high-performance, and reliable platform and ecosystem in .NET.

Summary

- F# is a robust, succinct, and performant general-purpose programming language.
- F# runs on top of .NET, a runtime that can target multiple operating systems and devices.
- F# can be used for a variety of application types, from console to web to cloud applications.
- F# has a lightweight and interactive scripting mode that is ideal for exploration.
- F#'s syntax is simple enough that nontechnical people can read it, making it a useful tool for collaboration.
- F# is highly productive, rewarding, and fun to use.
- F# makes it easy for you to do the right thing and, conversely, gives you guardrails to stop writing code that is likely to fail.
- F# has a basic model of data and functions, which is simple to learn yet made powerful through composition.

Hands on with F#

2

This chapter covers

- Writing code the F# way
- F# and .NET
- Creating your first F# program
- Getting started with Visual Studio (VS) Code
- Configuring VS Code
- Working with the REPL and scripts

F# may be different than other languages you've used, but it's powerful and useful. In this chapter, we'll get started coding and dive into what makes F# great.

2.1 Writing code the F# way

Let's start by considering some of the principles behind F# with a quick compare-and-contrast with typical so-called curly-brace languages such as Java and C#. It's worth doing before we start diving into the code so that you're mentally prepared for some of the differences you might observe when doing F#. In some ways, much of what you read in this section is similar to what I said in chapter 1, except this is a more code-focused examination.

> ## How much of a functional programming language is F#?
> We'll cover this in more detail later, but in a nutshell, F# encourages what I consider the two most important parts of functional programming (FP): expressions and immutability. It also has many other features that support flexible functions (such as composition and currying), and numerous recently added features have made their way into many other languages, such as lambdas and pattern matching. However, it doesn't support or enforce more hardcore FP features such as pure functions, type classes, or higher kinded types.

2.1.1 What, not how

Imperative code can be thought of as the low-level "how"—how you want to implement something—typically a set of lower-level instructions. Conversely, declarative code concentrates more on expressing the "what"—what you want to achieve and leaving the low-level details to another party—in this case, a compiler. Here's an example of an imperative way of filtering out odd numbers from a list using both imperative code (I'm using C# syntax here) and the equivalent declarative variant (written in F#):

```
IEnumerable<int> GetEvenNumbers(IEnumerable<int> numbers)
{
    var output = new List<int>();
    foreach (var number in numbers) {                        Imperative
        if (number % 2 == 0)                                 code
            output.Add(number);
    }
    return output;
}

let getEvenNumbers =                                         Declarative
    Seq.filter (fun number -> number % 2 = 0)                code
```

Both samples do the same thing. However, while the declarative version is focused on stating *what* we want and leaving the compiler to work out the nitty gritty, the imperative version takes ownership of *how* we want to filter the numbers—by creating an intermediary list, iterating through each item one by one, etc.

Of course, most languages have libraries to support a declarative model, such as LINQ in C#, Streams in Java, and so on. In F#, this is the de facto way of working and is much more pervasive than you might be used to. If you're used to the imperative model of developing, this can feel a little like giving up control. However, once you're used to it, it's very difficult to go back!

2.1.2 Composability

F# also emphasizes composition rather than inheritance to achieve reuse, with support for this baked into the language. Functions are the main component of reuse rather than classes, so expect to write small functions that plug together to create powerful abstractions. Individual functions are nearly always easier to understand and reason about than entire sets of methods coupled together through state in a class. As such, making changes to existing code is much easier to do with a greater degree of confidence.

Here's a simple example of how we might build behaviors into more powerful ones in C# and F#, trying to get all even numbers from a list and then square each. Again, in C#, I've deliberately kept things at the method level, but you should also consider the effort required when trying to compose more complex sorts of behaviors across classes and objects:

```
IEnumerable<int> SquareNumbers(IEnumerable<int> numbers) {
    // implementation of square elided...
}

IEnumerable<int> GetEvenNumbersThenSquare(IEnumerable<int> numbers) {
    return SquareNumbers(GetEvenNumbers(numbers))        ◁──── Composes two
}                                                               methods together

let squareNumbers = Seq.map (fun x -> x * x)
let getEvenNumbersThenSquare = getEvenNumbers >> squareNumbers    ◁────

                    Composes two functions together in F#
```

> **Where are the types?**
>
> F# is a *statically typed* language, just like languages such as Java and C#. But it has an extremely powerful *type inference* engine, which means it has the succinctness close to dynamic languages such as Python, yet with the backing of a strong type system and compiler, so you get the best of both worlds. More on this later.

I'm not going to explain what the >> symbol does yet. But if you look at the F# version of code, you can visually observe that we're somehow plugging the `getEvenNumbers` and `squareNumbers` functions together. This mode of design is, again, very common—building small functions and bits of code that do a single thing well and then composing them together into larger, more complex parts later.

2.1.3 *Data and behavior*

Another key pattern you'll commonly see in F# is a clear separation of data and behavior. If you're coming from a language that uses object orientation (OO) as the key mechanism for organizing code, you'll find this a little different. Instead of having classes that have both state and behaviors fused together, F# encourages you to design code with simple data types with modules of functions that act on those types.

For example, in the OO world, in a retail web application, you might have a `Basket` class with methods such as `AddItem`, `Clear`, and `Checkout` on them plus the internal *encapsulated* state (what the items in the basket are, etc.). When you call methods on them, they would perform some action and modify that internal private state. In the FP world, you'd have an *immutable* record that stores the *current* state of the basket (e.g., what the items in it are) and a module with *stateless* functions such as AddItem, Clear, and Checkout. Each function would do some action and then return an updated version of the basket. This generally leads to much simpler code that's easier to write, understand, and test and is more flexible and simpler to maintain. Of course, you'll learn exactly why that is in this book.

2.1.4 Working with a smarter compiler

F# as a language inevitably changes how you write code. I think of myself as a lazy developer: I like having things *done* for me. F# helps a great deal in this regard, especially for boilerplate activities that in other languages need more care to ensure you've done the right thing.

Let's take a simple example in which you're a developer working on a small change to an existing application. Imagine you decide to add a new field to an existing class; you find the class and add the new field to it. Your code compiles, and you carry on with your day. Unfortunately, while you can reference this new field elsewhere, you forgot to account for all the code paths that *create* objects of this type and, unfortunately, left a code path where this field is not initialized.

Later, you run the application and receive a null reference exception somewhere further down the call stack. Or, perhaps you're unlucky and don't notice the bug because it's in a particularly obscure branch of code. Instead, a few months later, your users hit that code path, crashing the application and forcing a costly new release.

You could, of course, write unit tests to force this issue to the surface sooner. Unfortunately, developers often don't write unit tests, particularly for seemingly innocuous changes such as this. After all, who has time to write unit tests like this when there's real work to be done for our customers and deadlines to hit!

Wouldn't it be nice if the language itself could support us here to prevent this kind of situation from occurring? In the F# world, adding a new field will instantly stop your code compiling until you explicitly set the value of the new field at initialization time, everywhere. You can only deal with how that new field is being used after you've fixed all the assignments and usages. Nulls aren't allowed for F# types either, so you can't set it as such. Instead, F# has the notion of *optional values,* which force you to account for the possibility of missing values.

The net result? You'll spend slightly more time fixing compiler issues and evaluating possible branches of code but a whole lot less time testing and fixing runtime issues. In this example, you don't need to write any unit tests to guarantee consistency of the type, nor is there a risk of getting a null reference exception at run time—and you won't need to debug it to prove that you won't get one.

You may feel an instinctive negative reaction to what I've just told you. After all, why would you want a compiler to get in the way of writing code and slow you down from running your application? Don't worry; this is a normal reaction and part of the learning curve in trusting the compiler to help us write correct code in a much richer way than we're used to, which saves us a lot more time further down the road.

As an example, imagine you're a developer meeting a customer for a first discovery workshop. They're looking for you to build an IT system that can manage their train stock and inventory, and the first question you want answered is "What is a train?" What information needs to be captured? What kind of carriages does a train have? After talking for a while with your customer, you end up with the following model. It captures things like the carriages that a train is made up of, including what class they are, what features each carriage has, and the stops that the train will make.

Listing 2.1   A domain model of a train system

```
open System

type Feature = Quiet | Wifi | Toilet          ◄──
type CarriageClass = First | Second           ◄──

Type CarriageKind =                  ◄──
    | Passenger of CarriageClass
    | Buffet of {| ColdFood : bool; HotFood : bool |}

type CarriageNumber = CarriageNumber of int          ◄──

type Carriage =                      ◄──
    {
        Number : CarriageNumber
        Kind : CarriageKind
        Features : Feature Set
        NumberOfSeats : int
    }

type TrainId = TrainId of string
type Station = Station of string
type Stop = Station * TimeOnly          ◄──

type Train =                ◄──
    {
        Id : TrainId
        Carriages : Carriage list
        Origin : Stop
        Stops : Stop list
        Destination : Stop
        DriverChange : Station option
    }
```

- **A train carriage can have a number of different features.**
- **A carriage can be either first or second class.**
- **Carriages can be either for passengers or buffet carts.**
- **A carriage has a unique number on the train.**
- **A carriage is composed of all of these things.**
- **Each stop is a station and a time of arrival.**
- **A train has a unique ID, and a list of carriages. It always has an origin and destination and a list of stops in between. It might also have a station where the driver changes.**

Obviously, as this may be your first exposure to F#, some of the symbols, keywords, and concepts here may be unfamiliar to you. Nonetheless, hopefully, you can see how F#'s syntax is lightweight and easy on the eye compared to some other programming languages and how something like this could be read and understood by a domain expert.

2.2   *F# and .NET*

.NET is the runtime, or platform, that F# code primarily executes on (although that's not the only platform that F# can target). .NET is free to use, open source, cross-platform, and capable of running on Windows, Mac, and Linux.

Although the majority of .NET is written in (and primarily designed for consumption by) C#, F# has great support for interacting with C# code. .NET provides a great deal of functionality and capabilities that you can directly use from F#, whether it's working with the file system, automated memory management, web development, or databases. In addition, you can download over 200,000 ready-made packages from the official NuGet website. .NET and the set of libraries it comes with are fully open sourced by Microsoft and free to use.

I thought .NET was Windows only!

The original incarnation of .NET, the .NET Framework, was indeed Windows only, although it had an open source cross-platform sibling called Mono. Today, .NET Framework is effectively in maintenance mode and has been replaced by what was initially known as .NET Core (and now simply .NET). The latest long-term supported version of .NET at the time of writing is .NET 6.

You can reference any .NET assembly from F#, and vice versa. F# has interoperability features to allow seamless interaction across languages while also taking advantage of F#-specific features to make dealing with .NET libraries more convenient. You can consume and create classes with inheritance, interfaces, properties, and methods. Indeed, one of the strengths of F# is that it permits the developer to mix both FP and OO styles where appropriate.

So, if you're already a .NET developer, you're not going to have to give up the libraries that you already know or the knowledge you've learned over the past years regarding the Common Language Runtime (CLR), garbage collection, reflection, and so forth. And if you're not a C# expert, the documentation you read about .NET, even if the samples are written C#, will generally be just as applicable to F#.

Figure 2.1 shows how the three main languages (C#, F#, and VB .NET) running on .NET today can work together in a single application. All three compile into the same interoperable *Intermediary Language* (IL), and exist on top of the same CLR.

In terms of tooling, the main integrated development environments (IDEs), such as Visual Studio, Visual Studio Code (VS Code), and JetBrains Rider all have very good F# tooling. If you're coming from a C# background, the experience won't have quite as many bells and whistles (after all, C#'s tooling is probably best-in-class), but if you're coming from other languages, F# might be a pleasant surprise, with editor autocompletion, type hints, semantic navigation, and refactorings plus excellent command-line tooling through the .NET command-line Interface (CLI).

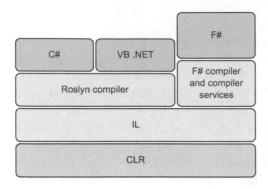

Figure 2.1   A simplified view of the .NET language and runtime landscape

In short, F# has all the pieces in place for you to take full advantage of the .NET ecosystem and allow you to write basically anything you want.

2.3   Creating your first F# program

There's one thing I've learned from teaching F# for some years now, and that's that you won't learn it unless you do it. So let's start as we mean to go on and write some basic F# together.

2.3.1   Installing F#

As an integral part of .NET, F# can be installed on Linux, Mac, and Windows operating systems. To install it, navigate to https://dotnet.microsoft.com/en-us/download/dotnet/6.0 and follow the instructions to install version 6 of the .NET SDK (not just the runtime!) for your operating system. Once you're done installing, congratulations! You've now successfully installed F#!

2.3.2   The .NET CLI

Historically, .NET was very much a thing that was highly coupled to Microsoft's own IDE, Visual Studio. Today, things are very different: .NET can be installed without any IDE and has a rich and extensible command-line tooling platform known as the .NET CLI. The CLI lets us perform many actions that historically would only have been possible through Visual Studio, such as creating, building, running, and testing your applications.

Wherever possible, we'll be using the .NET CLI that is included with .NET 6 for all such activities. There are many benefits to this approach; for example, it works consistently across all operating systems (which makes my life as an author much easier!) and can be much more easily automated than using a GUI. However, if you prefer a point-and-click approach, the main IDEs all support the ability to create applications via menus and wizards.

2.3.3   *Hello World in F#*

Let's create a basic F# console application using the .NET CLI. Start by opening a terminal window and enter the following commands:

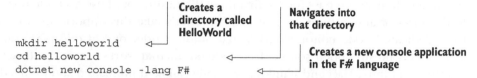

Creates a directory called HelloWorld

Navigates into that directory

Creates a new console application in the F# language

```
mkdir helloworld
cd helloworld
dotnet new console -lang F#
```

Can I create other application types?

The dotnet new command can create a whole host of different application types (e.g., web apps, class libraries, etc.), called *templates*. You can see all the available templates using the `dotnet new --list` command. What's especially good is that the templates stored in dotnet are extensible, so you can build your own and share them on .NET's NuGet package management system.

The very first time you run this, you'll get a bunch of text, but at the end, you should see something like the following:

```
Processing post-creation actions...
Running 'dotnet restore' on
C:\Users\isaac\code\helloworld\helloworld.fsproj...
  Determining projects to restore...
  Restored C:\Users\isaac\code\helloworld\helloworld.fsproj (in 151 ms).
Restore succeeded.
```

If you now get a directory listing using, for example, the `dir` or `ls` commands, you'll see that two files have been created:

```
helloworld.fsproj
Program.fs
```

Why do I need to specify F#?

Don't forget that .NET supports three languages: C#, F#, and Visual Basic (VB) .NET. C# is the default language for the .NET CLI, so you need to specify `-lang F#` whenever you want to create a new template that supports both F# and C#. However, you can switch F# to be the default language instead by setting the `DOTNET_NEW_PREFERRED_LANG` environment variable to the value `F#`. Doing this means you won't have to enter `-lang` ever again.

We'll investigate the contents of those files in a short while, but for now, let's just run the application using the command `dotnet run`. After a short delay, you should see the following output:

```
Hello world from F#
```

Congratulations! You've now created and run your very first F# application!

2.4 Getting Started with Visual Studio Code

It's time to look at some F# for the first time. While you could use a simple text editor to do this—F# applications are just text files—let's take this opportunity to install a free, dedicated code editor called Visual Studio Code, or VSCode. VSCode is an extensible, (mostly) open source, free code editor that works across the three main OS choices: Linux, Mac, and Windows. VS Code can be downloaded and installed from https://code.visualstudio.com/; follow the appropriate installation guide for your operating system.

> **What IDEs can I use with F#?**
> There are three main options for F# IDE that I would recommend today: Microsoft Visual Studio, which is Windows-only and has a free community edition and paid licenses, as well as a sibling for Apple, VS For Mac. Second, JetBrains Rider is a commercial IDE that works across all three OSs. Lastly, there's VS Code.

2.4.1 The Ionide extension

Out of the box, VS Code doesn't support F#. That's not a surprise or a problem because VS Code is designed to be an extensible and language-agnostic code editor. To add F# support, you need to install the Ionide extension. This free extension provides rich F# support, including code completion, type hinting, navigation, and refactorings:

1 Navigate to the Extensions panel (View Menu > Extensions).
2 In the search box, search for Ionide.
3 Find the Ionide-fsharp extension and click the Install button.

After a short delay, the extension will install. You're now good to go!

2.4.2 Exploring F# with VS Code

Let's start by loading the HelloWorld application that you created earlier into VS Code. One way to do that is by navigating within a terminal into the helloworld directory you created earlier and entering the command

```
code .
```

Note the period (.) at the end, which tells VS Code to open in the current directory. You'll now be looking at a window something like figure 2.2.

Double-click the `Program.fs` file to open it in the main editor pane:

```
// For more information see https://aka.ms/fsharp-console-apps
printfn "Hello from F#"
```

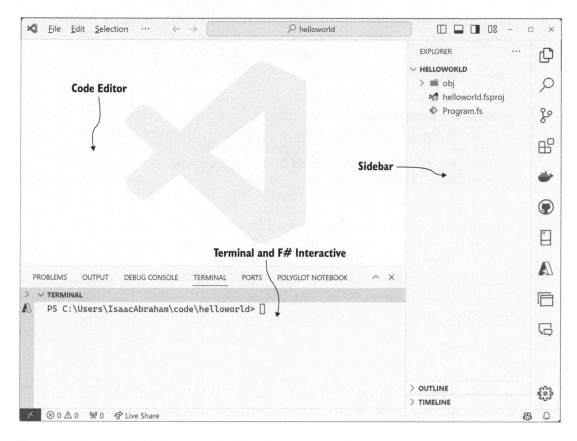

Figure 2.2   The VS Code window. Note the default sidebar position is on the left of the code editor.

Pretty simple, right? No need for classes or `static void main` or opening namespaces or importing modules—just some simple code.

The first line is a comment that starts with `//`. The second line is actual F#: `printfn` is a function that prints some text to the console (it actually does more than that, but for now, that's sufficient).

There's also an `.fsproj` file, which isn't necessary to look at just yet. It contains the manifest of your application, such as what type of project it is (e.g., an executable or reusable library), and the explicit list of all the F# files to compile (this is unlike some platforms, where all files in the folder are automatically used).

2.4.3   Writing your first F#

Let's make a quick change to the application so that it prints your name and the current date and time:

```
let name = "isaac"
let time = System.DateTime.UtcNow
printfn $"Hello from F#! My name is {name}, the time is {time}"
```

The first line assigns the value `isaac` to the symbol `name`. Note that I didn't use the word *variable* but *symbol*. There's a good reason for that, which will become clear later! The second line gets the current date and time in UTC format using the `DateTime` type, which lives in the `System` namespace.

> **What's a namespace?**
>
> A namespace is a way to logically group types in a system. Many of the core types in .NET live in the `System` namespace, including primitive types, such as `String` and `Int32`, and common classes such as `Environment`, among others. We'll come back to namespaces later.

The third and final line has also changed in several ways from our original application: we've prepended the $ symbol at the start of the string, which allows us to inject any value directly within the string as long as it's surrounded by {} (this is known as *string interpolation*). We've used this to inject `name` and `time` into the string.

Launch the program again using `dotnet run` and observe that the output has changed as expected:

```
Hello from F#! My name is isaac, the time is 04/11/2021 19:59:36
```

Congratulations! You've now actually written your first F# code. You should now take the time to configure VS Code to your liking. As VS Code is always changing with new features and extensions, you should also take some time to see what else is out there that suits the way you like to work.

2.5   *REPL and scripts*

You've now seen how to work with console applications, a concept that I expect is familiar to you regardless of which language you're coming from. However, there's another side to developing F#, which you may or may not be familiar with: scripting. You might already be familiar with some languages that have good support for scripting, including Python and Clojure; others, such as Java and C#, have more limited or even nonexistent scripting modes.

2.5.1   *The F# REPL*

A core part of scripting is having a great REPL. REPL, which stands for read–evaluate–print–loop, is a mechanism that allows you to enter arbitrary, ad hoc code into a standalone environment and get immediate feedback without compiling and building a dedicated application. Instead of being used when *running* an application, a REPL is used when *developing* it. You send code to the REPL, which evaluates the code and prints the result. This feedback loop, depicted in figure 2.3 is a tremendously productive way to develop. Here are some example uses for a REPL:

- Writing new business logic that you want to add to your application
- Coming up with a new data model for your domain
- Testing existing production code with a predefined set of data
- Exploring a new NuGet package that you've heard about in a lightweight exploratory mode
- Performing rapid data analysis and exploration

Read   Evaluate

Print

Figure 2.3 The REPL cycle in action

The emphasis is on short, rapid exploration cycles: trying out ideas in a low-cost manner and getting cheap feedback before pushing that into the application code base. What's nice about F# is that because the language allows you to encode business rules succinctly and with a powerful type system, you can often have a great deal of confidence that your code will work without first running it. Instead, you'll find yourself working in the REPL more, trusting the compiler and focusing on writing code that delivers business value. In F#, the tool for the REPL is known as F# Interactive, or FSI.

2.5.2 Trying out FSI

FSI is an application that is bundled with .NET. To run it, open a terminal and type `dotnet fsi`. You'll see a response that looks something like the following:

```
Microsoft (R) F# Interactive version 12.0.0.0 for F# 6.0
Copyright (c) Microsoft Corporation. All Rights Reserved.

For help type #help;;

>
```

The prompt at the end is where you can start typing in F#. Let's test it out:

1 Type `1 + 2;;` and press Enter (don't forget the two semicolons!).
2 You'll see the response, `val it: int = 3`.
3 Enter `System.DateTime.Now;;`.
4 You'll get a response with the current date and time, plus various other fields that .NET's `DateTime` object captures.

FSI is a stateful REPL. This means that you can store data in one command and reference the result in the next. Try this out:

1 Enter `let version = 6;;`.
2 Enter `$"F#{version} is cool!";;`.

You'll see the output, `val it: string = "F#6 is cool!"`. You can write functions, load data, and even reference other F# files or packages in FSI. In other words, you can write entire programs in it.

The two semicolons (;;) at the end of each command tell FSI to execute the text currently in the buffer. Without this, FSI will continue to add that command to the buffer until it encounters ;; and will then execute all the queued commands together. When you want to quit the REPL, type `exit 0;;`.

> **What is "it"?**
> You probably noticed `val it` in FSI for the commands that you executed. What is it? `it` is the default symbol that any expressions are bound to if you don't explicitly supply one using the let keyword. So executing `1 + 1;;` is the same as executing `let it = 1 + 1;;`.

2.5.3 *Moving to interactive scripts*

If you've tried the preceding exercise, your first thought was probably something like, "Well, this is quite useful, but it's all in a basic command prompt!" You get no syntax highlighting, no IntelliSense support—no nothing, really. Working directly in FSI isn't great fun.

Luckily, there's a much better way to work with FSI that does give you IntelliSense and syntax highlighting: F# scripts. Scripts are standalone F# files that have the extension `.fsx`. They don't require a project file and can be executed either as a single file of sequential commands or in an interactive mode where you can write code in a file with full editor support but send F# code, line by line, to the FSI and observe the results. Let's try it out:

1. In VS Code, create and open a new file called `Scratchpad.fsx`.
2. In the code editor, type `1 + 2`.
3. With the cursor still on that line, choose FSI: Send Selection from the command palette (I recommend learning the keyboard shortcut for this, which is, by default, ALT + Enter on Windows and Option + Enter on Mac).
4. A new terminal in VS Code will appear called F# Interactive. In there, you'll see the same introductory text and the same result from the exercise in section 2.5.2.
5. Create a new line and perform the same action for `System.DateTime.Now` and observe the following:
   a. In a script file, you get full syntax highlighting and autocomplete, so typing `System.` provides a dropdown with all possible types in that namespace.
   b. If you repeatedly execute this line, the current time is continually recalculated and sent to the console.
6. If you highlight both lines and use the Send Selection command, FSI will send both lines, one after the other, to FSI.

2.5.4 State in the REPL

One big benefit of REPL over a console test harness application is that it is stateful. Thus, as we saw earlier, you can bind values to symbols using `let`. You can then use these values in subsequent commands, just like a program, but because you can access the data and arbitrarily interrogate and create new values from them, it's much more flexible and powerful. Do the following:

1. Enter `let version = 6` and send it to FSI. (henceforth, I will refer to this action as simply "execute").
2. Execute `$"F# {version} is cool!"`

You should have the correctly executed expression `F# 6 is cool` showing in the terminal.

There's a catch, however. The state of FSI isn't automatically kept in sync with your script: you must ensure that you've executed the correct expressions in the correct order. Let me show you what I mean:

1. Restart FSI using the FSI: Start VS Code command or by executing `exit 0`. This kills the current FSI session, losing all state. Observe that your code in the script still remains as is.
2. Execute the line of code from step 2 again (but *not* step 1).
3. You will now get a compiler error from FSI:

```
$"F# {version} is cool";;
------^^^^^^^
error FS0039: The value or constructor 'version' is not defined.
```

This result is because although your script has the previous expression to create the `version` value, you never sent it to FSI, so it is unaware of it.

2.5.5 Creating your first function

To finish this chapter, let's create and test a function in our script that takes in someone's name and age and returns a string that's a greeting of the person. After all, F# is a functional language, right? Enter the following code in the script file that you already have open or create a new one (it doesn't matter):

```
let greetPerson name age =
    $"Hello, {name}. You are {age} years old"
```

Whether you use a tab or spaces, make sure that the body of the function is indented at least one space from the definition. Most people use four spaces. Now, execute the function into FSI again using the Send to FSI command. You'll notice no result is displayed; all we've done is compile the function into FSI:

```
val greetPerson: name: 'a -> age: 'b -> string
```

The `'a` and `'b` represent *generic types*. We'll cover this later in more depth, but this is saying that name and age can be any type—string, integer, or customer. It doesn't matter at this point; the function will work with anything.

Back in the script, call the function, which will correctly generate the correct string as an output:

```
greetPerson "Fred" 21
val it: string = "Hello, Fred. You are 21 years old"
```

You can now change the values of the parameters to the function and prove that it correctly executes each time.

2.6   *Development flows*

Now that you've had a quick play with scripts, I want to compare them to other development flows that we commonly use today so that you can gain an understanding of where they are best utilized. Scripts are a great way to use F# in an interactive and lightweight fashion, and much of what we do in this book will focus on them. For many F# developers (including myself), scripts form an integral part of the development lifecycle, particularly in the exploratory phase of development, when you're trying out different ways of representing data, experimenting with third-party packages, etc., and I would highly encourage you to use it. They can enhance or replace several other development flows:

- *Application-oriented development*—When you develop your application and prove to yourself it works by running it and navigating to that section of the app to stress the code you've just written. It's inefficient, nonrepeatable, and not always possible (e.g., you have code that only runs on a certain day of the year).
- *Console test rigs*—When you create a console application to test your application. These are challenging to maintain and can be expensive to develop.
- *Automated unit tests*—Automated tests are great for regression tests but are nowhere near as efficient as scripts for exploratory development. Additionally, they require a great deal of experience to do correctly. I still use automated tests after the fact, but I have completely stopped any form of test-driven development since moving to F#.

2.7   *Where scripts and the REPL fit in*

F# scripts are an extra tool in the development lifecycle through which we can change how we develop. Figure 2.4 illustrates some of the different scenarios.

As you can see, a great deal of development can be done in scripts, particularly in the exploratory phase of developing a project. By this, I mean any time you want to create a new module or component in your application and want to start by sketching out a rough idea before formalizing it.

Figure 2.4 represents my view of how you should use scripts and what a typical development cycle in F# might look like. You'll typically start in a script, trying things

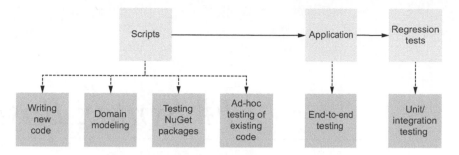

Figure 2.4   The different types of uses for F# scripts

out; once you're happy with the result, you'll port it into a full application (whether a console application, background service, web application, etc.). Once done, you might do a quick end-to-end test just within the app to validate that things work in an integrated fashion; perhaps you'll even automate that integration test. Finally, you may opt to write some regression tests to prove that the behavior of your code isn't accidentally changed in the future. In terms of creating new code or validating that something is working in the first place, as far as I'm concerned, the idea of console test rigs and test-driven development is out for most use cases.

Until now, you've been taking my word for all of this, so the rest of this book will prove it through practical examples. I want to give you one last piece of advice before going any further. To fully benefit from learning F# in the most effective manner, to quote Yoda, "You must unlearn what you have learned." If you can resist the temptation to see F# as an alternative syntax for designing code in the way you do today and trust that there's an alternative way to solve the same kinds of problems, you're halfway there.

Summary

- F# encourages you to focus on composable, declarative code that promotes the separation of data and behavior.
- F# changes the relationship between you and the compiler.
- F# is a part of the .NET platform, which runs on Mac, Linux, and Windows.
- You can write F# in Visual Studio Code with the Ionide extension.
- The REPL and FSI are key tools for learning and working with F#.
- Scripts are great ways to create snippets of code and can be reused for multiple purposes.
- You can easily migrate from scripts into full-blown applications, so scripts are a natural starting point for applications.

F# Syntax Basics

Now that you've gained a basic understanding of F# tooling and have spent a little time writing some (admittedly simple) F#, it's time to learn about the core elements of the F# language. Many of the concepts and elements that you learn in this chapter are what I would call "cross-cutting"—they don't have specific effects in any one type of application or use case but form the underpinnings of almost everything else in the language. So, it's important to make sure you learn these concepts thoroughly. The first two, syntax and type inference, will give you an insight into the structure and look and feel of the language, while the second half of this chapter will help you understand how you'll be structuring and composing applications together and building basic routines at a fundamental level.

3.1 F# syntax basics

The core syntax rules of a language say a lot about the "feeling" of the language. For example, some languages may focus on being highly explicit and verbose (I would, for example, put Java into this category); others may be terse and powerful but require more investment up front to understand what's going on (Haskell, perhaps). Others might be lightweight with the intention of getting out of your way but don't allow you to easily define the rules of what you're trying to achieve (Go and, perhaps, Python).

3.1.1 Characteristics of F# syntax

I would say that F#'s goal as a language from a syntactic point of view from day one has generally been to be highly succinct and highly safe. Most fans of dynamic languages complain that the syntax of statically typed languages is too verbose, which gets in the way of actually getting stuff done. And in some languages—I'd suggest Java as one—it's possibly true (The C# team has made a big effort to improve matters here, although I'm not entirely sold on the latest revisions of the language). Meanwhile, the C#/Java folks—those coming from a static type system—point out that refactoring is difficult without a type checker and compiler and potentially affects scaling a team without writing a large number of unit tests.

F# hits a real sweet spot here: it's lightweight, readable, and type-safe all at the same time. Don't believe the myth that you can't have a programming language with all these three factors because F# proves it's possible. I'd like to cover just a few points regarding these language characteristics, as it'll help you get into the right mindset when looking at F# code samples, and will probably bring into question some accepted fundamentals that you might be used to from other languages!

I've heard people use the word *terse* to describe F# syntax. However, this is misleading: it causes people to fear that F# is full of arcane symbols, with the goal being some kind of "code golf" to reduce the number of characters used in a program. That's totally incorrect. *Succinct* is a far more appropriate term: it refers to F#'s stripping away of unnecessary symbols and keywords that other languages rely on, resulting in your code having a far greater percentage of text relating to business logic than syntax.

READABILITY

F# code is generally very pleasing to the eye. Of course, I'll acknowledge that this is a somewhat subjective matter, but it's been my observation that compared to other languages I've worked in, it's far easier to write code in F# that is easy to understand. For example, F# has a relatively small number of symbols and characters needed for different features (far less than, say, modern C#). Many operators you might see in other languages don't exist in F#, instead replaced with human-readable functions (e.g., instead of negation being ! at the start of an expression, F# has a function called not). The lightweight syntax helps, while F# also has some nice tricks up its sleeve to make it easy to create *domain-specific languages* (DSLs) and write code that can be read by non-technical people, which is very useful when you're trying to validate that your model aligns with the business purpose.

SENSIBLE DEFAULTS

F# has defaults optimized to the most common cases, meaning that we need to type less to get the same thing done as in many other languages. In effect, this means that your code will generally have a much higher amount of code that relates to the problem you're trying to solve rather than code that's there to satisfy the compiler.

A good example of this is public versus private status. In many other languages, members are private by default, and you must explicitly mark members on classes as public, even though more often than not, members are public rather than private. F# flips this around, so public is the default. (Don't be alarmed if you're coming from languages such as C# or Java; you'll see in upcoming chapters why it's perfectly safe in F#.)

CONSISTENCY

Where possible, F# uses a core set of language constructs and symbols that can be applied in many places. For example, functions and simple values are declared using the same pattern and syntax:

```
                                    A function definition, myFunction, taking in two
                                    arguments, arg1 and arg2 (implementation omitted)
let myFunction arg1 arg2 =  ◄───┘
let mySimpleValue = 99      ◄───   The definition of
                                   mySimpleValue, an integer
```

Notice both use the same `let xxx =` pattern. In this way, you can think of simple values as being the same as functions except that they happen not to take in any parameters.

This philosophy of consistency is replicated in many places in the language. There are very few one-off language keywords for specific features but rather flexible and general-purpose ones that cover many different situations. For instance, the `type` keyword is used to define records, classes, interfaces, and unions instead of having multiple keywords for each. Another example is the `async/await` pattern prevalent today in many other languages (which, interestingly, was originally modeled on F#'s `async` blocks). In F#, `async/await` is replaced with a general-purpose language feature that can be used in many different situations, not just for asynchronous code.

A WORKED EXAMPLE

Listing 3.1 contains a typical F# code snippet showing the definition of a function that takes in a number as input, adds 10 to it, and then doubles it. It then prints out a description of what it's done before returning the answer to the caller.

Listing 3.1   F# syntax basics

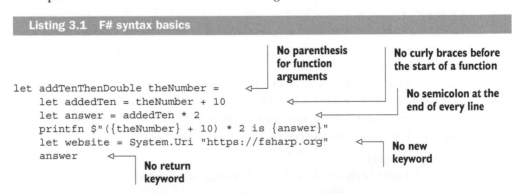

```
                                    No parenthesis          No curly braces before
                                    for function            the start of a function
                                    arguments
let addTenThenDouble theNumber =  ◄──┘                      No semicolon at the
    let addedTen = theNumber + 10  ◄──────────────┘         end of every line
    let answer = addedTen * 2  ◄────────────────────┘
    printfn $"({theNumber} + 10) * 2 is {answer}"
    let website = System.Uri "https://fsharp.org"  ◄──┐  No new
    answer  ◄───┐                                        keyword
              No return
              keyword
```

Here are some of the things to watch out for:

- *No parentheses*—F# uses parentheses in a few places, but they are usually not required to signify the start and end of arguments to functions that you define or call (as can be seen when creating the `Uri` object).
- *No curly braces*—F# is whitespace sensitive and expects all lines within any scope to start at the same column. Try indenting any line in listing 3.1 by a space, and you'll receive a compiler error.
- *No semicolons*—F# doesn't require semicolons to end a line. Simply forget that they were ever needed: F# doesn't need them for this.
- *No* `new` *keyword*—The `new` keyword can generally be omitted when creating objects. F# thinks of the constructor on a type as a static function and lets you treat it as such instead of as some kind of unique construct in the language.
- *No* `return` *keyword*—The last expression of a function is automatically the return value. Therefore, there's no need to use the `return` keyword.
- *No type annotations*—F# mostly doesn't require any guidance from you for the types of values (known as type annotations), yet it is a highly type-safe language.

These features all work together to make the F# syntax what it is. For example, consistency and simplicity are only feasible because the syntax is generally concise, whereas some other languages need custom keywords or features as shortcuts for different specific scenarios. Compare listing 3.1 with an alternative (mostly valid F#) version in the following listing that adds in the extra baggage that was omitted.

Listing 3.2 A verbose version of F# syntax basics

Parenthesis for function
arguments and return type

Curly braces
before the start
of a function

```
let addTenThenDouble (theNumber : int) : int =
{
    let addedTen : int = theNumber + 10;
    let answer : int = addedTen * 2;
    printfn $"({theNumber} + 10) * 2 is {answer}";
    let website : System.Uri = new System.Uri ("https://fsharp.org");
    return answer;
}
```

Semicolon at the
end of every line

New
keyword

Return keyword

This code is no more type-safe or readable than the original; the only thing we've achieved is to increase the cognitive overhead by adding more symbols and words to wade through that have given us very little. It's more code to write, more to read, and more to maintain.

3.1.2 *The let keyword*

Let's move on and look at the `let` keyword. This is the most important keyword you'll use in F#. It allows you to bind values to symbols. We can illustrate its use in this arbitrary example:

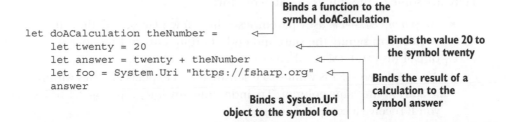

```
let doACalculation theNumber =
    let twenty = 20
    let answer = twenty + theNumber
    let foo = System.Uri "https://fsharp.org"
    answer
```

Binds a function to the
symbol doACalculation

Binds the value 20 to
the symbol twenty

Binds the result of a
calculation to the
symbol answer

Binds a System.Uri
object to the symbol foo

> ### Functions are just values
>
> F# treats both functions and simple values in the same way: they're just values. Some values take in arguments (in other words, functions), and others don't (numbers, customers, strings, etc.). But you can treat them the same way in your application insofar as, for example, you pass them around your application as arguments, bind them to symbols, and so on.

A good way to understand `let` is to think of it as a copy-and-paste instruction: wherever you see this symbol used in code, replace it with the value on the right-hand side of the equals sign. This code sample may illustrate this idea a little:

```
let isaac = 42
let olderIsaac = isaac + 1
let youngerIsaac = isaac - 1
```

Binds the value 42 to
the symbol isaac

References the symbol
isaac to get the value 42

This is the same as

```
let olderIsaac = 42 + 1
let youngerIsaac = 42 - 1
```

Using find and replace to
use the value 42 directly

> ### var and let
>
> Some languages use the `var` keyword to perform what appears to be the same thing as `let`. Don't confuse `let` with `var`. While they might seem similar, there's one major difference: `var` declares variables, which can vary by being assigned different values later or by being mutated, whereas `let` (by default) creates an immutable reference to a value. Once you've bound a value to a symbol, you can't change it to reference another value later.

3.1.3 Scoping

I touched briefly on *scoping* earlier. What does scoping mean? Generally, it means the lifetime in which other parts of code can reference a symbol. We've already seen a scope used when declaring the definition of a function, but let's take a step back and start by illustrating a couple of different styles of scoping.

CURLY BRACE VS. WHITESPACE INDENTATION

We'll start with a fictional curly-brace version of F# in which we create a function `foo` with three arguments plus some arbitrary implementation that I've omitted:

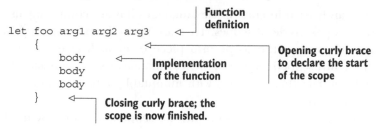

You may have seen this style before, too:

There are many different styles people adopt when using curly braces. And although you don't have to indent code—the curly braces are all the compiler needs—everyone does anyway so that humans can visually make sense of things. F# takes a different approach: it says that since everyone indents code anyway to visually indicate scope, let's just use that. Here's the equivalent F# example illustrating it:

```
let foo arg1 arg2 arg3 _
    body
    body
    body
```
Function definition

Implementation of the function indented

End of scope

That's it! If all the lines in the body are indented by the same amount, you won't go wrong. Most people in the F# world use four spaces at a time for each nested scope; I'd advise sticking to that. You can also use the tab key to make them (e.g., four spaces at a time), but they'll need to be saved as spaces; F# doesn't allow the use of tabs as a valid token.

I see a lot of people get emotional about curly brace versus whitespace. Trust me, as someone who spent the first 15 years of their career working exclusively in curly brace languages, it's not a problem. The popularity of Python today and historically Visual Basic as one of the first programming languages should tell you that (like much of F#) it's not hard, but it may be different.

EXERCISE 3.1

Create a function that takes in three numbers as input arguments. Add the first two together and bind it to a symbol `inProgress`. Then, multiply that by the third argument and bind it to a symbol `answer`. Finally, return a string that says `The answer is` `{answer}` using string interpolation.

NESTED SCOPES

Nested scopes are rarely used in curly brace languages but are commonly used in F# to create arbitrary scopes inside of scopes. They are useful because they allow you to clearly indicate to the reader the scope of a piece of data. It's also good practice because the more tightly scoped a value is, the less chance of it being misused, leading to bugs (although the fact that F# works with immutable data by default minimizes this risk tremendously anyway).

Let's look at an example of some code with no scope and then rewrite it to one with clearly defined nested scopes:

```
let fname = "Frank"
let sname = "Schmidt"
let fullName = $"{fname} {sname}"          Uses the two previously-
let greetingText = $"Greetings, {fullName}"   defined symbols to
                                               create a third

                                               Uses the previously defined
                                               symbol to create a fourth
```

We're only using `fname` and `sname` to create `fullname`; it's never required elsewhere. Similarly, `fullName` is only used to construct `greetingText`. So, let's rewrite this code with some more clearly defined scopes to formalize those observations:

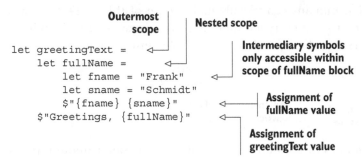

Notice that the nested scope of `fullName` is declared simply by indenting code further in. Once we outdent again, the scope goes back up a level automatically.

Although this is a relatively simple example, imagine this in a larger function. If everything was declared at the same scope, it would rapidly become very difficult to understand how and where a specific symbol was used. By using intelligent scoping, we don't have to, for example, use comments or similar; instead, it becomes clear from where we're defining symbols how they're being used. So `fname` and `sname` are now only accessible within the block that defines `fullName`. They can't be accessed before defining or after declaring `fullName`. Armed with that knowledge, you can now see the intention and use of those values. You don't even need to ask your development environment to find all references or ask yourself where else this value is being used. It's right there in the code!

> **Understanding the importance of scoping**
>
> You probably have heard the phrase: "Global variables are bad." Most rules like this are true, although greatly lessened by using immutable data (which is a first-class citizen in F#). Nonetheless, I would suggest reading the excellent *Code Complete* (2nd ed., O'Reilly, 2004) by Steve McConnell, which has some great research and illustrates in detail how and why the lifetimes of variables are directly related to the number of bugs found in codebases (i.e., the larger the scope of something is, the more likely it will be involved in a bug).

NESTED FUNCTIONS

Because functions are just values, F# has no problem with you creating nested functions—that is, functions that are defined inside of other scopes or even inside other functions. Let's see how we might rewrite the previous sample so that the creation of `fullName` is done via a function:

```fsharp
let greetingTextWithFunction person =
    let makeFullName fname sname =          // Defines a function makeFullName
        $"{fname} {sname}"                  // Implementation of the function
    let fullName = makeFullName "Frank" "Schmidt"   // Calls the function and assigns the result to fullName
    $"Greetings {fullName} from {person}."
```

`makeFullName` is only available within the definition of `greetingTextWithFunction`. This capability makes it quick and easy to create arbitrary functions as and when needed (although, in this simple example, the nested function is only called once).

ACCESSING OUTER SCOPED VALUES

Because you can create functions and scopes so easily, it's worth pointing out that while you can't access symbols that are declared within a scope afterward, you can do the opposite: if you declare a symbol before a nested scope starts, that scope will have access to it.

Listing 3.3   Accessing outer scoped values

```fsharp
let greetingTextWithFunction =
    let city = "London"                     // Declares the symbol city in an outer scope
    let makeFullName fname sname =
        $"{fname} {sname} from {city}"      // Accesses city within the inner scope
    let fullName = makeFullName "Frank" "Schmidt"
    let surnameCity = $"{sname} from {city}"    // Won't compile
    $"Greetings, {fullName}"
```

You can do this inside nested functions or simple blocks.

NOTE   Referencing outer scoped values inside a function, as in listing 3.3, is known as *capturing* the value. In other words, we're implicitly capturing the value of `city`. You don't need to worry about doing this yourself; the compiler handles it all for you. However, it's worth being aware of it, as it can have implications in high-performance scenarios.

CYCLICAL DEPENDENCIES

You may have noticed in the previous section that I specifically used the word *before* when referring to captured values from outer scopes. That's because, except in certain advanced scenarios, F# does not allow you to reference a symbol unless you've already declared it:

```
let description = $"{employee} lives in New York."     ◄——| Compiler error: the value
let employee = "Joe Bloggs"                                 | or constructor employee
                                                            | is not defined.
```

Now, this might be a complete shock to you if you've worked in a language that does nothing to prevent this kind of code. Stick with me, though: I am a firm believer that this feature is part of the sweet spot of F#. This doesn't only make many other features of F# easier to work with, but it also results in much, much simpler code for us as developers:

- You can't write so-called spaghetti code where A references B, which references C, which references A (although if you really need to do it, there are some escape hatches, but you really shouldn't need it!).
- Code is much easier to navigate. Want to know what the dependencies on a specific function are? Just look up the page. Want to know the potential callers? Just look down the page.

Also, be aware that this restriction exists across files as well. Remember the project file we talked about in chapter 2? Well, that contains a list of every F# file in your application in which the order matters: files declared earlier in the project file cannot reference code that lives in files declared later in the file.

   If you're getting a little scared or suspicious by this, trust me—it's not worth worrying about. In F#, you'll use far fewer files than you're used to in other languages and quickly get used to this way of organizing code. And, once you've written a few multi-file programs and had to go back and make some changes later, you'll appreciate the simplicity and trust that you gain from this way of working.

Errors in VS Code

There are a few ways to display errors in VS Code. There's the Problems panel, which shows all errors in a list. Clicking any error will navigate the Editor window straight there. Alternatively, you can cycle through all errors by executing the Go To Next Problem command (F8 by default), which will also display the error underneath the code in a pleasant overlay. Lastly, the Error Lens extension, which I highly recommend installing, will show errors as you type on the same line.

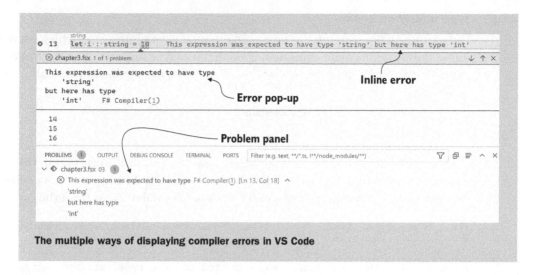

The multiple ways of displaying compiler errors in VS Code

3.2   Type inference

Type inference is one of the features of F# that cuts across virtually all of the language, and it's something that without explaining now would lead to much confusion later. The general idea behind type inference is relatively simple: instead of you having to explicitly tell the compiler the type of every symbol (remember that F# is statically typed), the compiler should be able to figure this out for itself.

3.2.1   Benefits of type inference

There are many benefits of using type inference (I also highlight some challenges with it later in this chapter):

- *Easier to read*—There's less extraneous code to read, allowing you to focus on what's important. This is particularly important with generics, as we'll see later.
- *Quicker to write*—You type less when you're developing; as the compiler deduces what you're doing, it automatically specifies the types for you.
- *Quicker to refactor*—You can make changes to your application that ripple through your codebase without having to make boilerplate changes throughout; the only changes you need to make are where actual clashes between old and new code occur.

Many mainstream statically typed languages already have some form of type inference (e.g., C# and Scala), usually symbolized with the `var` or `val` keywords. However, F# has a type inference implementation known as the Hindley–Milner method (also found in other ML–derived languages such as Ocaml, Haskell, and Elm) that is a level ahead of most other languages and much more powerful.

3.2.2   *Type inference basics*

Let's look at a few examples in F# of code that uses type inference (which we've been doing thus far) and some equivalent code that uses type annotations, which allows you to explicitly tell F# the type of a symbol. This first example binds the value 10 to the symbol i:

```
let i = 10            ⟵──| No type annotation
let i : int = 10      ⟵──┐ Type annotation
```

Both versions are the same from a compiler point of view: it's just that in the second example, we've explicitly marked our intention for I to be an integer. Try changing the annotation to a string, and you'll receive a reasonable error from the compiler:

```
let i : string = 10;; C:\Users\IsaacAbraham\Code\helloworld\Program.fs
-----------------^^

error FS0001: This expression was expected to have type 'string' but here has
    type 'int'
```

> ### Annotations: Before or after?
>
> In F#, a type annotation goes *after* the name of the symbol, and most new languages today seem to be following suit (e.g., Go, Rust, TypeScript, Kotlin). Older languages that derive from C (e.g., Java, Javascript, C#, C++) don't follow this pattern.

IDE SUPPORT FOR TYPE INFERENCE

This book is about F# the language, but CodeLens and LineLens are two IDE features that are so useful from an educational point of view that I can't ignore them. They're officially supported at the time of writing in various guises in both VS Code and JetBrains Rider (there's an experimental implementation in Visual Studio, which I don't recommend). Figure 3.1 shows a screenshot of the previous code snippet in VS Code.

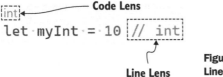

Figure 3.1   CodeLens and LineLens in VS Code

Both CodeLens and LineLens are features provided by VS Code and integrated with the F# compiler as you type. I've turned on both in this screenshot for illustrative purposes, but I recommend you pick one. They essentially provide you with a look at what the F# compiler has inferred, and because it's provided in real time, you can see how it reacts to what you're doing with a rapid turnaround cycle. For example, figure 3.2 shows what a string, a floating-point number and a `System.DateTime` will show.

```
int
let myInt = 10 // int
string
let myString = "Hello" // string
float
let myFloat = 123.456 // float
System.DateTime
let myDate = System.DateTime.Now // System.DateTime
```

Figure 3.2   Further examples of CodeLens and LineLens in VS Code

Try changing the right-hand side of the equals sign to a string, float, or a built-in value in .NET, such as a `Uri` or `DateTime`, and watch how the compiler immediately updates the annotation. This isn't some built-in list; it will work for any type, even your own custom-defined types, including functions. I will be referring to this elsewhere in this book; it's an invaluable learning tool, and I highly recommend you use it when writing in F#. I wish it had existed when I started learning the language!

However, type inference can go much further in F# than this simple example. Function inputs and return types for any F# types are also supported. Any evidence available to the compiler will be used to infer types such as usage and comparison. It's very smart and will surprise you with just how much it can figure out on its own.

Here's another example, which I encourage you to work through side by side. I start with a function `add` that takes in two numbers, `a` and `b`, and returns their sum.

Listing 3.4   Working with type annotations

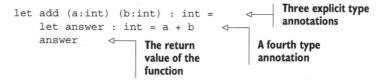

```
let add (a:int) (b:int) : int =        ◄─┤ Three explicit type
    let answer : int = a + b     ◄──       annotations
    answer    ◄─┐              A fourth type
              │ The return     annotation
              │ value of the
              │ function
```

The interesting bits here are on the first line. We're not going to dive in-depth into functions until later, but for now, suffice it to say that a function in F# has the following components:

- The `let` keyword
- The function name `add`
- One or many arguments (in this case, two integers `a` and `b`)
- The return type `int`

In our case, we've explicitly annotated the two function arguments as integers and stated that the function returns an integer. The function signature is notated as `int -> int -> int`. The first two `int`s refer to the functions' arguments; the final `int` is the return type.

If you're wondering why we need the parenthesis around every argument here, it's because of the type annotations. Consider the following definition of a function `foo`, which takes in a single argument `bar`:

```
let foo bar : int =
    ...
```

What does `: int` signify here—the type of `bar` or the return type of the function `foo` itself? The correct answer is the return type of the function `foo`. Therefore, you must wrap each function argument in parenthesis whenever you want to type annotate them so that the compiler is clear about what the annotation is (we'll come to *tupled* function arguments later in the book, which is the one exception to this rule).

EXERCISE 3.2

Complete the following steps to see some basic type inference in action:

1. Enter the code from listing 3.4 into an empty F# script file.
2. Observe that the CodeLens correctly identifies the type signature of the `add` function.
3. Remove the return type annotation (`: int`) so that the function declaration is `let add (a:int) (b:int) =`.
4. Observe that the CodeLens still correctly indicates that the function returns an integer.
5. Remove the type annotation from `answer`.
6. Observe that the CodeLens still correctly understands that the function returns an integer.
7. Remove the type annotation from `b` (you can also remove the parenthesis around it).
8. Observe that the CodeLens still correctly understands that `b` is an integer.
9. Remove the type annotation from `a` (you can also remove the parenthesis around it).
10. Observe that the CodeLens still correctly understands that `a` is an integer.

You should be left with something like figure 3.3.

```
int -> int -> int
let add a b = // int → int → int
    let answer = a + b
    answer
```

Figure 3.3   F# type inference for function arguments and return types

How has F# inferred all the type annotations? It's not magic. Here's how:

1. When you remove the return type annotation in step 3, the compiler can deduce it because it knows the type of `answer` is an integer. Therefore, the return type must be an integer since that's the type of what's being returned.

2 When you remove the type annotation from `answer` in step 5, the compile infers `answer` as an integer since `a` and `b` are both integers, and adding two integers together must produce another integer.

3 When you remove the annotation from `b` in step 7, the compiler can infer `b` to be an integer since it was being added to `a`. As F# does not permit implicit conversions (under normal circumstances; there are some exceptions as of F# v6), there's no other type that `b` could be.

4 When you removed the final annotation from `a` in step 9, the compiler had one final trick up its sleeve. You added `a` and `b` together: if there's no other evidence, F# assumes addition to be against integers for the purpose of type inference. However, if you had annotated one of the elements as, say, a string (which supports addition), then the compiler would use that to infer everything else as a string.

At this point, you should experiment with the type-inference engine using the final (annotation-free) function (not as sequential steps but as separate exercises) by adding type annotations or adding constant values to the function body to see how the type-inference engine works.

EXERCISE 3.3

1 Add the string `hello` to a + b on line 3. What happens?

2 Add a type annotation of `string` to the return type of the function. What happens?

3 Explicitly annotate `b` as an integer again and add 13.34 (which is a float, not an int) to a + b on line 3. What happens?

3.2.3 *Inferring generics*

F# has support for a feature in .NET known as *generics*. Generics are common in most modern languages (Go was a notable exception that resisted generics until recently). Generics allow you to create types and functions that can operate on any type rather than being bound to a specific concrete type. A common example of this is a list: it's a data structure that should be able to operate on any type of data; in the first version of .NET, there were no generics, so you had to either cast everything into an Object (the top type in .NET that everything inherits from) or construct wrappers so that you had a `CustomerList`, `IntList`, `StringList`, etc. as required. Generics solved this in .NET 2 (around 2005) with deep integration into the platform.

It's no surprise that F# has excellent support for generics since the author of F#, Don Syme, also lead the research team that created the implementation of generics for .NET in the first place! Let's take a quick look at generics and type inference support with a set of code samples.

WORKING WITH EXISTING GENERIC TYPES

This first one shows you how to create a `ResizeArray`, a .NET list that will automatically resize as you add new items to it, of integers using an explicit type annotation or leaving it for the compiler to infer. For those coming from C#, ResizeArray is just a type alias for the System.Collections.Generic.List<'T>:

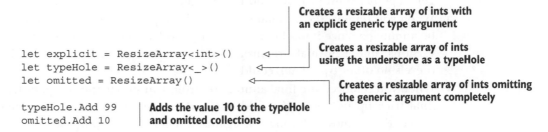

Creates a resizable array of ints with an explicit generic type argument

Creates a resizable array of ints using the underscore as a typeHole

```
let explicit = ResizeArray<int>()
let typeHole = ResizeArray<_>()
let omitted = ResizeArray()
```

Creates a resizable array of ints omitting the generic argument completely

```
typeHole.Add 99
omitted.Add 10
```

Adds the value 10 to the typeHole and omitted collections

The first expression explicitly states that the collection stores integers, as specified by the <int> (generic arguments in C# and F# are always specified with angle brackets). The other two let the compiler determine the type of the list based on the usage (in this case, based on the call to Add).

EXERCISE 3.4

Change the value 10 to a string. What happens to the type of omitted? Note that if the compiler can't infer the generic type argument because there's no usage of the list, it will infer the type argument as Object, although the compiler will actually throw an error forcing you to add type annotations.

AUTOMATIC GENERALIZATION

F# will automatically generalize your functions. This means that if it determines that an argument to a function is generic, it will automatically do that for you. Here's an example of a generic function that takes in three values of the same type, 'T, and combines them into a resize array. In this first example, I've put in an explicit type argument, as can be seen with the proliferation of 'T throughout the function:

```
let combineElements<'T> (a:'T) (b:'T) (c:'T) =
    let output = ResizeArray<'T>()
    output.Add a
    output.Add b
    output.Add c
    output

combineElements<int> 1 2 3
```

Specifies a generic type argument, <'T>, on the function

Creates a resize array of the type 'T

Calls the function to combine three numbers

Note the 'T annotation here, which is used as a placeholder that we can use to refer to the generic type in the function (as we've done when creating the ResizeArray). This function can be used with any type—strings, ints, your own types, etc. It's important to understand that this is not some kind of weak/dynamic typing. You can't do the following:

```
combineElements<int> 1 2 "test"
// Error: This expression was expected to have type 'int' but here has type
    'string'
```

However, automatic generalization means that we can do away with all the type annotations and let the compiler do this all for us:

```
let combineElements a b c =          ←──┐  Lets the compiler generalize
    let output = ResizeArray()          │  the function for us
    output.Add a
    output.Add b
    output.Add c
    output
                            ┐ Calls the automatically
combineElements 1 2 3    ←──┘ generalized function
```

My recommendation is to let the compiler automatically generalize your functions for you. On the rare occasion that you don't want it to generalize your functions, you can add explicit type annotations as required.

The only difference between the generalized and nongeneralized samples (and you can see this from CodeLens) is that the compiler uses 'a as the generic type argument rather than 'T. Why did I show 'T in the initial example, then? Because in the .NET framework class libraries, and in C#, that's what's used. This is an unfortunate divergence between F# and C#, but there's no difference aside from that (it's worth noting that these are just conventions; it's perfectly fine to use 'Foo or 'Bar).

There are times when you'll need to use generic type arguments yourself (although in F# it's fairly rare). In such cases, I would recommend using 'T, at least as a prefix (e.g., 'TElement or 'TItem). Then, if you see 'a anywhere, you'll know that the compiler automatically created it for you.

3.2.4 *Diagnosing unexpected type inference behavior*

Here's a practical exercise that's a great way to gain more confidence in trusting the F# type inference engine and to learn how to guide the compiler when it infers something unexpected and you can't figure out why.

Consider the following completely arbitrary and random code sample: two functions, calculateGroup, which takes in an age and determines whether the person is a child, adult, or retiree, and sayHello. sayHello to call calculateGroup with some arbitrary logic:

```
                                 ┐ calculateGroup function has
                                 │ the signature int -> string.
let calculateGroup age =   ←─────┘
    if age < 18 then "Child"
    elif age < 65 then "Adult"
    else "Pensioner"
                              ┐ sayHello function has the
                              │ signature float -> string.
let sayHello someValue =  ←───┘
    let group =
        if someValue < 10.0 then calculateGroup 15   ←──┐ The string
        else calculateGroup 35                          │ result of calling
    "Hello " + group                                    │ calculateGroup

let result = sayHello 10.5    ←────────  Example call site
```

EXERCISE 3.5

Copy the previous code sample into an empty script file in VS Code. You'll see that the type inference engine correctly figures out all the types for the functions; for example, `age` is an `int`, and `sayHello` returns a string. Let's now make what appears to be an obvious semantic mistake and see how the compiler behaves in an unexpected way.

On the second line, change `18` to the string `"test"`. Clearly, this value is incorrect from a semantic point of view, yet the compiler will now suddenly show error messages in several other places (figure 3.4).

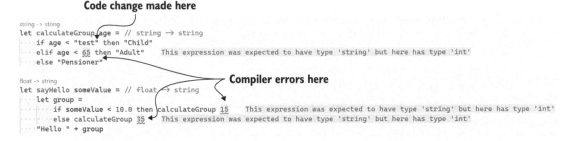

Figure 3.4   Type Inference behaving in a way that may be unexpected

Let's look at two things: where (and why) all the errors have shown up and why it's happening in the first place. We'll start by focusing on the first error on line 3:

```
This expression was expected to have type 'string' but here has type 'int'
```

In other words, the compiler thinks that `age` is a string, and you can't compare a number with a string (at least not in F#). We can also confirm this by looking at the Code-Lens above the `calculateGroup` function, which now reads `string -> string`, whereas it was `int -> string` before. The errors on lines 8 and 9 should now be relatively simple to understand: `calculateGroup` now expects a string as input and, therefore, shows errors at these call sites because we're supplying integers.

So, why does F# think `age` is now a string rather than an int? Because of line 2—we're comparing `age` with the string `"test"`, so the compiler says, "`age` must be a string." In other words, the F# compiler uses the first opportunity it gets to infer the type of a value. Since we know better, we can guide the compiler by temporarily putting in an explicit integer type annotation against `age`. As you can see in figure 3.5, this then shows the error in exactly the right place.

Now, the compiler correctly shows a compiler error on the comparison with `test`, since we've told the compiler that `age` is an integer. Once the error has been fixed, you can safely remove the type annotation again.

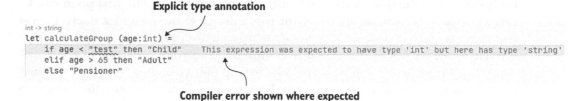

Figure 3.5   Using a temporary type annotation to guide the compiler

> **Fixing compiler errors efficiently**
>
> If you are overwhelmed by a large number of confusing errors that all appear at once, always try to locate the first error that's been identified rather than being concerned that there may be several error messages. Remember, since F# enforces file and symbol ordering, the first error will nearly always be the first error in the first file in the project. Particularly with a type system that relies heavily on type inference, it's not uncommon to fix many downstream compiler errors at once by solving the first error.

3.2.5   *Limitations of type inference*

There are a few areas where type inference won't work, and you'll have to put in some explicit type annotations. These are almost all around the object-oriented half of F#, which we'll not really be focusing on in this book. So, any classes that you create or reference from C# won't be inferred based on member access. This includes essentially all the framework class library. That means types like `String` or `DateTime` can't be inferred based on member access. However, once the compiler has identified a type, whether it's one from C# or not, it can use that information for inference further downstream. See this example:

```
let addThreeDays (theDate:System.DateTime) =        ⟵—┤ Type annotation
    theDate.AddDays 3                                      required

let addAYearAndThreeDays theDate =                  ⟵—┤ Type annotation
    let threeDaysForward = addThreeDays theDate  ⟵—┤ not required
    theDate.AddYears 1
                                                       Usage point for type inference
```

In this example, the `addThreeDays` function requires a type annotation to access the `AddDays` member. However, the `addAYearAndThreeDays` function doesn't require one since we use `theDate` by calling `addThreeDays` , and the compiler can use that to infer the type of `theDate`.

3.2.6   *Criticisms of type inference*

It would be unfair to ignore some of the criticisms of type inference. Some developers do shy away from it, although 99% of the time, in my experience, this is more out of fear or misuse. The most common complaint I hear is that it's "magic" or that one can't determine the type of a variable without an annotation. The first point can be easily dispelled by reading the rules for type inference: the compiler doesn't guess types but instead uses a clearly defined set of precedence rules. All the issues with type inference can be followed through until one point in your codebase where a type clashes and leads to a compiler error. The second point can also be dispelled by the number of excellent IDEs that give you both tooltips or a code lens (including VS Code) that serve as excellent educational guidance.

Another concern I occasionally hear is that you lose semantic meaning without an annotation (i.e., you can't easily see the intent or meaning of the code without types). I'm not convinced by this. The following code snippet shows three different ways of describing the same operation.

```
                              No type annotations,        Type annotation,
                              poor naming                 poor naming
let x = getData ()     ←
let x : Customer list = getData ()      ←
let customersToRemind = loadOverdueCustomers ()     ←    No type annotations,
                                                         good naming
```

As you can see, the issue generally isn't around type annotations but poor naming of functions and symbols. If you use human-readable names that describe their contents and intent, you will very rarely require type annotations. There are, of course, exceptions to this rule, but they are very rare. My advice is to not bother with type annotations (especially with the support of VS Code) by default; the benefits massively outweigh any costs.

It's well worth spending the time to understand type inference in F# because it's a crucial part of the flavor of the language. Type inference fits with the "more with less" philosophy and another side of F# discussed at the start of this lesson, which is trusting the compiler. You need a different mindset to create functions and arguments without type annotations and let the compiler fill in the gaps, and as you saw, at times, it's important that you understand what the compiler is doing under the hood. But as you'll see, type inference is incredibly useful in writing succinct, easily refactorable code without needing to resort to a third-party tool to "rewrite" your code for you.

3.3   *Exercise answers*

EXERCISE 3.1

```
let exercise31 a b c =
    let inProgress = a + b
    let answer = inProgress * c
    $"The answer is {answer}"
```

EXERCISE 3.3

1 The arguments a and b are now inferred as strings.
2 The arguments a and b are now inferred as strings.
3 The compiler gives an error because you cannot add a float to an integer.

EXERCISE 3.4

Omitted is now a list of strings.

Summary

- The philosophy behind the F# syntax is about succinctness and simplicity.
- F#'s syntax does away with a lot of the boilerplate that you might expect to see in a programming language.
- The `let` keyword is the most important keyword in F# and allows you to bind values to immutable symbols.
- F# allows you to make scopes for your code simply by indenting it.
- Scoping allows you to more carefully control the lifetime and accessibility of symbols, which aids readability and intent.
- Type inference is a powerful feature of F# that dramatically reduces the amount of code you need to write and aids in refactoring.
- IDEs such as VS Code offer flexible support for F# errors, while CodeLens allows you to see type inference in action.

F# Fundamentals

4

This chapter discusses two of the core features of F# that will have a large effect on how you write and design code: Expressions and immutability. Both features go hand-in-hand: without one, the other wouldn't be especially useful. Both are designed to change the way you write code into one that's oriented around working with values and applying transformations to those values as the basic mechanism of implementing any logic. That might sound complicated but don't worry; it's not.

4.1 Expressions

Expressions and statements are two sides of the same coin. They're sometimes described in all sorts of complicated or vague ways but in F# it's quite clear, as table 4.1 shows.

Table 4.1 Expressions vs. statements

	Returns something?	Has side-effects?
Expressions	Always	Occasionally
Statements	Never	Always

4.1.1 Purity and side effects

It's worth spending a couple of minutes clearly defining the terms *purity* and *side effects* for later. A pure function is a function that doesn't have any side effects and is guaranteed to always give the same output for a given input. Such functions are typically easy to test; you only have to worry about giving it some inputs and checking the return value that it gives back. You don't have to check whether some internal, encapsulated state has been modified or a file has been written; it's just inputs and outputs. Functional purity is something you'll see enforced in some functional programming languages such as Haskell. F# doesn't provide any guarantees over pure functions, but it does have some features that help you identify functions that are not pure (i.e., impure functions), as we'll see later.

A side effect is typically some effect that a function has on data that exists outside of itself. This could be writing to a database table or modifying some global mutable state. Side effects can't be observed from a function's signature (i.e., its inputs or outputs) and so can be harder to test. Instead, you might need to observe side effects by, for example, calling other methods on an object and confirming that its behavior has changed or looking to see if a row was added to a database table.

EXERCISE 4.1

Let's look at some simple examples of statements and expressions. Which of the following do you think is which?

1 A method on an Employee class, `SetSalary()`, that takes in their new salary and modifies its private state to the new salary. It returns nothing (known as `void` in some languages).
2 A function `Add`, which takes in two numbers and returns the sum of them.
3 A function `SaveCustomer`, which takes in a customer and saves it to a database. The function returns nothing.
4 A function `SaveCustomer`, which takes in a customer and saves it to a database. The function returns `true` if it succeeded and `false` if the customer already exists.

4.1.2 Difficulties with statements

Many languages today, especially those in the object orientation world, are what I would call *statement-oriented*: the primary way you compose code is through statements and functions, which behave as statements. But there are several issues with statements that allow all sorts of bugs to creep in. Listing 4.1 shows some code that attempts to describe the age of a person supplied as input. I'm using C# syntax here, but any statement-oriented language will have a fairly similar design (newer versions of C# have introduced some slightly different syntax, but this is still perfectly valid).

Listing 4.1   Working in a statement-oriented language

```
using System;

public void DescribeAge(int age)          Initializes a
{                                         variable with a
    string ageDescription = null;         default value
    var greeting = "Hello";               Creates a variable
    if (age < 18)                         to use later
        ageDescription = "Child";         First if branch
    else if (age < 65)
        greeting = "Adult";               Second if branch

    Console.WriteLine($"{greeting}! You are a '{ageDescription}'.");
}
```

This code has several issues, all caused by the fact that `if/then` in most languages is a way of controlling program flow with a set of arbitrary, unrelated statements (see figure 4.1):

- There's no handler for the case when `age` ≥ 65. As you're not accessing any properties on the string, you won't get any null reference exceptions. Instead, the code will simply print out null for the description.
- The code accidentally assigned the string to `greeting`, rather than `ageDescription`, in the second case.
- `ageDescription` needed to be declared with a default value before assigning it. This opens the possibility of all sorts of bugs for more complicated logic.

> **Null reference checking**
>
> More recent versions of C# have an optional powerful (and complicated) feature called non-nullable reference types, which makes it possible to create values that can never be set to null (a few other languages have something similar). We'll discuss this in more detail later in the book, but don't worry about it here, as it doesn't really affect statements and expressions.

Figure 4.1 illustrates listing 4.1 as a flow diagram.

Your initial instinct might be to say that no one really makes mistakes like this, but you'd be amazed how many bugs creep in from situations just like this, particularly as a code base grows and all sorts of minor bugs and issues, or "code smells," begin to manifest themselves in strange ways.

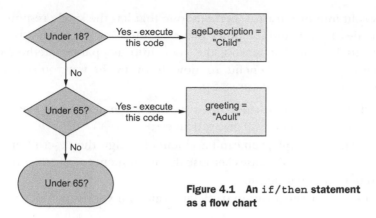

Figure 4.1 An `if/then` **statement as a flow chart**

4.1.3 Expressions to the rescue

In the previous example, you saw several issues with code that is considered perfectly valid from the compiler's perspective yet contains mistakes that you were (hopefully!) able to identify quickly and easily. Why can't the compiler fix these things for you? Why can't it help you get these things right the first time?

The answer is that statements are weak. Compilers have no understanding that there's any relationship between all the branches of the `if/else` block. Instead, they're simply different paths to go down and execute; the fact that they're all supposed to assign a value to the *same* variable is purely coincidental. The fact that you didn't handle the catch-all branch is irrelevant.

What we need is a construct that's a little bit more powerful for the compiler to understand what we're trying to achieve. As it turns out, you can fix all of these problems in one fell swoop by rewriting your code as expressions instead. The following listing illustrates this.

Listing 4.2 Working with expressions in a statement-oriented language

```
using System;

private static string GetDescription(int age)        Expression with
{                                                     signature int ->
    if (age < 18) return "Child!";                    string
    else if (age < 65) return "Adult!";
    else return "OAP!";
}

public void DescribeAge(int age)
{                                                     Call site to
    var ageDescription = GetDescription(age);         function
    var greeting = "Hello";
    Console.WriteLine($"{greeting}! You are a '{ageDescription}'.");
}
```

The code is now split into two distinct methods: one that has the single responsibility of generating the description and the other that calls and uses the result it provides. There's the obvious benefit that moving the code into a separate method might improve readability, but the real benefits are now shown by the way you're naturally forced to structure your code (see figure 4.2):

- It's impossible to forget to include the `else` case when generating the description; if you do, the compiler will give you an error.
- As in the previous example, you can't accidentally assign the description to the wrong variable in half of the cases because the assignment to `ageDescription` is performed in only one location.
- You don't need to create an arbitrary default value for your variables, either.

Figure 4.2 shows listing 4.2, again as a flow diagram.

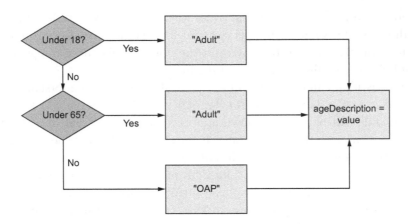

Figure 4.2   Expressing the same flow but using expressions

Even though this is a trivial example, it's worth taking a moment to consider it a little more and its main implication. There's now a clear separation between working with data transformations and assigning the result to a variable (`ageDescription`). In other words, the first half of the diagram is focused on simply the relationship between the person's age and the resulting description; we're not thinking about the bigger picture here, just the calculation itself. Compare this to the previous example, where both activities were intermingled: if the age was under 18, not only did we decide that the text is `child`, but we also assigned that to `ageDescription` at the same time. This mixing of calculations and assignment leads to all kinds of bugs and is something you should avoid; you'll see this distinction time and again in F#—series of data transformations followed by a final state modification.

You might be scratching your head, wondering why you are making an effort to differentiate expressions and statements. So, let's see how things work in F#.

Switch/case and pattern matching

Many languages have other branching mechanisms, such as switch case (C# even has
two variants), most of which are statement oriented. Some use expressions, which is
great; the point here isn't to criticize other languages and pretend none have expressions but to highlight the distinction between statements and expressions in general.

4.1.4   Expressions in F#

F# is an expression-oriented language. This means that virtually everything is an
expression; there are no statements, or functions that return `void` (although F# has a
nifty escape hatch for cases where you don't have any result). This also is why you
don't need the `return` keyword in F#: since every scope of code must return something,
the `return` keyword isn't needed. Even branching logic constructs such as `if/then` are
expressions. To illustrate how things look in an expression-based language, let's look
at the following listing, which is the previous example but now in F#.

Listing 4.3   Working in an expression-oriented language

```
let describeAge age =
    let ageDescription =                    Value binding with
        if age < 18 then "Child"            a nested scope
        elif age < 65 then "Adult"          if/else expression
        else "OAP"                          branches
    let greeting = "Hello"
    $"{greeting}! You are a '{ageDescription}'."
```

The key thing to observe here is that the `if/then` block of code has a result that's
assigned to `ageDescription`. Here, each branch of the block acts more like a function in that it has an (implicit) input (`age`) and an explicit result (either `"Child"`,
`"Adult"`, or `"OAP"`), which is then assigned to `ageDescription`. And, as an expression, each branch of the `if/then` block must return a value of the same type (in this
case, a string).

By moving to this way of working with expressions, you get the same benefits that
you did in listing 4.2, except here they're a first-class part of the language. You don't
have to create arbitrary methods or functions to benefit from the extra safety that
expressions provide; they're baked into the language.

As a second point—which we'll discuss more in the next section—also notice that
this sample no longer relies on modifying (*mutating*) any data: `ageDescription` and
greeting are never modified, but only set once.

Lastly, I've changed the function to return the generated string rather than print it
to the console. This again makes the overall function an expression as it now returns a
string, rather than if I had printed it out (in which case, it would return something
called `unit`, which we'll see shortly).

4.1.5 *Composability*

A further benefit of expressions is that they naturally compose. By this, I mean that they tend to create more flexible codebases that you can more easily refactor or repurpose later on without much effort.

For example, imagine you want to support writing the result to disk rather than print to the console. In the following listing (a repeat of listing 4.1), this would be quite tricky: it's writing to the console as an integral part of the single method.

Listing 4.4 Working in a statement-oriented language

```
using System;

public void DescribeAge(int age)
{
    string ageDescription = null;
    var greeting = "Hello";
    if (age < 18)
        ageDescription = "Child";
    else if (age < 65)
        greeting = "Adult";

    Console.WriteLine($"{greeting}! You are a '{ageDescription}'.");
}
```

Console output as an integral part of this function

But if you separate the method into two parts, one that generates a string and another that outputs to the console, you can reuse the first part much more easily (as well as make `unit` testing simpler). In listing 4.3, this would be a trivial task to do since the logic to generate the string is decoupled from the printing to the console.

REFACTORING TO FUNCTIONS

Let's take a quick practical look at how we might refactor listing 4.3 so that the code that calculates the `ageDescription` is its own function rather than a nested scope so we could easily use it with other outputs such as the filesystem. Doing this is a common activity in F# and, thanks to the type inference and lightweight syntax that we've already seen, is usually very simple to do.

EXERCISE 4.2

1 Identify the scope you wish to move into a function of its own.

2 Cut that code out and paste it above the function that it's currently in, taking care to correct the indentation so that it's within the same scope as the function you extracted it from.

3 Identify any required symbols and add them as inputs to the function. For example, in listing 4.3, this is the `age` symbol. Don't worry about type annotations; the compiler can normally infer them for you.

4 In place of the code in the original function, replace it with a call to the newly created function.

As a practice exercise, I'd encourage you to try this out yourself: observe where you get compiler errors and how to fix them (the correct solution is found in the following listing).

Listing 4.5   Refactoring to functions

```
open System

let calculateAgeDescription age =          Newly defined function with
    if age < 18 then "Child"               signature int -> string
    elif age < 65 then "Adult"
    else "OAP"

                                           Calls the
                                           newly defined
let describeAge age =                       function
    let ageDescription = calculateAgeDescription age
    let greeting = "Hello"
    printfn $"{greeting}! You are a '{ageDescription}'."
```

It's well worth doing this yourself, even if it seems easy and/or obvious to do: F# makes it very easy to create functions, and you'll be doing it on a regular basis, so it's good to get into the habit early on.

4.1.6   Unit

I mentioned earlier that F# insists that every function you create returns something. How do we then handle the cases when our code doesn't return any value (e.g., a function whose result is simply to print something to the console or write to the file system)?

The answer is that F# has a built-in value called `unit` that represents nothing. However, unlike `void` in many other languages, `unit` acts like a regular value that can be returned from any piece of code or even bound to a symbol. In this way, you can say that every function always returns a value, even if that value is `unit`. Here's an example:

```
let printAddition a b =                     The last expression of the
    let answer = a + b                      function prints to the
    printfn $"{a} plus {b} equals {answer}."  console. The function
                                            result is a unit.
```

> **Interoperating with void**
>
> How does F# work with the .NET Framework Class Library (FCL), the set of core functionality in .NET that is all written in C# and has thousands of methods that return `void`? The answer is that F# implicitly converts `unit` to `void` for us, so anywhere you see .NET code listings etc. that say they return `void`, it'll be represented in F# as `unit`, and vice versa.

In listing 4.5, the `describeAge` function fits exactly this: a function that prints to the console as the final action it performs. There's no return value. Sure enough, if you enter this function in VS Code, you'll see the code lens shows that it has a signature of `int -> unit`. In other words, it takes in an integer (the age) but has no meaningful output.

UNIT AS AN INPUT

You can also use `unit` as an input to a function. This is useful if you want to have some code that is executed every single time it is called. Observe the following code:

```
let getTheCurrentTime = System.DateTime.Now    ◁⎤  Calculates the current time
let x = getTheCurrentTime                         and assigns to a symbol
let y = getTheCurrentTime        ⊢ Copies the value of getCurrentTime
                                   to another symbol
```

The problem is that once you've executed it, `getTheCurrentTime` will always return that initial value. It won't recalculate itself once it's been bound, no matter how long you wait. It's just a simple value, so you'll be copying the value to another symbol. However, if we change the definition to take `unit` as an input, signified by `()`, this will change the behavior:

```
let getTheCurrentTime () = System.DateTime.Now    ◁⎤  Creates a function that will
let x = getTheCurrentTime ()                          return the latest time
let y = getTheCurrentTime ()     ⊢ Calls a function and assigns
                                   the current time to a symbol
```

Think of this as us telling the F# compiler that every time we call this piece of code, the state of the world has changed, and therefore it should re-evaluate the function.

UNIT AND SIDE EFFECTS

Seeing `unit` in a function signature, either as input or as output, is a tell-tale sign that this function has some kind of side effect in it and that calling it multiple times will probably have different results every time:

- *Unit as input*—Probably calling some impure code that will affect the result (e.g., getting the current time, generating a random number, etc.)
- *Unit as output*—Probably writing to some I/O as the final action in the body (e.g., print to console, write to filesystem, save to database etc.)

However, since F# doesn't enforce purity, it's still possible that code that doesn't take in or return `unit` still has a side effect. For example, the following code has two side effects but does not have `unit` anywhere in its type signature:

```
                         Function has signature float ->                Invisible side
                         DateTime; unit is nowhere to be seen.          effect to get the
let addDays days =    ◁                                                 current date
    let newDays = System.DateTime.Today.AddDays days    ◁
    printfn $"You gave me {days} days and I gave you {newDays}"   ◁
    newDays
let result = addDays 3                    Invisible side effect to
                                          print to the console
```

4.1.7   *Ignore*

There are times when you call a function that returns a value that you're not interested in. This is common with a function like addDays that we just saw: a function with
some side effect (in this case, printing to the console) and a return value (the calculated DateTime). Let's assume that we're calling this function because of its ability to
print to the console. We're not interested in the actual DateTime object that it returns,
and we write the following code:

```
let addSeveralDays () =        ←⌐     Defines a function
    addDays 3
    addDays 5                      Calls addDays several times and
    addDays 7       ←⌐            implicitly ignores their outputs

                      Final call: the result from this
                      call is returned back out.
```

You'll see that F# provides a warning for the first two call sites (lines 2 and 3 of this
snippet):

```
The result of this expression has type 'DateTime' and is implicitly ignored.
Consider using 'ignore' to discard this value explicitly, e.g. 'expr |>
ignore', or 'let' to bind the result to a name, e.g. 'let result = expr'.
```

Don't worry about the |> referred to in the warning message. We'll cover that in a
later chapter.

What does this warning mean, and why are we getting a warning in the first place?
Well, remember that F# is an expression-oriented language. In such a language, you
compose code by plugging together functions that take in some data and return a
result, which can be acted on by another piece of code. So, throwing away the result of
a function makes no sense unless, of course, your code executes some side-effect that
the compiler is unaware of (as is the case with addDays).

In such a case, you need to explicitly tell F# that this function returns something, but you know better and are happy to ignore the result. We do this using the
built-in function in F# called (unsurprisingly) ignore. It simply takes in any value
and gives back a unit value (which the F# compiler understands can be discarded
without a warning):

```
let addSeveralDays() =
    ignore (addDays 3)        Explicitly ignores results
    ignore (addDays 5)        from function calls
    addDays 7
```

Creating statements in F#

Although I don't advise it and it's completely atypical in F#, you can do statement-based evaluation in F#. Essentially, just make sure that all of your code returns `unit` (using `ignore` where necessary). In addition, you'll need to use mutable data throughout your codebase—something we'll see very shortly—which is deliberately more work than using *immutable* data.

4.2   *Immutable data*

If expressions are the one part of the core of how you architect and organize your code in F#, immutability is the other half that is almost mandatory once you accept that you want to develop using expressions. Immutability can, in some ways, be one of the more challenging concepts to get used to, but once you "grok" it, you'll be pleasantly surprised at how little you need mutable data structures. In fact, in my experience as a trainer and coach, it's remarkable how quickly people develop an aversion to mutable data. It's almost like the same fear a developer used to static typing feels when moving to a dynamic language.

4.2.1   *The problem with mutability*

Immutability is the concept of working with data whose state never changes. You create data with a value, and that's it; the value is set for the lifetime of the symbol. We'll discuss the obvious questions, such as how you could write applications only using immutable data in a little bit. However, to start, I'd like to give a few real-world examples of some of the everyday issues we face when working with mutable data—examples that I've seen first-hand or fallen foul of myself. We don't tend to think of these as problems simply because working with mutable data is so common. So, instead, we often just accept it as the way things are.

THE UNREPEATABLE BUG

Say you're developing an application, and one of the test team members comes up to you with a bug report. You walk over to that person's desk and see the problem happening. Luckily, your tester is running in Visual Studio, so you can see the stack trace and so on. You look through the locals and application state and figure out why the bug is showing up. Unfortunately, you have no idea how the application got into this state in the first place; it's the result of calling several methods repeatedly over time with some shared mutable state stored in the middle. You go back to your machine and try to get the same error, but you can't reproduce it. You file a bug in your work-item tracking system and wait to see whether you can get lucky and figure out how the application got into this state.

MULTITHREADING PITFALLS

How about this one? You're developing an application and have decided to use multi-threading because it's cool. You recently heard about the Task Parallel Library in .NET, which makes writing multithreaded code a lot easier; you also saw that there's a `Parallel.ForEach()` method. Great! You've also read about locking, so you carefully put locks around the bits of the shared state of your application that are affected by the multithreaded code. You test it locally and even write some unit tests. Everything looks good! You release but, two weeks later, find a bug that you eventually trace to your multithreaded code. You don't know why it happened, though; it's caused by a race condition that occurs only under a specific load and a certain ordering of messages. Eventually, you revert your code to a single-threaded model.

ACCIDENTALLY SHARING STATE

Here's another one. You're working on a team and have designed a business object class, while your colleague has written code to operate on that object. You call their code, supplying an appropriate object, and then carry on. Sometime later, you notice a bug in your application: the state of the business object no longer looks as it did previously! It turns out that the code your colleague wrote modified a property on the object without you realizing it. You made that property public only so that you could change it; you didn't intend or expect other areas of code to modify it! You fix the problem by making an interface for the type that exposes the bits that are really public on the type and give that to consumers instead.

TESTING HIDDEN STATE

Maybe you're writing unit tests. You want to test a branch of a specific method on your class, but unfortunately, to do that, you first need to get the object into a particular state by calling other methods on the class. You mock out any dependencies required by these other methods and then try to assess whether your actual method under test worked as expected. However, you only then realize that the only way to do this is to access some private state of the class, which is not visible to your unit test. Your deadlines are fast approaching, so you simply change the accessibility of the private field to be public.

SUMMARIZING THE CHALLENGES OF MUTABILITY

All these problems are real issues that occur regularly and are nearly always due to mutability. They all boil down to a single truth: working with mutable data is hard. It's hard to reason about the lifetime of data, and changes of state can happen in ways that are hard to trace or predict, especially in larger and/or more complex systems.

The problem is often that we simply assume that mutability is a way of life, something we can't escape. So we look for other ways around these sorts of issues, including encapsulation, hacks, or one of the many design patterns out there, which add more code, effort, and complexity. It turns out that working with immutable data solves many of these problems in one fell swoop.

4.2.2   *Modeling with mutable and immutable data*

It's worth first comparing the basic ways we structure and design programs using mutable and immutable data. Working with mutable data structures in the object orientation world follows a relatively simple model: you create an object and then modify its state through operations on that object, as depicted in figure 4.3. What's tricky about this model of working is that it can be hard to reason about your code: calling a method such as `UpdateState()` will generally have no return value; the result of calling the method is a side effect that takes place internally on the object on some encapsulated state.

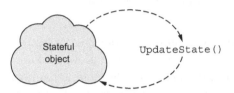

Figure 4.3   Modifying mutable state on an object by calling a method. Every call to `UpdateState()` modifies that single object over time.

Let's compare figure 4.3 with how this looks in the immutable world in figure 4.4. Here, you cannot modify any data. Instead, every time you want to apply an operation, you create a new copy of the data with any updates applied to that, which is then given back to the caller. That state then becomes the new, current state, which is passed on downstream.

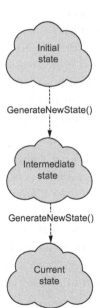

Figure 4.4   Generating new states on every operation with immutable data. Every call to `GenerateNewState()` creates a new object rather than modifying a single item.

> **Performance of immutable data**
>
> A common but nearly always unsubstantiated concern of immutable data is that it must be slow. After all, we're creating copies of data rather than making changes to a single version, right? My advice is, like any optimization problem, unless you can back up that concern with real evidence, don't worry about it. In my experience you simply won't notice any difference except for very specific use cases. Yes, it's more work to copy an object than to make an in-place update to it. However, unless you're in a tight loop performing millions of updates per second, the cost of doing so is negligible compared to, say, opening a database connection or deserializing some JSON data. Many languages (including F#) also have data structures designed to work with immutable data in a highly efficient manner, as well as some compiler tricks that help to keep garbage collection to a minimum.

4.2.3 Optimizing and opinionated languages

All languages are opinionated and optimized in some way. One of the things F# is optimized for is working with immutable data. While F# can (and does) work totally fine with mutable data, the syntax is more verbose than for immutable data. The inverse is true in many other languages. Here's a quick comparison of C# and F# for creating immutable and mutable values as well as assignment and comparison. First, the C# version, which, even from those coming from other languages, should be standard fare:

```
                                        ┌─ Declares an immutable value
const string name = "isaac";    ◁──┘   ┌─ Declares a mutable variable
var age = 42;                    ◁──────┘
age = 43;                        ◁──────── Performs an assignment
if (age == 43) { …              ◁──┐
                                    └─ Performs a comparison
```

Here's the F# version. Note the use of the <- operator, which is the mutate operator. This is F#'s equivalent of assignment in many other languages, which is normally an =:

```
                                    ┌─ Declares an immutable value
let name = "isaac"          ◁──┘   ┌─ Declares a mutable variable
let mutable age = 42        ◁──────┘
age <- 43                   ◁──────── Performs an assignment
if age = 43 then …          ◁──┐
                                └─ Performs a comparison
```

There are a couple of things to note here:

- F# optimizes for creating immutable data: it's less code to write than for a mutable variable, where you need an extra keyword. This is the opposite of C#.
- F# optimizes for working with immutable data: when it comes to equality comparison, the equals symbol = is used for, well, equality checks; a new operator <- is used for mutation/assignment. In C# (and many other languages), = is used for assignment, and == is used for equality comparison.

WORKING WITH IMMUTABLE DATA: A WORKED EXAMPLE

Let's take a relatively simple scenario that we'll try to model using both mutable and immutable data—write some code that can simulate the gas tank in a car:

- We would like a function called `drive`. It takes as an input the distance driven, which is a string of either far, medium, or near.
- The gas tank starts at 100.
- If driving far, reduce the amount of gas by half the amount of gas in the tank.
- If driving a medium distance, reduce the amount of gas in the tank by 10.
- Otherwise, reduce the amount of gas in the tank by 1.

Those who are more eagle-eyed may ask, "What if you enter another string for this exercise?" Ignore that for now, but later in this book, we'll look at several features in F# that will force us to deal with this.

DRIVING A MUTABLE CAR

Let's start with the mutable version. Create a new script and enter the code in the following listing.

Listing 4.6   Managing state with mutable variables

Creates a mutable variable
and sets its value to a float

```
let mutable gas = 100.0        ◁─┘
let drive distance =           ◁──     Creates a function that is
    if distance = "far" then gas <- gas / 2.0        dependent on the mutable state
    elif distance = "medium" then gas <- gas - 10.0      Mutates state
    else gas <- gas - 1.0      using the <-
                               operator
```

There are several interesting things to note about this listing:

- Look at the type signature of the `drive` function: string -> unit. It's "dishonest" in two ways:
  - It's dependent on two pieces of data, but only one is shown as an input. gas is implicitly utilized, but you can't see that from the type signature. This is similar to a method on a class that uses some encapsulated private state.
  - `drive` has no outputs. You call it, and it silently modifies the mutable gas variable; you can't know this from the type signature, which returns unit.
- Methods are nondeterministic. You can't know the behavior of a method without knowing the state. If you call `drive "far"` three times, the value of gas will change every time by a different amount, depending on the previous calls.
- You have no control over the ordering of method calls. If you switch the order of calls to `drive`, you'll get a different answer at the end.

You can test out the code by compiling it (remember: highlight the lines and press ALT + Enter [or Option + Enter on a Mac] or use the Send to FSI command) and then call the function with arbitrary arguments to check the mutable state:

```
drive "far"
drive "medium"       Repeatedly
drive "near"          modifies the state
gas                  Checks the current
                     the state
```

NOTE Note the last line of the previous snippet, which is just the word `gas`. Compiling that line will simply evaluate it and send the result to FSI, so you can easily check the state at any point in time. This is a really important lesson when working with scripts: don't think of them as linear, noninteractive programs. Think of them as living documents that you're building up piece by piece in which you can inspect data at any point in time: you can highlight `gas` at any point and execute that line to inspect its value.

DRIVING AN IMMUTABLE CAR

The following contains the equivalent example using immutable data.

Listing 4.7 Managing state with immutable values

```
let drive gas distance =                    Function is explicitly
    if distance = "far" then gas / 2.0      dependent on the state.
    elif distance = "medium" then gas - 10.0
    else gas - 1.0
                                            Stores the initial start state
let gas = 100.0                             Stores the result of each function
let firstState = drive gas "far"            call in a separate symbol
let secondState = drive firstState "medium"
let finalState = drive secondState "near"   Manually chains
                                            calls together
```

There are now a few changes to the code. The most important one is that there is no longer a mutable variable representing `gas`, but an initial state of `100` and then a set of immutable values threaded through each function call. There are several benefits to this:

- You can reason about behavior much more easily. This function is "honest" and easily understandable from the type signature: the function takes in `gas` and `distance` and returns the updated `gas`. Also, rather than hidden side effects on private fields, each method or function call can return a new version of the state that you can easily understand. This makes unit testing much easier, for example.

- Function calls are repeatable. You can call `drive 50 "far"` as many times as you want, and it will always give you the same result. This is because the only values that can affect the result are supplied as input arguments; there's no global state that's implicitly used—in other words, a pure function.

- The compiler can protect you from accidentally misordering function calls because each function call is explicitly dependent on the output of the previous call.

- You can also see the value of each intermediate step as you work up toward the final state.

> **Passing immutable state in F#**
>
> In the previous example, we manually stored the intermediate state and explicitly passed it to the next function call in the chain. That's not necessary in F#, and you'll see later on how F# has language syntax designed specifically to avoid having to do this.

EXERCISE 4.3

Spend some time experimenting with this code, calling the functions in different orders to appreciate the differences. Also, it's a good opportunity to apply some of the concepts we covered earlier in the chapter. Here's a quick exercise to test out some of those skills:

1 Instead of using a string to represent how far you've driven, use an integer.
2 Instead of far, check whether the distance is more than 50.
3 Instead of medium, check whether the distance is more than 25.
4 If the distance is > 0, reduce gas by 1.
5 If the distance is 0, make no change to the gas consumption. In other words, return the same state that was provided.

4.2.4   *Other benefits of immutable data*

Immutable data has a few other benefits that aren't necessarily obvious from the preceding example:

- When working with immutable data, encapsulation is no longer as important as with mutable data: since everything is read-only, you don't have to live in fear that some other part of code will pull the rug from underneath you and change the value of your precious data. At times, encapsulation is useful to have (e.g., as part of a public API), and F# has access modifiers such as public, private, and internal, but generally making your data read-only eliminates the need to hide data values.
- You don't need to worry about locks within a multithreaded environment. Because there's no shared mutable state, you never have to be concerned with race conditions. Every thread can access the same piece of data as often as it likes, as it can never change.

4.3   *Exercise Answers*

EXERCISE 4.1

Answers 1 and 3 are statements: they run some code and change some state somewhere but return nothing. The only way that they can affect the application is by modifying some state or calling external systems. It's impossible to know their output from the type signature since both return nothing (in some languages, this is known as void). Answers 2 and 4 are expressions: both take in some values and give back something in return.

EXERCISE 4.3

```
let drive gas distance =
    if distance > 50 then gas / 2.0
    elif distance > 25 then gas - 10.0
    elif distance > 0 then gas - 1.0
    else gas
```

Summary

- F# is optimized for working with expressions and immutable data rather than statements and mutable data.
- F# encourages but does not enforce the use of pure functions.
- F# has a value called `unit`, which represents a function that has no value for its inputs or outputs.
- Expressions and immutability are much safer ways of writing code, removing entire classes of bugs.
- Using immutability means that there's much less need to encapsulate your data.
- Immutability and expressions make it much easier to observe what is happening, especially in a chain of function calls.

Shaping data

Up until now, we've only dealt with primitive types, such as integers or strings, or built-in .NET types, such as System.Uri. Of course, F# needs a way to compose primitives together to make our own types: customers, orders, etc. F#'s type system has several ways to do this, and we'll cover most of them in this chapter.

5.1   Composing types in F#

F# has a few more options and capabilities than many (although not all) languages. F# runs on the .NET platform, which means that it has to be able to understand all of the core .NET types and capabilities. This book ignores *most* of those features—things like classes and enums—not because you can't use them (indeed, classes still do have an occasional part to play in certain edge cases in F#) but more because they are not typically required or used in everyday F#.

In this chapter, we will look at what are known as *product* types. These types let you compose other types together by "anding" them together: for example, a customer has a name *and* an address. Classes can be considered product types, so if you're coming from an object-oriented language, you'll most likely be quite used to this. F# has two ways to model product types: tuples and records. Later in this book, we'll also look at s*um* types, which provide the ability to say, "A customer can have an email address *or* a telephone number." Figure 5.1 shows an example of these two different modeling techniques side by side.

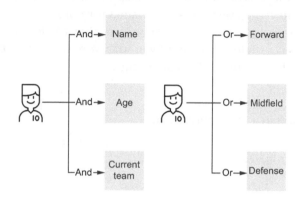

Figure 5.1   Illustrating product (AND) and sum (OR) types. A soccer player has a name, age, *and* a team, but their position on the field is either forward, midfield, *or* defense.

5.1.1   *Data and functions in F#*

One question that people often have when looking at F# types is "Where do we put our behaviors?" F# strongly encourages the separation of data and behavior from one another; in an object-orientated sense, this can be thought of as not having methods on classes but, instead, having data transfer objects (DTOs) and classes of static methods. You rarely have a type in F# with a method on it (although you can do this if required; they're called *members*), and it's extremely rare that it modifies its state in the same way a method on a class does.

In this chapter, we'll focus on how to store and access *data*, and in the next chapters, we'll focus on the behavior side of things.

5.2   *Tuples*

Tuples are the quickest way to compose multiple fields together in F#. They're lightweight, easy to create, and quick to use. Tuples are a great solution for when you have some code and want to, for example, return more than one piece of data back to the caller or simply group some data within your code but don't want to pay the cost of creating a specific class or type just for this one situation.

5.2.1 *Tuple basics*

Here's an example of how to capture a person's first name and last name as a tuple:

```
let name = "isaac", "abraham"        ⟵┐ Constructs a tuple
let firstName, secondName = name     ⟵   formed of two strings
                                         Deconstructs a tuple back
                                         into its constituent parts
```

The first line shows how to bind multiple values into a single symbol—in this case, name; the second line shows how to *deconstruct* a tuple back out into multiple values again. Notice that when deconstructing, we must assign names for both symbols of the two elements—in this case, firstName and secondName. Note that F# doesn't allow you to specify names for fields in a tuple, so it's up to you what you call them; F# only knows that this tuple has two values, both of which are strings.

5.2.2 *More on tuples*

Let's look at some parts of tuples in a little more detail.

TYPE SIGNATURES

Tuples have a type signature as follows:

```
Type1 * Type2 * … TypeN
```

The type signature for name in the previous code snippet would be string * string. You can have tuples of any length; they aren't restricted to only two items. So, a tuple that stores first name, last name, age, and town might have a type signature of string * string * int * string. VS Code will automatically show you the type signature of a tuple, as shown in figure 5.2.

```
string * string * int * string
let name = "isaac", "abraham", 42, "london"
```

Figure 5.2 Creating a tuple of four items with a type annotation. The types relate to each element of the tuple in order.

WILDCARDS

If there are elements of a tuple that you're not interested in, you can discard them while deconstructing a tuple by assigning those parts the underscore symbol:

```
let nameAndAge = "Jane", "Smith", 25    ⟵┐ Creates a tuple
let forename, surname, _ = nameAndAge   ⟵   of three items
                                            Discards the third element of
                                            the tuple when deconstructing
```

This is especially useful when you want to extract only certain sections of a tuple, and it's better than assigning it to arbitrary values such as x or y. The underscore is a specific symbol in F# that tells the type system (and the developer) that you explicitly don't want to use this value.

TYPE INFERENCE

We've already seen how F# will infer the structure of a tuple when binding to a symbol. However, F# can do much more; for example, it can infer tuples as both inputs and outputs of functions. In the following listing, a function takes in a tuple of someone's name, deconstructs it, and returns just their surname and a title.

> **Listing 5.1   Type inference of a function taking a tuple as input**

```
let makeDoctor name =                    Deconstructs
    let _, sname = name        <──────   the tuple
    "Dr", sname        <──────┐
                              └──  Returns a new tuple
```

It's worth looking at the type signature of this function in a little bit of detail as it's a good example of a few type inference features that we discussed in the previous chapter:

```
'a * 'b -> string * 'b
```

This type signature shows that the type inference has correctly determined that both the input and output are tuples of two elements. However, the compiler has also automatically *generalized* this function for us: since we never actually do anything with the first element and merely return the second one, the compiler essentially says: "Well, I know for sure that name is a tuple of two items, but I haven't seen any evidence of what types they are. I'll make this function generic so the developer can pass in anything for them." Obviously, from a business point of view, we might want to specify that the incoming tuple must be string * string, so once again, we could provide a type annotation:

```
let makeDoctor (name:string * string) =
```

The compiler can now deduce the output to also be string * string.

It's also important to note the use of parentheses here. If you don't use them, the compiler will think that the type annotation refers to the *return type* of the function itself:

```
let makeDoctor name : string * string =     <──┐  Input of name whose type is inferred.
let makeDoctor (name : string * string) =   <──┐  The return type is string * string.
```

Input of name whose type is string * string. The return type is inferred.

INLINE DECONSTRUCTION

You can also deconstruct a tuple that's supplied to a function inline. Here's the same example as listing 5.1, except this time we unwrap, or deconstruct, the tuple within the function declaration:

```
let makeDoctor (_, sname) =     <──┐  Deconstructs the tuple inline
    "Dr", sname                      of the function argument
```

NESTING

You can also nest, or group, tuples together. The preceding three-element examples treated all items as *siblings*, but you can change that by creating a nested tuple within a larger tuple by grouping the inner part with parentheses:

```
let nameAndAge = ("Joe", "Bloggs"), 28          ⟵   Creates a nested tuple
let name, age = nameAndAge                      ⟵   Deconstructs the tuple
let (forename, surname), theAge = nameAndAge    ⟵   Deconstructs the tuple
                                                    and the nested element
                                                    simultaneously
```

EXERCISE 5.1

1. Create a function, `buildPerson`, that takes in three individual values as input arguments: `forename`, `surname`, and `age`. As an output, return just the forename and surname elements as a tuple.
2. Now, ensure that all the inputs are annotated as strings or ints so that the signature is no longer generalized. What signature does the function have?
3. Use a wildcard on the unused age argument.
4. Now remove the wildcard again and return a two-part nested tuple. The first part should contain the forename/surname. The second part should contain the age and a string that is either a "child" if the age is less than 18 or "adult" otherwise.
5. Call this function within your script file and experiment with assigning the result to a single value or a deconstructed tuple.

TUPLE AND VALUE TUPLE

By default, F# tuples compile into a .NET type called `System.Tuple`. These values are known as *reference types*: they are passed by reference, and their values are stored on the heap and thus are subject to garbage collection.

When C# gained language-level support for tuples some years later, rather than use this same type, the C# team opted to create an alternative known as the `ValueTuple`. Value tuples are value types, passed by *value*, and are generally stored on the stack and thus not subject to garbage collection.

You can create or consume value tuples in F# by preceding type annotations with the keyword `struct`. Struct annotations are somewhat viral in that you need to use them when deconstructing as well as constructing them:

```
let makeDoctor (name : struct (string * string)) =     ⟵   Struct keyword
    let struct(_, sname) = name        ⟵   Struct keyword       on tuple type
    struct ("Dr", sname)               ⟵   on tuple             annotation
                                           deconstruction
                   Struct keyword on
                   tuple construction
```

Which type should you favor? There are performance implications for both reference and value tuples: reference tuples need to pay the cost of garbage collection, while value tuples pay the cost of copying a tuple whenever you need to pass it from one function to another. Both of them work within C#, so you don't need to worry about interoperability.

My advice is to stick to reference tuples in F# unless you have a specific performance requirement to use a `ValueTuple` based on evidence that proves it's worth the cost of the extra keywords and boilerplate. I've probably felt the need to try to use it perhaps just once or twice since they came out—that is, very rarely indeed. Table 5.1 illustrates some of the differences between the two kinds of tuples as a useful reference.

Table 5.1 Comparing `System.Tuple` and `System.ValueTuple`

	`System.Tuple`	`System.ValueTuple`
Pass by	Reference	Value
F# support	Default option	Needs extra struct keyword
C# support	Not normally used	Default option
Performance costs	Garbage collection allocation	Copying when passed from function to function, especially if tuples have many fields

OUT PARAMETERS IN F#

C# contains a feature known as *out parameters*. I won't bother explaining them in detail because they're a bad compromise that was made in the early days of .NET (before tuples in C# were a thing). Luckily, F# silently turns these into tuples for us: any time you see a method in .NET called `TryParse`, which parses a string into some type (these exist on `Int32`, `DateTime`, etc.), F# renders them as a tuple result for us:

```
                                                    Uses the in-built
                                            DateTime.TryParse method in F#
open System
let parsed, theDate = DateTime.TryParse "03 Dec 2020"    ◄
if parsed then printfn $"Day of week is {theDate.DayOfWeek}!"   ◄

                                                    Consumes the tuple to
                                                    print out the date
```

A tuple of a Boolean and the parsed `DateTime` is returned. The first element represents whether the parsing operation was successful (if it's false, the second element will be `DateTime.Min`).

5.2.3 Costs and benefits of tuples

Tuples are a simple way to combine values that can be passed from one section of code to another. They're quick to construct and, due to their simple nature, quick to learn how to use. However, there are some shortcomings to them that you should be aware of.

First, you can't assign names to tuple elements. This makes it difficult to provide semantic information as to what information a tuple represents. For example, a tuple of `string * string` could store a first name and a last name but equally could store a town and a country. There's no way to know from a type system point of view. For this reason, try to avoid long-lived tuples that store multiple values of the same type or of basic types such as ints or strings unless it's particularly obvious from either the symbol or function name what the contents of the tuple are, such as this example:

```
let a, b = data                              ←┘  Poor naming
let a, b = bankDetails                              ←┘  Improved naming
let sortCode, accountNumber = sortCodeAndAccountNumber   ←┘  Better naming
```

Second, they offer only one way to "get at" the fields in them: deconstruction. For more complex types with multiple fields, this can result in lots of boilerplate code to access a single field in a tuple or to replace a value in a tuple with a new value. Lastly, their type signatures can appear quite complex for anything more than just two or three elements.

They are excellent for simple values (two or three elements at the most) that are relatively short-lived (e.g., within a function or two) and for simple exploration; there's nothing stopping you from using them for more complex types but be aware of the costs you'll have to pay if you do.

5.3   Records

Records are the second way to compose multiple values together but provide a more structured way to do so than Tuples, fixing their limitations along the way. Like tuples, records are a simple mechanism to safely compose multiple values in a single object and pass them around your application. Unlike tuples, however, records allow you to specify names for each value, known as *fields*.

> **NOTE** Although not commonly required, you can also define behaviors on records using members such as properties and methods. This isn't possible with tuples.

5.3.1   Defining, creating, and consuming records

Unlike tuples, you need to first define a record before you can use it. Let's define a record that can capture your first and last name as well as your age:

```
                              | Name the type
type Person =      ←┐
    {                 └── Starts declaring fields
                ←┘
        FirstName : string          Field
        LastName : string           definitions
        Age : int
    }        ←┐
               └── Ends field
                   declarations
```

> ## Declaring records with other styles
>
> F# is quite flexible on how you declare and define records; for example, you can put the first field on the same line as the opening curly and the last field on the same line as the closing curly. You just need to ensure that all fields start on the same column.
>
> You can also define the record on a single line (useful for simple records) by using a semicolon as a separator (e.g., type `Address = { Line1 : string; Line2 : string }`).
>
> While taking up the most whitespace, this style makes it easier to add or remove fields or merge in code from branches that modify the record.

Now, let's see how you create an *instance* of that record:

```
                                    │ Symbol binding
                                    │
let isaac =         ←───┐
    {               ←───┘└─│ Starts record creation
        FirstName = "Isaac"    ←─┐
        LastName = "Abraham"     │ Field
        Age = 42                 │ assignments
    }   ←───┐
            │ Ends record
            │ creation
```

Finally, how do you consume one of these? Using standard dot member notation:

```
let fullName = $"{isaac.FirstName} {isaac.LastName}"
```

Bear in mind, records and tuples can be composed with each other without a problem. Like we did with nested tuple before, you can nest a record inside another record or make a tuple of records or a record with a tuple as a field. The following listing shows how we might define a person, consisting of their first and last name and address.

Listing 5.2   Constructing a nested record in F#

```
type Address =      ←───┐ Defines an
    {                    │ Address type
        Line1 : string
        Line2 : string
        Town : string
        Country : string
    }

type Person =                     ┌ Defines Name
    {                             │ as a tuple of
        Name : string * string  ←─┘ two strings
        Address : Address   ←───┐ References the
    }                            │ Address type
                                 │ as a field
```

> **Mutually recursive records**
>
> In listing 5.2, we had to define the `Address` type *before* the `Person` type so that the `Person` type could make use of the `Address`. There is a feature in F# called *mutually recursive records*, which allows you, in limited circumstances, to have a type reference another type *before* defining it. This also means you can set up infinite cycles of records. Indeed, a record can have a field on it of its own type; this is sometimes useful for defining certain types of data structures, such as trees. I'm mentioning this so that you're aware that there is an escape hatch if you really need it, but it's something that you shouldn't require often.

F# has one constraint on records that may appear to be a huge limitation at first glance: you must set all fields on a record when creating them. If you try to create an instance of the `Person` type defined in listing 5.2 and forget to assign a value to any of the fields, you'll receive a compiler error (not a warning!), as shown in figure 5.3.

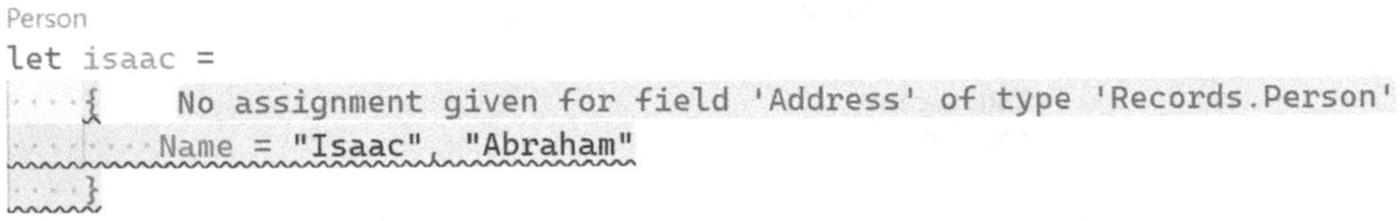

```
Person
let isaac =
    {       No assignment given for field 'Address' of type 'Records.Person'
        Name = "Isaac", "Abraham"
    }
```

Figure 5.3   A compiler error for a missing field on a record

One nice thing about having to set all fields of a record is that when you decide to add a new field to an existing record, the compiler will immediately notify you about every location in your codebase where you create an instance of that record. This means you can never accidentally create a record with half of it uninitialized.

You might wonder how you can deal with cases that only have some values of a record upfront. Or perhaps you want to use only some of the fields in the record some of the time and other times use all of them. In many languages, it's common to reuse a class like this for multiple purposes by omitting to set some fields under certain circumstances and then testing later on which version it is based on which fields are null and which ones aren't. In F#, records are so cheap to define and work that the cost of having different records for different purposes, even if they look similar, is so low that it nearly always pays to "do the right thing" and define different types for different use cases. Plus, you can factor out the parts of multiple records that are truly common, as we did in listing 5.2 with the `Address`.

This is again part of F# trying to guide you down the road of being explicit about this sort of thing and ultimately encoding these sorts of business rules or situations within the type system. We'll cover the most common solution to these questions (i.e., *discriminated unions*) in a later chapter. However, the main point is that this behavior may be different than what you're used to with classes in many languages, but it brings with it several benefits that are not immediately apparent.

EXERCISE 5.2

Repeat the steps in exercise 5.1, but instead of returning data as tuples, create a record to return the data.

5.3.2 More on records

Now that you've seen how they work with some simple examples, this section expands to illustrate some further features that records offer that make them even more powerful to work with.

TYPE INFERENCE

F# records are, naturally, statically typed. You can't accidentally access a field that doesn't exist or assign the wrong type of data to a field. They also support type inference. If you look back at figure 5.3, you'll see the code lens clearly says "Person" above the `let` keyword. The compiler infers the type based on the fields assigned in a record. This also applies within a function, both for inputs and outputs. The following listing shows a function that takes in an `Address`, checks the `Country`, and then returns a `Person`. Notice that no type annotations are required.

Listing 5.3   Using type inference for records within a function

```
let generatePerson theAddress =                    ◁──────────    Function with input
    if theAddress.Country = "UK" then     ◁─────               of type Address
        {                                 ◁─────
            Name = "Isaac", "Abraham"                 Accesses the
            Address = theAddress                      Country field on
        }                                             the Address
    else
        {                                    Returns a value
            Name = "John", "Doe"             of type Person
            Address = theAddress
        }
```

The compiler is able to correctly infer these types based on their usage—by assignment of and/or accessing fields on the record or by supplying to another function that takes a certain type as input. If the compiler can't figure it out, it'll tell you—for example, if you use fields from two different records when defining a value. Rest assured: it's impossible to create half a type or similar. The only catch is that if you have two records with exactly the same fields, the compiler will infer the most recently defined type. In any case, you can always explicitly supply a type annotation to tell the compiler what type you're trying to create. This also has the added benefit of getting type-ahead suggestions and/or refactoring support immediately. The following listing provides two alternate ways of type annotating a record.

Listing 5.4   Using explicit type annotations when creating a record value

```
let isaac : Person =                    ◄─────────┐   Annotates the record
    {                                              │   via the right-hand
        Name = "Isaac", "Abraham"                  │   side of the equals
        Address = theAddress
    }

let isaacTwo =
    {                                                        Annotates the
        Person.Name = "Isaac", "Abraham"        ◄────┤       record when
        Address = theAddress                                 assigning a field
    }
```

My advice is to not bother with annotations unless you need to.

> **NOTE** You'll be surprised at just how often the compiler is able to infer the types for you. Even in relatively large codebases I've worked on, I've very rarely needed to explicitly annotate records.

COPY AND UPDATE

Like regular value bindings, fields on F# records are immutable by default. If you try to modify a value using the mutate operator (`<-`), you'll get a compiler error. Of course, in the real world, we often need to model the case where a value changes its state over time. How can you do this without mutating fields on a record? F#'s answer to this is to provide what is known as *copy-and-update* syntax. Let's see how to change the `Country` of an existing `Address`.

Listing 5.5   Using copy-and-update syntax to clone a record

```
let theAddress =             ◄─────────┐   Defines an
    {                                   │   address
        Line1 = "1st Street"
        Line2 = "Apt. 1"
        Town = "London"          ┌──────  The copied
        Country = "UK"           │        record
    }
let addressInDE =            ◄────┤       Starts a copy-and-update
    {                                      operation
        theAddress with          ◄────
            Town = "Berlin"            ┌──  Supplies modifications
            Country = "DE"            │     to the source record
    }
```

The `theAddress with` syntax is used to tell the compiler that we want to use `theAddress` as the source of the copy operation; after this, every update that we want to apply is written underneath, which is then applied as a copy into a new symbol (in this case, `addressInDE`). This gives you the best of both worlds: On the one hand, you still get the capability of what appears to be mutation through a simple and readable syntax. On the other hand, you gain the safety of immutability: you can safely supply a record value to another part of your codebase without fear that someone will modify it somehow. And more than that, you don't have to worry about tracking the state of this value ever again: nothing can change it, and each mutation is explicitly tracked by creating a new object.

Real mutation

If you absolutely must—and this should be the exception to the rule— you can override immutable behavior on a field-by-field basis by adding the `mutable` modifier. You might want to do this if you have a record that will be used in a tight loop, mutating itself thousands of times a second, for example. But I recommend that the default be to use immutable data structures initially, test performance, and *only if you see an issue*, reconfigure the definition of the record. Certainly, in all the applications I've written, this has never been an issue for me. Bottlenecks are far more likely to occur with other parts of your application (e.g., a database query).

EQUALITY CHECKING

Both records and tuples support *structural equality* by default. This means that when you compare two different values of the same type, they are considered equal if the data they both store is the same. This is different from the default behavior in .NET, in which reference equality is the default—that is, if two values reference the same underlying memory space. Consider the following listing.

Listing 5.6   Using explicit type annotations when creating a record value

```
let isaac =
    {
        Name = "Isaac", "Abraham"
        Address = theAddress
    }
let isaacTwo =
    {
        Name = "Isaac", "Abraham"
        Address = theAddress
    }
```

Creating a second record that has the same contents as the first round

Annotates the record when assigning a field

If you were to compare `isaac` and `isaacTwo` from listing 5.6, .NET would consider them to be equal:

```
let areTheyTheSame = (isaac = isaacTwo) // true
```

Equality checking for records and tuples will navigate the entire graph of fields, so nested records, tuples, etc. will all get checked for free. Figure 5.4 illustrates checking two `Person` records, each with the same `Name` but a slightly different `Address`. F# will diligently follow the graph of the entire record, checking every field against one another until it finds a difference between them.

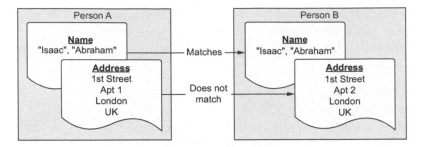

Figure 5.4   F# will perform a deep structural equality check on records. If all fields match, the two records are equal.

If you're coming from a C# background and use classes a lot, you'll never have to use a code-generation or IDE tool such as Resharper to generate equality for you again because it's built into F#!

> **Turning off structural equality**
>
> Typically, when developing applications, structural equality is exactly what you want. But sometimes, you don't want (or need) to compare an entire object graph for equality checks. F# allows you to disable it by decorating a record with the [<NoEquality>] and [<NoComparison>] attributes. You can also set your own custom equality comparison by using the [<CustomEquality>] and [<CustomComparison>] attributes. There are a few hoops to jump through to make it happen, and it's beyond the scope of this book to document it, but it's good to know that there is an escape hatch if needed.

5.3.3   *Records and .NET*

For the .NET developers out there, F# records compile down to .NET classes. This means that you'll have the standard methods present on all .NET objects, such as `ToString()` and `GetHashCode()`. Record fields are represented as `Get`-only properties, while a constructor is defined that requires each field as a mandatory argument. To conduct the equality checks, a number of interfaces, such as `IEquatable` and `IComparable`, are automatically implemented for you. In other words, you can quite happily consume and create instances of F# records from C#.

C# records, which are a relatively new addition to the language, are not really the same as F# records (even though they share a common name). For example, F# records were included in the initial release of F# (in the mid-2000s) and, as such, are the de-facto way of modeling structured data, whereas in C# classes are still (and probably always will be) the most popular choice for C# developers. C# records are also much closer to classes, supporting features such as inheritance, with multiple ways to define and initialize them, and without guaranteed immutability (at least, at the time of writing). One of the strengths of F# records is that 95% of the time you will only need the features I've outlined here, making them a very simple yet powerful language feature.

Lastly, F# records are *reference types*. However, if you wish to declare them as value types (and therefore on the stack, with pass-by-value semantics), simply add the [<Struct>] attribute onto the record:

```
[<Struct>]
type Address =
    {
        Line1 : string
        ...
    }
```

That's it! The record will now be created as a value type. As with tuples, be careful before you decide to move to a value-type records. Performance test thoroughly first.

EXERCISE 5.3

Imagine we have been asked to develop a system to capture details on our customers and suppliers. Both customers and suppliers have names and addresses, but customers need to store a credit rating, which is an integer. Meanwhile, a supplier needs to record the outstanding balance we owe them and the due date for the next payment. Can you model this? Have a try and see what you come up with and then compare your work to the following listing.

Listing 5.7 Modeling similar types through composition

```
type Address = { Street : string; Country : string }     Reusable and common
type Name = { Forename : string; Surname : string }      parts of our domain,
                                                         defined as dedicated
type Customer =                                          records
    {
         Name : Name                    Uses
         Address : Address              common
         CreditRating : int      <—    types to
    }                                   quickly
                               Adds fields onto construct
type Supplier =                a record that  a record
    {                          are unique to
         Name : Name           that model
         Address : Address
         Balance : decimal      <—
         NextDueDate : System.DateTime
    }
```

The main thing to note here is that I've resisted the temptation to try to combine the notion of Customer and Supplier into a single record to keep things simple; instead, I've taken the time to identify the common parts of our domain that I've factored out. An alternative implementation that tried to merge it all into one record might look like this:

```
type Person =
    {
        Forename : string
        Surname : string
        Street : string
        Country : string
        CreditRating : int
        Balance : decimal
        NextDueDate : System.DateTime
        IsCustomer : bool
    }
```

This approach has many problems: you can't easily see what the data stored here is for (`Customer`? `Supplier`? Both?), and it's difficult to see the forest for the trees. You have to look at all the fields to really "grok" what's being stored here. Even worse, we have an extra field, `IsCustomer`, which would tell the system which kind of `Person` we're dealing with. This sort of code is heading for trouble. Don't do it!

Instead, I've made dedicated types for `Customer` and `Supplier` and then factored out the common `Name` and `Address` into dedicated types. Not only does this save typing, but it's also much quicker and easier for someone looking at the `Customer` or `Supplier` records to understand what they're composed of. You could even go further if you wanted. For example, you could make a record (or perhaps a tuple) for `Name` and `Address` together if you felt that this was a common pattern in your domain and worth showing that `Name` and `Address` always "travel together." Records are cheap, and the semantic value that they bring helps immeasurably.

5.4   *Anonymous records*

A relatively recent addition to F# is *anonymous* records. An anonymous record looks very similar to a record as just explained, except it doesn't require a formal definition first. Instead, you can define it as needed. The only syntactical difference from "proper" records is that you construct them with vertical bars:

```
let company =
    {|                          ◀── Defines an anonymous
                                     record value
        Name = "My Company Inc."  ◀─┐ Field
        Town = "The Town"          │ definitions
        Country = "UK"             ┘
        TaxNumber = 123456
    |}
```

This type has no formal name; it's defined simply based on the fields it contains. If you look at the code lens for a definition such as the previous one, you'll see that instead of, for example, `Person`, it shows the name and type of each field.

5.4.1 Anonymous record tricks

Anonymous records also have some unique features that standard records don't. One is that copy-and-update syntax allows you to not only update existing fields but also add new fields simultaneously:

```
let companyWithBankDetails =
    {|
        company with
            AccountNumber = 123
            SortCode = 456
    |}
```

Anonymous records can also be returned from functions, and type inference will work correctly for them, too. However, there's no such thing as a free lunch, and anonymous records have several shortcomings:

- The compiler doesn't support type inference when they are used as inputs to functions.
- You can't place attributes on them.
- You can't pattern-match on them. We've not seen pattern matching yet, but it's a core part of program flow in F#, and anonymous records don't play especially well with it.

Even so, anonymous records have some very good use cases:

- *Exploration and scripts*—If you're testing out some code and trying out a new way of modeling, rather than create a full record, you can use an anonymous record to see whether it fits nicely with your existing code. If it works out, consider promoting it to a full record.
- *Replacing tuples*—If you want to move from tuples but aren't sure if it's worth moving over to records, anonymous records are a nice halfway house: you can create them inline, just like tuples, but they allow you to dot into them and have proper named fields, just like records.
- *Nested types*—If you have a record inside another record, you can define the nested record inline. Compare listings 5.2 and 5.8; in the latter, you don't need to define a type for the `Address` explicitly first; it's simply declared as part of the `Person` type.

Listing 5.8 Nesting anonymous records inside a full record

```
type Person =           ◄─────── Normal record definition
    {
        Name: string * string
        Address :                ◄──────  Defines the
            {|                            address
                Line1: string            inline
                Line2: string
                Town: string
```

```
        Country: string
    |}
}
```

This is very useful for one-off types, but if you find yourself defining the nested anonymous record again and again, you should factor it out into a full record.

- *Serialization*—Anonymous records are a great fit for serialization and deserialization to, for example, JSON. Instead of decorating your types with custom attributes for your serialization framework, you can map your domain types into a set of anonymous records that maps 1:1 to the target JSON; serialization then becomes a trivial matter.

5.5 *Tuples or records*

Let's finish with a quick wrap-up of when and where to use tuples or records. The short answer is as follows:

- Use tuples for very simple groupings of data that are typically short-lived—perhaps within the implementation of a function rather than exposed as part of an API.
- Use records for more complex types that require formal definition or for a public API definition.
- Use anonymous records when you feel that tuples aren't sufficient for your needs but also feel that defining a record would be overkill. They're designed in such a way that promoting them to full records is relatively easy. They're also very useful for working with over-the-wire serialization structures, in which creating full records might be overkill.

Table 5.2 outlines some of the key differences and similarities.

Table 5.2   Distinguishing between tuples, records, and anonymous records

	Tuples	Records	Anonymous records
Best for?	Short-lived, simple values	Everyday data modeling	Prototyping, serialization, nested types
Weaknesses?	Fields have no names	Formal construction	Limited type inference; no pattern matching
Structural equality?	Yes	Yes	Yes
Immutability?	Yes	Yes, with optional mutability at field level.	Yes
C# Interop?	Yes	Yes	Limited
Struct support?	`struct` keyword	`[<Struct>]` attribute	`struct` keyword
Accessing fields	Destructuring only	Dot-notation	Dot-notation
Copy-and-update?	No, manually destructure and recreate	Yes, `with` keyword.	Yes, and can add new fields at the same time!

5.6   *Exercise answers*

EXERCISE 5.1

```
let buildPerson (forename:string) (surname:string) (age:int) =
    let description = if age < 18 then "child" else "adult"
    (forename, surname), (age, description)

let person = buildPerson "Isaac" "Abraham" 42
let nameDetails, ageDetails = buildPerson "Isaac" "Abraham" 42
let (fname, sname), (age, description) = buildPerson "Isaac" "Abraham" 42
```

EXERCISE 5.2

```
type Person = {
    Forename: string
    Surname: string
    Age: int
    Description: string
}

let buildPersonRecord (forename: string) (surname: string) (age: int) =
    let description = if age < 18 then "child" else "adult"

    {
        Forename = forename
        Surname = surname
        Age = age
        Description = description
    }
```

Summary

- F# typically favors a clear separation of data and behavior.
- F# supports product (Name AND Address) and sum types (Red OR Yellow).
- There are three main ways to create product types in F#: tuples, records, and anonymous records.
- All three product types support immutability by default.
- You can use copy-and-update syntax to safely simulate mutability.
- Records allow you to turn off immutability at a field-by-field level if required.
- Tuples are a simple way to start with, but they have several limitations.
- Records are the most common way of modeling data in F# and, despite their simplicity, are very powerful.
- Anonymous records are useful for exploration and can act as a halfway house between tuples and records.

Functions and modules

This chapter covers

- Different ways of declaring functions in F#
- Chaining functions together
- Making flexible functions
- Organizing code
- Moving from scripts to applications

We're on chapter 6 of a book on a programming language that's primarily functional in nature, and yet only now are we looking into functions! In this chapter, we'll learn more about how functions work in F#, and I'll be throwing a couple of language features and concepts at you that you might not have seen before in other languages, so strap in!

6.1 Functions

Much of what you've seen in this book has glossed over function arguments, so this section is designed to clarify it for you. There's a little reference material–style content here, but it's backed by exercises, so you'll get some hands-on experience, too.

6.1.1 The truth behind F# functions

In most mainstream programming languages such as Java, JavaScript, or C#, we consider arguments to a method as a *list* of inputs (which might be empty) with either one or no return value (indicated by `void`). In F#, things are a little different: every function in F# *always has only one input and one output.* How can this be true when the F# function in listing 6.1 appears to have two arguments (x and y)?

Listing 6.1   Example of method and functions calls in different languages

```
void Foo (int x, int y) { … }          ←      Declares a
let foo (x:int) (y:int) : unit = …     ←      method in C#

                                               An equivalent function
                                               declaration in F#
```

All F# functions obey several simple rules:

- Any function that requires no specific input takes in the unit `()` value.
- Any function that has no specific output returns the unit `()` value.
- Any function that appears to have multiple inputs (as x and y in listing 6.1) is actually something different: it's a function that takes a single argument and returns a new function that takes in the remaining arguments.

In listing 6.1, it's a function that takes in just x, and itself returns a function that takes in just y and returns `unit`. It doesn't look like that from the syntax, but look at a function like in the following listing.

Listing 6.2   Calling an F# function

```
let add (firstNumber:int) (secondNumber:int) =     ←    Creates a function
    firstNumber + secondNumber
let addFive = add 5        ←    Calls add with just the first argument
let fifteen = addFive 10   ←    to get back a new int -> int function

                                Calls addFive with the remaining argument
```

What's happened here? With a function defined like `add`, when you call it with just the first argument (`firstNumber`), F# realizes this and gives us back a new function that requires the remaining arguments (in our case, `secondNumber`). Indeed, if you look at the signature of the three values in VSCode yourself, you'll see the following:

- Signature of `add`: int -> int -> int (firstNumber -> secondNumber -> return value)
- Signature of `addFive`: int -> int (secondNumber -> return value)
- Signature of `fifteen`: int (return value)

The important bit is the `->`, which indicates a function. You can achieve this sort of behavior, known as *currying*, in most languages by hand, but it requires a lot of boilerplate and often complicated syntax. In F#, you get it for free. Figure 6.1 visually illustrates the

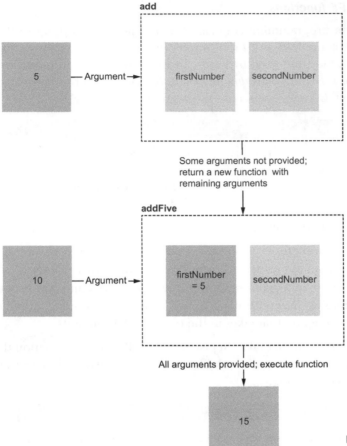

Figure 6.1   Calling an F# function in two stages

code in listing 6.2. Of course, you don't have to call each argument one by one; it's perfectly acceptable to call `add` with both values at once (e.g. `add 5 10`); F# will take care of everything for you.

EXERCISE 6.1

Before we go further, I would advise you to open up VS Code if you haven't already and experiment with the following exercises:

1. Using the function `add` defined in listing 6.2, create a function `addTen`, and test that this new function works as expected.
2. Create a function `multiply` that works in a similar fashion to `add`.
3. Create a function, `addTenAndDouble`, that takes in a single number. It should add 10 to it before and then double the answer.
4. Create a dedicated `timesTwo` function based on `multiply` and use that in the `addTenAndDouble` function.

There are several benefits of working with functions that support this kind of one-at-a-time processing. Let's look at a few of them now.

6.1.2   Partially applying functions

Partially applying functions is a way of describing fixing several of the arguments to specific values before calling the returned function multiple times with different arguments. For example, let's say you had a class that knew how to send emails to a customer; it can be parameterized by the email type (welcome letter, payment overdue, etc.) and the customer to whom it is being sent. Depending on how you're working with this, in the object-oriented (OO) world you might elect to design a class as follows:

```
class EmailSender {
    public EmailSender(string customerAddress)...        ⟵┘ Constructor
    public void SendEmail(LetterType letterType)...      ⟵┐ Public method
}
```

Notice that the SendEmail method doesn't require the email address each time because you supplied it via the constructor: you only need to supply the type of letter you want to send. You can think of each email sender object as being constrained to a specific customer. A curried function allows you to do this at the function level rather than at the object level:

```
let sendEmail customerAddress letterType = ....          Calling sendEmail with only
let sendEmailToFred = sendEmail "fred@email.com"     ⟵┘  the customerAddress supplied
sendEmailToFred LetterType.Welcome                   │   Calling the partially applied function
sendEmailToFred LetterType.PaymentOverdue            │   with the letterType argument
```

F# allows you to have as many curried arguments as you like, and you can fill in more than one at a single call site:

```
let sendEmail sender letterType emailAddress postDate = …
let sendOfficeWelcome = sendEmail "office@firm.com" LetterType.Welcome
sendOfficeWelcome "fred@email.com" System.DateTime.UtcNow
sendOfficeWelcome "joanne@email.com" (System.DateTime.UtcNow.AddDays 1.)
```

6.1.3   Pipelines

One of the nicest things that curried functions really enable is a feature called *pipelines*. It's designed to make it easy to chain functions together in a pipeline of operations, as shown in figure 6.2.

In most languages, when you're faced with a pattern like this, one option is to manually thread data from one function into another. This is a little verbose and harms

Figure 6.2   An example pipeline of functions

readability: you have temporary placeholder symbols (or a mutable variable) that act as a way to pass data from one function to another (this is similar to what we did in the earlier car gas exercise).

Listing 6.3 Manually threading values in a chain of functions

```
let add a b = a + b          ⟵┐ Defines two functions
let multiply a b = a * b

let firstValue = add 5 10
let secondValue = add firstValue 7       Manually threads values
let finalValue = multiply secondValue 2  through three function calls
```

Alternatively, you can chain functions together directly using parentheses:

```
let finalValueChained = multiply (add (add 5 10) 7) 2
```

The problem with this is that you have to invert the flow so that the left-most function in the diagram ends up as the right-most function in code and works backward. If you compare this to figure 6.2, you'll see that the code is read in the exact opposite of the diagram.

Luckily, F# has a special operator called the forward pipe, which is a simple yet powerful feature. It looks like this: `arg |> function`. That doesn't look like much, so let's explain it another way: take the last argument to a function and flip it over to the left-hand side of the pipe. In other words, given a function called `addFive`, instead of calling it as `addFive 10`, you can call `10 |> addFive`. The result is the same; it's simply another way of expressing the same code. If you have multiple arguments, you can use the pipeline to flip the last argument over, so `add 5 10` can become `10 |> add 5`.

> **NOTE** Some languages have a similar concept to the pipeline, but most mainstream languages don't, mostly because they don't support currying. At the time of writing, there are ongoing open issues in languages such as JavaScript and C# to try to find a good way to incorporate it into those languages.

The beauty of this is that so long as the *output* of one function matches the *input* of the next one, any function can be chained with another one. They don't have to be explicitly designed to work together, and you don't have to declare them with a special syntax (as is required with, for example, C# extension methods). The following listing shows the same code as listing 6.3 but uses pipelines. As you can see, you can use pipelines on a single or multiple lines.

Listing 6.4 Chaining function calls using the pipeline operator

```
let pipelineSingleLine = 10 |> add 5 |> add 7 |> multiply 2   ⟵┐ A pipeline
                                                                on a single
let pipelineMultiline =          ⟵┐ A multiline                line
    10                             pipeline
    |> add 5
```

```
|> add 7
|> multiply 2
```

Notice how this pipeline reads virtually identically to figure 6.2. You'll find that the pipeline is extremely useful for composing code into a human-readable *domain-specific language* (DSL). And because pipelines operate on the last argument of a function, you can quickly create code that looks like the following listing.

> **Listing 6.5   A fictional pipeline to send an email to a customer**

```
customerId
|> loadFromDb            ⟵──┐  Constructs a pipeline
|> reviewCustomer            │  of business operations
|> createEmail EmailTemplate.Overdue
|> send
```

If you're worried about not being able to check the intermediate states, you have a few options:

- If you're in a script, you can simply highlight a subset of the pipeline (e.g., just the first two or three lines) and execute just that part into F# Interactive (FSI).
- If debugging an application (which we've not seen yet but uses standard .NET techniques, such as breakpoints, etc., across all IDEs), you can set breakpoints on individual pipeline stages. The debugger should stop there and show you the current state at that point.

A word on fonts

There are some popular fonts that support *ligatures*. Ligature support enables your code editor to provide slightly nicer-looking characters when a specific combination of characters is placed next to each other. For example, the |> (pipeline) operator is rendered as though it's a single character (i.e., without a gap between the two characters, etc.). Examples of such fonts include Cascadia Code and Fira Code, but plenty of other ones are out there, too.

EXERCISE 6.2

I'd like you to try to update the `drive` function from the exercise we worked on in chapter 4 to use pipelines. Currently, it looks like the following, but can you make it a single pipeline that takes in the gas as the input to the pipeline and returns the `finalState`?

```
let gas = 100.0
let firstState = drive gas 55
let secondState = drive firstState 26
let finalState = drive secondState 1
```

Remember, to pipeline functions, the last argument in the function is the one that gets pipelined (in our case, the gas). Have a try. The solution is at the end of this chapter.

Composing functions

F# has another built-in operator called `compose`, represented by `>>`. It allows you to compose two functions together into a new one if the first's output matches the second's input. It's not used especially often and is just a shortcut for manually plugging two functions together by hand, but it's worth being aware of its existence in case you see it elsewhere. As an example, these two functions do the same thing:

```
let addFiveAndDouble input = input |> add 5 |> multiply 2
let addFiveAndDoubleShort = add 5 >> multiply 2
```

If you made it, you'll notice that the function itself is exactly as it was earlier. The only difference is how we're calling it: instead of manually binding the intermediate states to symbols and manually threading them through, we're now using the pipeline operator to do it for us. As you can hopefully see, this essentially reads as intended: you start with 100 units of gas, then drive 55, then another 26, and then another 1 unit.

When should I use the pipeline?

You may be tempted to use the pipeline everywhere for all arguments to functions, even when you have just a single function. Avoid falling into the trap of using it dogmatically. I advise using the pipeline operator when there is a logical flow of operations or at least when seeing data going into a function visually makes sense. I do occasionally use it for single-function calls, but it always depends on factors such as the name of the function, the specific situation and the type of data being threaded through.

6.1.4   *Using records and tuples with functions*

You've already seen that you can, of course, supply records and tuples as inputs to functions in F#. As an example, here's a function that takes two input arguments: a connection to a database and a customer value:

```
let saveCustomerToDb connectionDetails customer : unit =
    let (server:string, dbName:string) = connectionDetails
    ...
```

The `connectionDetails` value is a tuple of `string * string`, while the `customer` value is a `Customer` record. The signature might look something like this:

```
(string * string) -> Customer -> unit
```

We could then supply a connection to a specific database up front, but then call the resulting function repeatedly for each customer that we want to save to the database:

```
let saveCustomerToTestDb = saveCustomerToDb testDbDetails
for customer in customers do
    saveCustomerToTestDb customer
```

This is a simplistic example, but it is invaluable as a way of mocking and abstracting implementation details. We'll see more of this later when we look at higher-order functions.

6.1.5 Tupled functions

You will sometimes see functions in F# look like they take in multiple arguments without spaces—for example,

```
let add (x,y) = x + y
```

Don't be fooled into thinking this is some other way of defining functions in F#: it's identical to everything we've seen so far. All we're saying here is that this function takes in a single value, which happens to be a tuple of int * int.

When should you use which style? I tend to prefer curried functions as a default. They have support for being partially applied and require less typing at the call site: you need no parentheses or commas, just spaces, for each argument. Curried functions also work much more nicely with pipelines.

I use the tupled style occasionally—generally, if I want to enforce a certain set of arguments being supplied together as a single value. However, I might use a record rather than a tuple in such a case.

6.1.6 Comparing functions and methods

This book is geared toward showing you the functional side of F#, but F# does have full support for classes and methods that exist in other languages, such as C#. There are a few differences between them in F# that you should be aware of, as table 6.1 illustrates.

Table 6.1 Comparing functions and methods in F#

	Method	Function
Normally lives in	Classes	Modules or other Functions
Static or instance level?	Both	Static only
Currying / Partial application	No	Yes
Overloading	Yes	No
Type Inference	Limited	Full
Optional arguments	Yes	No
Pipelines	Limited	Yes

If some of the terms don't mean much to you, don't worry: it's mainly targeted at developers coming from languages that support features such as overloading, so they don't wonder where those features have gone. For those of you who do know what those features are and are thinking it's a lot to give up, trust me when I say you'll do just fine. Features such as optional arguments and (especially) overloading can occasionally be useful, but they can also be extremely complicated to reason about. In exchange for losing those features, you gain a set of (in my experience) far more powerful and useful features: full pipelining, currying, and type inference.

6.2 Organizing code

In this second half of the chapter, I want to break away from individual functions for a little bit and start to talk about how we organize our code—in other words, our types (tuples, records, and the yet-to-be-discussed discriminated union), which are used to store data, and functions, which model behavior on that data. F# has two basic constructs for this: namespaces and modules. These features allow us to easily group related code elements so that it's easier to manage and maintain and make it simpler for other developers to navigate our code.

6.2.1 Namespaces

Namespaces are ways of logically organizing types. As an example, the most common namespace in .NET is called `System`. If you open an F# script file in VS Code and type the `System.`, you'll see a pop-up menu appear with a whole host of entries (figure 6.3).

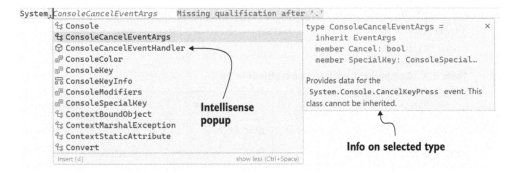

Figure 6.3   Navigating the list of children of the `system` namespace in VS Code

These are types that exist in .NET, as well as sub-namespaces—that is, namespaces that exist inside of this namespace. Think of this as a hierarchy; for example, the `File` type, which allows you to read and write from a file, lives in the `System.IO.` namespace, while the `ZipFile` type lives in the `System.IO.Compression` namespace. Listing 6.6 illustrates several features of namespaces.

Listing 6.6   Working with namespaces in F#

```
                        ┌─ Creates a
                        │  namespace, Foo        ┌─ Declares a type, Order,
namespace Foo  ◄───────┘                        │  in the Foo namespace
type Order = { Name : string }  ◄──────────────┘


namespace Bar.Baz  ◄──────┐ Declares a new namespace,
type Customer =           │ Baz, which lives in a
    {                       namespace Bar
        Name : string
        LastOrder : Foo.Order  ◄──┐ References Order
    }                             │ by fully qualifying
                                  │ its path
Declares a type, Customer,
that lives in Baz
```

As you can see, namespaces implicitly apply to all types declared after them until a new namespace declaration in the file is encountered.

You can also see in listing 6.6 that we refer to `Order` on the `Customer` record by fully qualifying its name. Repeatedly doing this would rapidly become verbose and annoying, so F# lets you open a namespace inside of the current namespace. Once you've done this, any types in that namespace can be accessed directly without qualification, as shown in the following listing.

Listing 6.7   Opening a namespace

```
                        ┌─ Opens the Foo            ┌─ References the Order
namespace Bar.Baz       │  namespace                │  type without fully
open Foo  ◄────────────┘                           │  qualifying its name
type Customer = { LastOrder : Order }  ◄───────────┘
```

Opening types

A relatively new addition to the F# language also lets you open a type itself. For everyday F#, it's generally not required, but when working with some C# types, it can be a useful tool. When you open a type using the `open type` syntax, you can access any static methods that exist on the type directly, without qualifying by the type at all. You can simply call the method as though it was globally available.

As namespaces are logical constructs, you can have multiple files in your application that contain types that all share the same namespace. Indeed, you can even share namespaces with other third-party applications or packages.

Namespaces are a great way to organize a large and complex set of types, but you probably won't need to create them very often for smaller applications. Namespaces also don't allow you to store values in them. For that, you'll need to create modules, which we'll discuss next. However, you'll certainly be accessing namespaces a great deal in F#, since you'll be utilizing types declared in other libraries and packages, as well as the core .NET libraries.

6.2.2   *Modules*

Modules are a general-purpose way to store both types *and* values. At first glance, they appear to behave like namespaces: You declare a module at the top of a file; anything declared after this point lives inside that module. However, once you dig in, you'll see a few key differences. Unlike namespaces, the biggest change is that modules also allow you to declare values inside them such as numbers, record instances, or functions. And just like a type declared in a namespace, the fully qualified name of a symbol declared inside the module is `Module.Symbol`.

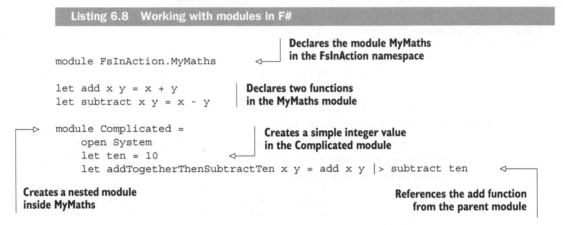

Listing 6.8   Working with modules in F#

```
module FsInAction.MyMaths          ◁─┐ Declares the module MyMaths
                                      │ in the FsInAction namespace

let add x y = x + y                │ Declares two functions
let subtract x y = x - y           │ in the MyMaths module

module Complicated =                  ┌ Creates a simple integer value
    open System                       │ in the Complicated module
    let ten = 10                   ◁──┘
    let addTogetherThenSubtractTen x y = add x y |> subtract ten    ◁──┐

Creates a nested module                                    References the add function
inside MyMaths                                                from the parent module
```

There are a few things worth observing here that are different from namespaces. First, if you declare a new module in a file, unlike namespaces, it becomes a child of the previously declared module. In the previous example, `Complicated` is nested inside of `MyMaths`. Also, nested modules don't need to open their parents, as can be seen by calling `add` in the last line. Finally, nested modules must have their contents indented.

One nice trick F# has up its sleeve, on the first line in listing 6.8, is that we declared `MyMaths` inside the `FsInAction` namespace in a single line. This is similar to what we did with namespaces, except here, the last element in the breadcrumb is the module (in this example, `MyMaths`); all the preceding breadcrumbs (just `FsInAction` here) become parent namespaces.

It's important to also note that modules are physical constructs (for the .NET developers reading this, modules are compiled into static classes at the MSIL level; the .NET runtime has no notion of modules, and F# doesn't support partial modules like C# has partial classes). This means you cannot declare the same fully qualified module in two files. Figure 6.4 shows how modules and namespaces co-exist in a typical F# application.

> **NOTE**   In scripts, which we have been working with almost exclusively so far, declaring the module is optional. If you leave it out, F# will use the name of the file as the module.

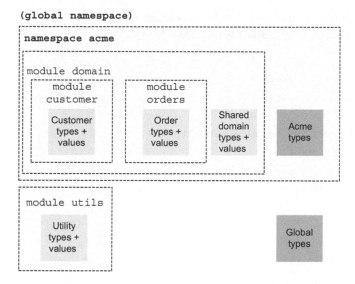

Figure 6.4 Namespaces and modules in a single application

The names are, of course, totally fictional in figure 6.4, but the key things to distinguish between the two structures should be visible, which I've also illustrated in table 6.2.

Table 6.2 Comparing namespaces and modules

	Namespaces	**Modules**
Can store types	Yes	Yes
Can store values	No	Yes
Can store child namespaces	Yes	No
Can store child modules	Yes	Yes
Can be declared in multiple files	Yes	No

6.2.3 *Moving from script to application: A step-by-step exercise*

You should do this exercise alongside me, step by step. It's designed to show a typical transition from modeling and exploration within a script into a full-blown console application.

We're going to take the car driving code that we developed earlier since it's hopefully fresh in your mind and use that to build a dedicated console application that will capture some input from the console and pass it into our code before printing out the results. It's not going to be the greatest application ever developed and won't hold a candle to the ones you can develop in whatever language you're most comfortable in. But it will show you how to move from scripts to applications and back again. We'll start with the `drive` function that you developed earlier in this chapter (if you didn't make it, a copy is available at the end of this chapter).

EXERCISE 6.3

1 In a terminal, create a new directory called `drivingapp`.
2 Create a new F# console application; see chapter 2 for details on how to do this if you can't remember.
3 Open up an instance of VS Code in this directory.
4 Create a new File, called `Car.fs`.
5 Create a module at the top of the file called `Car` and immediately below copy and paste in your car driving function. Your code should look something like this:

```
module Car

let drive distance gas =
    … // body elided
```

6 Now you need to add this file to the project so that F# knows to compile it and make it accessible to the rest of the program. In VS Code, with the command palette (CTRL + SHIFT + P), choose the F#: Add Current File to Project option.
7 Navigate to the `DrivingApp.fsproj`. Observe that there is an element in the file: `<Compile Include="Car.fs" />`. Every F# file in an application needs to be included in the project file like this.

At this point, I want to make something clear: in F#, not only must code be declared before you can access it within the same file, but the files themselves are ordered in the project file. Files that are declared in the project file first can't see files that are declared further down the list. In other words, declare the files that have no dependencies on other files first; the file that needs to tie everything together (typically `Program.fs`) needs to be declared last. Figure 6.5 shows this in a slightly larger project. In that file, `Program.fs` is declared last since it needs to access types and values declared in other files. Conversely, the lowest-level files decoupled from everything else (e.g., `Db.fs`) in the database access layer are declared first.

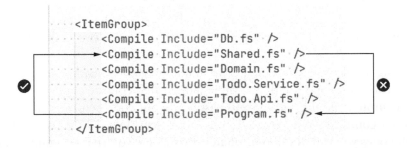

Figure 6.5   A typical F# project file, with the last file declared that can access all other files

This constraint is often seen initially as a limitation, but the restriction is actually very helpful: you basically can't have spaghetti code with recursive loops of code depending on each other. Instead, you simply have to look down the file (and project) to understand what depends on what. In VS Code, the standard file explorer shows files alphabetically, so you need to be aware that it doesn't reflect the project's file order. Instead, Ionide provides a second panel that you can use to view the logical order of files. Figure 6.6 illustrates this. Observe that the file order reflects the list of files from the project file in figure 6.5.

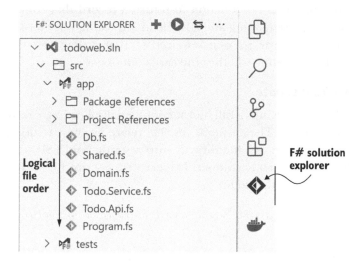

Figure 6.6 The F# Solution Explorer in Ionide shows the logical file order as defined within the project file, not the alphabetical file order.

With that out of the way, let's continue the exercise:

1 In `Program.fs`, enter the following code:

```
let remaining = Car.drive 2 8
printfn $"You have {remaining} gas left."
```

2 In the terminal, run the application using `dotnet run`. Observe the result: `You have 7 gas left.`

That's the basics done. Here are some challenges you can do on top of this (a full example is provided at the end of this chapter).

EXERCISE 6.4

1 Capture the distance to drive from the user. Use `printfn` and `System.Console .ReadLine()` as required to print and read from the console.

`System.Console.ReadLine ()` returns a string. You can use the built-in function `int` to convert this string into an integer (e.g., `int "123"` or `"123" |> int`). It's unsafe, though, so if you enter a string that isn't a valid number, the application will throw an exception and terminate (don't worry, there are much better ways to validate input in F# that we'll look at).

2 Remove the need for typing `System` in your main code by opening the `System` namespace at the top of the file.

3 Also, open the `Car` module so that you can simply type `drive` without fully qualifying it.

4 Change the output so that if your final gas is less than or equal to 0, it prints a message `you are out of gas!`

5 Test this by supplying a distance such as `35`.

6 Change the output of the `drive` function to return a record that contains two fields: the amount of gas remaining and a Boolean indicating whether the car is out of gas; change the `Program.fs` as required so that it now uses that field instead of manually calculating whether the car is out of gas.

6.2.4   *Referencing programs from scripts*

Now that you've moved your code into a full-blown compiled application, can you still work with scripts for exploration? The answer is yes. There are two ways to do it.

First, F# allows you to load an `.fs` file directly into a script (and FSI), using the `#load` directive. In the following code snippet, I've created a script file in the same folder as the project and entered this code:

```
#load "Car.fs"
let result = Car.drive 10 8
```

In FSI, you'll see something like the following when you execute the first line:

```
> #load "Car.fs"
[Loading C:\code\drivingapp\car.fs]
type DriveResult =
    {
      GasLeft: float
      IsOutOfGas: bool
    }
val drive: distance: int -> gas: float -> DriveResult
```

After that, you can simply make calls to the code in your script and reference it as though you had written it directly in the script.

For simple single-file applications like this, `#load` is fine. However, for larger multi-file applications, things get a bit more complicated. You'll have to call `#load` for each of the files in the same order as the project file (e.g., `#load "FileA.fs" "FileB.fs" "FileC.fs"`), and it can become a maintenance issue to keep this in sync with the project, as well as becoming quite slow with larger projects. A better option in this case is to reference the entire dynamic-link library (DLL) that you've built using the `#r` directive:

```
#r "bin/debug/net6.0/DrivingApp.dll"
```

The good thing with this approach is that you simply reference the DLL—all the files are already built—so it's quicker and easier to work with. If your DLLs themselves reference other libraries, FSI is generally smart enough to bring them in; third-party NuGet packages also have very good support, which we'll see later on.

Whichever option you use, you need to remember that whenever you make changes to the files or DLLs, even though the code editor will automatically reflect the changes to your types, etc., you must explicitly reload them into FSI by re-executing the `#load` or `#r` directives to pull in the latest version. My advice is to restart FSI whenever you do this and start your scripting session over from clean.

6.2.5 *Best practices for modules and namespaces*

Namespaces and modules work together nicely, and sometimes you'll use both—especially in larger applications that require a deeper hierarchy. However, normally, I would start my applications with modules only: they support both types and functions and allow submodules. You can open modules just like namespaces, and they also support nesting. These features are basically enough to develop applications with a good level of control of the organization of your types and functions.

On the other hand, as your application grows—especially if you're a library author—you may need to fall back to namespaces. For example, consider the case where you need to create two modules that share the same parent namespace *and* live in different files (e.g., `Contoso.WebApi.Orders` and `Contoso.WebApi.Customers`). Here, both the `Orders` and `Customers` modules would live in the `Contoso.WebApi` namespace.

Also, a word on files: my advice for working with modules and namespaces is not to get hung up on rules such as "one type per file" or similar. It's totally fine to start your applications in a single module in a single file. Many applications I've worked on started with just a few modules for the entire application in just a couple of files. I might start with something as simple as

- *Domain*—Contains all types (records, etc.) that I've defined
- *Logic*—Contains all functions that operate on those records
- *Program*—Orchestrates the whole application

I don't have single files for each type—that would be overkill. Instead, I'm quite happy to declare multiple types in a single file. Most IDEs (including VS Code) allow you to go to the definition and navigate to types and usages directly; you don't need to use file names as a convention or to help navigation. After a while, as it grows, I might remodel this out into logical groups or bounded contexts as, for example, the following:

- *Order management*—Types and functions relating to order management
- *Customer management*—Types and functions relating to customer management
- *Billing*—Types and functions relating to billing
- *Program*—Orchestrates the application

The point is that there's no perfect way to structure your application: do what works for you, but don't follow patterns from other languages, such as "single file per type," because it's generally not helpful in F#. The syntax is so succinct that you can often model your entire domain in a single screen of code. While it's easy to continue to follow rules that have served you well in the past, they'll likely not be required in F#.

6.2.6   *Tips and tricks*

Here's a few extra quick tips when working with modules.

ACCESS MODIFIERS

By default, modules, types, and functions are always public in F#. If you want to use a function within a module but don't want to expose it publicly, mark it as private (e.g., `let private x = 10`). You can also mark modules private, in which case only values declared in their containing module can access them. This can be useful if you have a large module but don't want consumers to be confused by a large number of functions.

AUTOMATICALLY OPENING MODULES

You can have a module automatically open itself without the need to use the `open` declaration by adding the `[<AutoOpen>]` attribute on the module. With this attribute applied, opening the parent namespace or module will also automatically open access to this module. You might use this if you have several modules that contain different functionality within the same namespace but would like to open them all automatically for the caller. `AutoOpen` is commonly used when defining domain-specific languages (DSLs), as you can open a single namespace or module and suddenly get access to lots of functions and operators without needing to open them explicitly. Just be careful of abusing this feature!

PREVENTING OPENING MODULES

You can also do the inverse of `AutoOpen` (i.e., prevent opening a module completely), meaning that you always need to qualify access to module members. Simply apply the `[<RequireQualifiedAccess>]` attribute on the module.

6.3   *Answers to exercises*

EXERCISE 6.1

```
let add a b = a + b
let addTen = add 10
let multiply a b = a * b
let timesTwo = multiply 2
let addTenAndDouble a =
    let firstResult = addTen a
    timesTwo firstResult
```

EXERCISE 6.2

```
let drive distance gas =
    if distance > 50 then gas / 2.0
    elif distance > 25 then gas - 10.0
    elif distance > 0 then gas - 1.0
    else gas

let gas = 100.0

let remainingGas =
    gas
    |> drive 55
    |> drive 26
    |> drive 1
```

EXERCISES 6.3 AND 6.4

Car.fs
```
module Car

type DriveResult =
    {
        GasLeft : float
        IsOutOfGas : bool
    }

let drive distance gas =
    let output =
        if distance > 50 then gas / 2.0
        elif distance > 25 then gas - 10.0
        elif distance > 0 then gas - 1.0
        else gas
    {
        GasLeft = output
        IsOutOfGas = output <= 0.0
    }
```

Program.fs
```
open System
open Car

printfn "How far do you want to drive?"          ◁─┐ Impure data
let distance = Console.ReadLine() |> int         ◁─┘ capture

let startGas = 8.0                               ┐ Pure
let remainingGas = startGas |> drive distance  ◁─┘ calculation

if remainingGas.IsOutOfGas then printfn "You are out of gas!"   ◁─┐ Impure data
else printfn $"You have {remainingGas.GasLeft} gas left."          │ output /
                                                                   └ presentation
```

Summary

- F# functions always take a single input and always return a single output.
- If you want to supply multiple values into a function, you can use tuples or records when you want to pass all the values together or curried functions if you want to be able to call functions one at a time.
- Curried functions are useful when you want to inject some arguments upfront but supply the rest later.
- If you want a function with no inputs or outputs, you can use the `unit ()` value.
- The pipeline `|>` operator is a great way to connect multiple functions in a lightweight fashion.
- Currying works hand in hand with pipelines.
- Namespaces and modules are two ways to organize your code into groups.
- Both namespaces and modules can be opened by callers to make it easier to access members.
- Both namespaces and modules have their strengths; you should start with modules and use namespaces if required.

Working with collections

7

This chapter covers

- Higher-order functions
- Functional collection pipelines
- F# Collections
- Aggregations

Until now, we've only really looked at individual items of data, also known as *scalars*. This chapter looks at how we work with multiple items of data at once. We do this all the time (e.g., working with a list of orders or customers, etc.). Collections are especially important in F# and functional programming languages in general because a lot of what we do involves thinking of things in terms of data transformations.

7.1 *Higher-order functions*

Before we dive into collections, there's a prerequisite to understanding them known as *higher-order functions* (HOFs), which are one of the ways you compose code in F# (there are others that we'll see toward the end of this book). These are functions that take *another* function as an argument. You will probably have seen this in languages that support even limited functional programming–style features.

One of the uses of HOFs is for implementing some common algorithm that operates over some varying logic. In the object-oriented world, you would probably use either the template or strategy design pattern. In the functional programming world, it's fairly easy to achieve the same thing with functions. Here's an example of a simple calculation function that logs its output to the console:

```
let executeCalculation a b =
    let answer = a + b
    printfn $"Adding {a} and {b} = {answer}"
    answer
```

Now let's imagine you want to vary the output channel. Instead of the console, you'd like to be able to output to a file or database. In F#, that's no problem:

```
let executeCalculation logger a b =
    let answer = a + b
    logger $"Adding {a} and {b} = {answer}"
    answer
```

The difference between these two code snippets is that `printfn` has been replaced with the `logger` function, which is now supplied as an argument. C# developers will be familiar with the idea of doing this using the `Func<T>` type; this is essentially the F# equivalent of that. If you hover over the `logger` value, you'll see that the type inference engine has correctly inferred that `logger` is a function of type (`string -> unit`). You'll notice the parentheses around the function argument: this makes it possible to distinguish arguments to the HOF itself and the arguments to the function being supplied (figure 7.1).

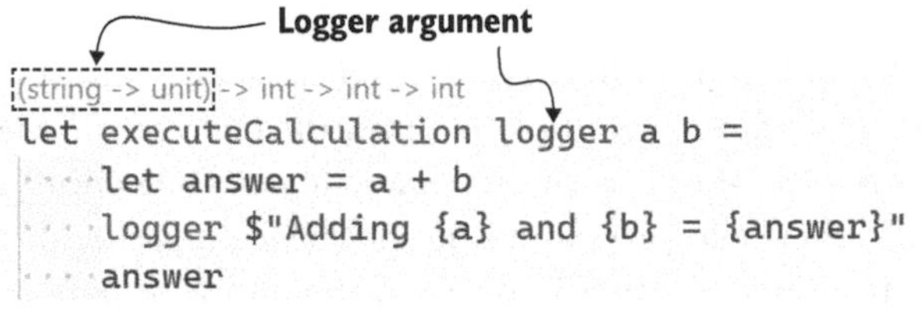

Figure 7.1   **The signature of an HOF, including arguments that are themselves functions**

HOFs, which are functions that take functions as arguments, are also simple to call. Let's call `executeCalculation` with a function that will write the output to a file:

```
let writeToFile text =
    System.IO.File.AppendAllText("log.txt", text)
executeCalculation writeToFile 10 20
```

If the signature of the supplied function matches the expected input argument, this will work; there's no need to use an interface or inherit from base classes. Of course, F# also allows you to pass a function body inline with what's known as a lambda function:

```
executeCalculation
    (fun text -> System.IO.File.AppendAllText("log.txt", text))
    10
    20
```

For very small functions, this sort of style is very common; for larger functions, I'd recommend declaring the function separately and supplying it as per the first example.

HOFs are a core part of working with collections, so it's important to understand what they are and how to consume them.

EXERCISE 7.1

Create an HOF `calculate` that takes in three arguments: a calculation function, such as `add` or `subtract`, and the two values it operates on. It should carry out the operation, print out the inputs, and answer and return the result. If you want to print out the name of the operation (e.g., `add`), you'll need to pass that in, too.

7.2   *Functional collection pipelines*

Armed with this knowledge of HOFs, let's now look at F# collections with an example dataset and challenge. Listing 7.1 creates a List of soccer results, declaring names of both teams and the number of goals they scored. We want to find out which team won the most away games.

Listing 7.1   Creating a sample dataset

```
type Result =                                    ◁──┐  Defines our domain type
    { HomeTeam : string; HomeGoals : int
      AwayTeam : string; AwayGoals : int }
let create home hg away ag =                      ◁──┐  A simple helper function
    { HomeTeam = home; HomeGoals = hg             │      to quickly create a record
      AwayTeam = away; AwayGoals = ag }
let results = [                                   ◁──┐  A List of results
    create "Messiville" 1 "Ronaldo City" 2
    create "Messiville" 1 "Bale Town" 3
    create "Ronaldo City" 2 "Bale Town" 3
    create "Bale Town" 2 "Messiville" 1
]
```

An F# List is denoted by `[ ]`, with the expression on each line representing an item. F# lists are generic, so the type of results is a `List<Result>` or `Result list`.

Creating lists

The compiler is fairly flexible in terms of the positioning of the opening and closing brace. You can put all elements on a single line if you wish and separate the elements with a semicolon—not a comma, as is common in many other languages, which is a tuple separator in F#. Watch out! If you're coming from a curly-brace language, you can essentially treat the formatting styles in a similar way.

7.2.1 *Imperative and declarative pipelines*

Let's assume you needed to find the team that had won the most away games in the season. How would you do this? Generally, there are two approaches to building any such query: *imperatively* and *declaratively*. The imperative approach would focus on a slightly lower-level how-to, step-by-step process, probably something like the following.

Listing 7.2 An imperative query implementation

```
type TeamSummary = { Name : string; mutable AwayWins : int }
let summary = ResizeArray<TeamSummary>()          ◁── A mutable List to store
                                                       intermediary results
for result in results do
    if result.AwayGoals > result.HomeGoals then   ◁── Filters results
        let mutable found = false                      based on away wins
        for entry in summary do
            if entry.Name = result.AwayTeam then
                found <- true
                entry.AwayWins <- entry.AwayWins + 1   Creates a new entry for
        if not found then                          ◁── teams that won away
            summary.Add { Name = result.AwayTeam; AwayWins = 1 }  for the first time

let mutable wonAwayTheMost = summary[0]            Gets the team that
for row in summary do                          ◁── won away the most
    if row.AwayWins > wonAwayTheMost.AwayWins then wonAwayTheMost <- row
```

Increases the number of matches for teams that have already found an away win points to the `for entry in summary do` line.

The problem with this approach is that it's difficult to read and immediately see what's going on. You need to read every line and think about it to track what's happening; that is, it's not immediately readable. It's also a lot of code to achieve something simple, and even worse, it's not *composable*: you can't easily extract the aggregation or the filtering portions of the code and reuse it elsewhere. And if the query grows in complexity, the maintainability would rapidly drop further. Lastly, as an observation, it's using mutable data and side effects: if you run the query portion of this code again, you'd find two sets of results in the summary collection (unless you explicitly cleared it first). Also, you cannot easily see what's happening from the type signatures—everything is essentially a statement that returns a unit. Let's see how it looks in the declarative world.

In contrast, let's see how things look in the declarative world. First, we need to change our perspective: instead of asking *how* we are going to solve the problem, we need to take a step back and express the problem in terms of *what* we're trying to do:

- Get all the results that were away wins (i.e., away goals are more than home goals).
- Count them up by the away team.
- Get the one that had the most wins.

The following listing shows how we might implement such a declarative solution in F#.

Listing 7.3 A declarative query implementation

```
let isAwayWin result = result.AwayGoals > result.HomeGoals
let wonAwayTheMost =
    results
    |> List.filter isAwayWin
    |> List.countBy (fun result -> result.AwayTeam)
    |> List.maxBy (fun (team, count) -> count)
```

Filters by away wins

Counts up rows by the away team

Picks the item with the greatest count

Don't worry too much about the individual pipeline stages just yet. Just note that we're using essentially the same type of pipeline approach we've done earlier in the book, except this time, we're working with a *list* of values rather than a single value. Again, the same core principles apply: data is immutable, and operations are expressions, not statements. Each pipeline stage outputs a result set, which is piped into the next stage until we reach the end. It's sometimes useful to visualize pipelines in terms of the data transformations happening, as shown in figure 7.2.

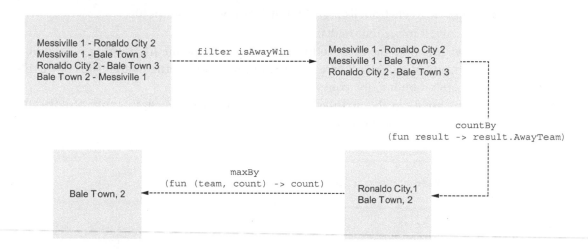

Figure 7.2 Visualizing the data transformations within a pipeline

As you can see, not only is it much less code than the imperative solution, but it's also more readable. It's also a much more composable or pluggable pipeline: we could inject another transformation in the middle without fear of affecting the others, as each stage is decoupled from each other. Finally, as each function creates a new List rather than modifying the existing List, you can repeat the code in this pipeline as often as you want, and you'll always get the same result.

The F# List type is one of the core collection types in F#. Not to be confused with the .NET generic List (which in F# is also known as a `ResizeArray`), its main characteristic is that it is an immutable linked list. This means you cannot add, remove, or replace items from a List once it's created. However, it has native support to combine two Lists to form a new List or append an item to the head (front) of the List, again creating a new List:

```
let a = [ 1;2;3 ]
let b = [ 4;5;6 ]
let c = a @ b
let d = 0 :: a
```

Combines the lists a and b into a new list, c

Creates a new list that starts with 0 and ends with the contents of list a

To be honest, I rarely use these operators, but it's good to know that they exist should you need them. Note that there is no operator (or way) to add a single item to the end of a List. You'll need to create a list of a single item and append that to the first List.

7.2.2 Debugging pipelines

Pipelines can quickly become powerful (and long) chains. That's why it's often useful to test out just a subset of it to see the intermediate results. Let's try that here:

1 Enter the code from listings 7.1 and 7.3 into a new script file.
2 Execute it to see the results.
3 Now, highlight the first two lines of the query pipeline from listing 7.3 (ending in the `filter`) and observe that FSI outputs the intermediate results of the filter operation into the console.
4 Now, highlight the first three lines (ending with `countBy`). Again, observe the output in FSI, as shown in figure 7.3.

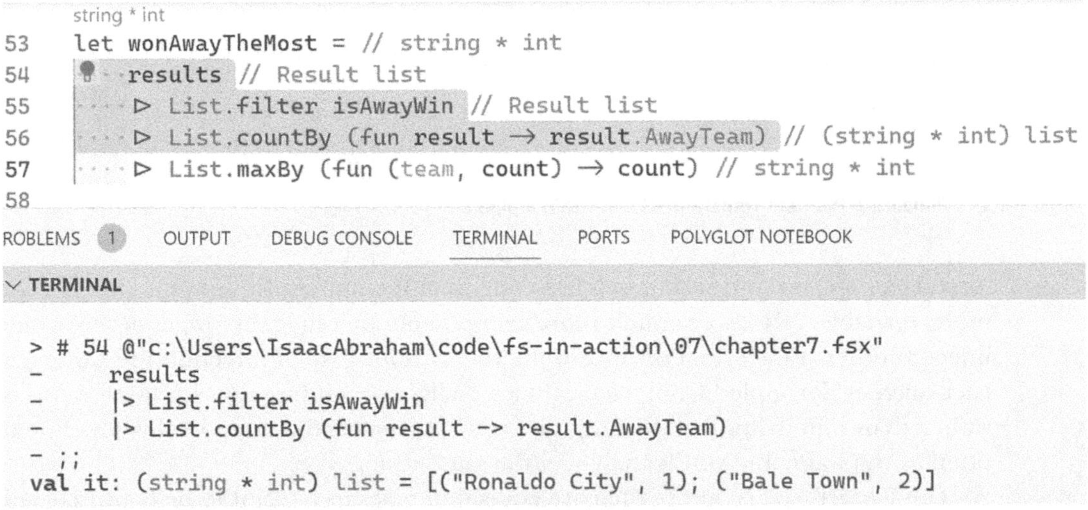

```
        string * int
53   let wonAwayTheMost = // string * int
54      results // Result list
55         ▷ List.filter isAwayWin // Result list
56         ▷ List.countBy (fun result → result.AwayTeam) // (string * int) list
57         ▷ List.maxBy (fun (team, count) → count) // string * int
58
```

ROBLEMS 1   OUTPUT   DEBUG CONSOLE   TERMINAL   PORTS   POLYGLOT NOTEBOOK

∨ TERMINAL

```
> # 54 @"c:\Users\IsaacAbraham\code\fs-in-action\07\chapter7.fsx"
-      results
-         |> List.filter isAwayWin
-         |> List.countBy (fun result -> result.AwayTeam)
- ;;
val it: (string * int) list = [("Ronaldo City", 1); ("Bale Town", 2)]
```

Figure 7.3 Executing a subset of a functional pipeline and observing the results

Another thing that some IDEs (e.g., Code and Rider) do is provide hints for the types at each stage of a pipeline. Observe in figure 7.3 at the end of each line are what appear to be comments such as `// Result list` or `(string * int) list`. These are actually generated automatically by the code editor so that you can see at a glance what kind of results you're generating. It's also helpful to help diagnose errors if you try to plug two incompatible functions together (in other words, the output of the first one doesn't match the input of the second).

EXERCISE 7.2

Create a List pipeline on the same dataset to answer the question, "How many games did Ronaldo City feature in?"

> **NOTE** The F# List is fine for everyday use and also has some nice optimizations up its sleeve. For example, when appending two Lists (or filtering a List), instead of copying all the items into a new List, it simply references the existing ones. Thus, you're not creating copies of objects (or even Lists); you're just reusing the existing space in memory. However, be careful when appending two lists together (either `List.append` or `@`), because the F# List is optimized for adding single items at the front. In isolation, `append` performs fine, but you'll run into performance issues if you start doing thousands of them in a tight loop. In such a case, consider one of the other collection data structures based on your needs.

7.2.3 Understanding the List module

What are these functions like `List.filter` and `List.countBy`? They are members of the `List` module, which comes included with F# and contains many useful functions for working with Lists. Many languages have similar functionality but are only accessible by dotting into the collection (e.g., LINQ in C# with extension methods); in F#, you call the function via its module explicitly. The only way to learn them is simply through practice. After a while, they'll become second nature, and you'll see all sorts of opportunities to use them where you wouldn't have noticed them before.

Probably one of the bigger areas I see people struggle with F# collections—particularly when collection functions don't seem to fit together—is that people don't take the time to learn how to read the function signatures and end up flailing around trying to randomly plug together list functions in the hope that they work together. This is especially important with functions in the `List` module (or any HOFs) because the signatures are a little more complicated than standard functions.

Let's look at a few common functions in the `List` module and break them down step by step (this is what I do when I see a function for the first time that looks a little scary). If you come from any language that has some kind of collection processing library, many of these will look familiar, except the names may be slightly different (e.g., C# calls map `Select` and filter `Where`), but the principles are the same.

Let's start with probably the most common collection function of all: `List.map`. If you type the function `List.map` into VS Code and hover over it with the mouse, you'll see the full type signature, description, parameter information, and, in most cases, a simple example of the function. You can also use Ionide's Info Panel in VS Code (ALT + ,), which opens a pane that continually displays contextual information as you move the caret around code elements. Figure 7.4 shows what I'm referring to.

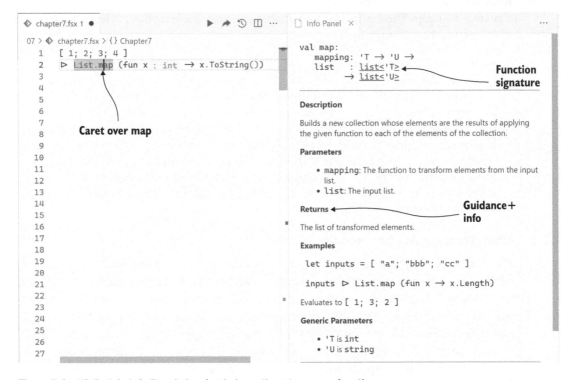

Figure 7.4   VS Code's Info Panel showing help on the `List.map` function

`List.map` has the following signature:

```
mapping : ('T -> 'U) -> 'T list -> 'U list
```

As you can see in figure 7.4, VS Code's Info Panel makes this a bit easier because it puts each argument on a separate line, but not all IDEs do this. Let's break down the function signature step by step:

1 We know that `->` is a separator for arguments in F#.
2 We also know that arguments that are themselves functions are shown with parentheses around them to distinguish them.
3 The last type in a function signature is the return type.

Therefore, this function takes in two arguments:

- `mapping`—Has a type `'T -> 'U` (in other words, a function)
- `list`—Has a type `'T list`

`'T` and `'U` are the generic type arguments of the function (if you provide the mapping function as I've done in figure 7.4, in the code sample, you'll see that the Info Panel shows the generic parameters `int` and `string`). The description of `List.map` says that it is designed to take in a List and apply some function against all the items in the List and return those transformed elements into a new List (see figure 7.5).

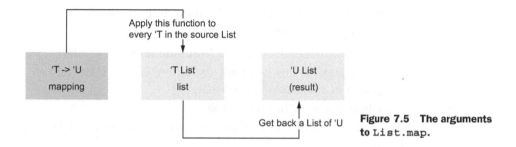

Figure 7.5 The arguments to `List.map`.

Let's apply this to the code sample in figure 7.4, which is reproduced here:

```
let output = [ 1; 2; 3; 4 ] |> List.map (fun x -> x.ToString())
```

The mapping function is `fun x -> x.ToString()`, which has a signature `int -> string`. The input List is an `int list` containing the integers 1 to 4. The output List is therefore `string list [ "1"; "2" .. ]`.

Remember that to work with pipelines, the piped argument is always the final argument, so the input List is the last argument. Figure 7.6 is the same as figure 7.5 but has real values to drill the example home.

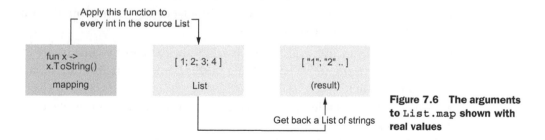

Figure 7.6 The arguments to `List.map` shown with real values

Many of the functions in the `List` module are HOFs with very similar signatures to `List.map`. For example, `List.filter` takes in a predicate function instead of a mapping function with a signature of `'T -> bool`. In other words, for every item in your

List, the function should return either `true` or `false`; items with `true` are kept in the new List; those that return `false` are discarded.

Most of the functions in the `List` module have good official online documentation along with examples available in your code IDE, as shown already. I'm not going to repeat that here. Instead, you should focus on learning the skills to read and "grok" the type signatures and documentation as easily as possible.

7.2.4   *Common List functions*

To finish this section, I want to highlight a few common `List` module functions that you probably want to learn before the others, as they're either very commonly used or very useful. Many of them have variants in the module (e.g., `map` has `mapi` and `map2`), but there are obviously many others you'll learn over time:

- `map`—Converts all the items in the List from one shape to another
- `collect`—A variant of `map` designed to flatten Lists-of-Lists; known in some other languages as `flatMap` or `selectMany`
- `filter`—Filters out some items in a List
- `skip` and `take`—Skips or takes a fixed number of items from a List
- `sort`—Sorts a List
- `groupBy`—Groups a List by a key that can be calculated from every item
- `windowed`—Performs a sliding window on a List; useful if, for example, you need to see the previous and next item in the List when performing a mapping
- `partition`—Breaks a List into two new Lists based on a predicate

This is just a subset of the operations provided by the `List` module—there are a lot of them. Over time, you'll naturally learn more and more and slowly learn a "muscle memory" where you instinctively learn the combination of functions to achieve a goal. Don't be disheartened if this takes a bit of time. If you've not worked in a language that uses collection functions in a functional style, it'll take practice to get used to it. The effort is worth it, though.

There are some red flags that you should watch for. For example, if you find yourself doing any of these things, you've inadvertently gone "off the rails" and should seriously reconsider your design:

- You're trying to use a `while` loop (they do exist in F#, but it's really going against everything we've been doing in this book; I probably use it maybe once or twice a year).
- You're using mutable data or trying to modify a collection in place after each operation.
- You find yourself trying to do multiple operations at once.

EXERCISE 7.3
Going back again to the soccer dataset at the start, construct a query that calculates the team that scored the most goals. You'll need to use `collect` to flatten out the List

of matches so you can get a single List of team/goal combinations, as well as `groupBy`, `map`, and `maxBy`.

What about LINQ?

LINQ is a technology introduced in C#3 (way back in 2008) that provided a whole bunch of features, mostly from the functional programming space, into the language. Together, they allowed collection operations that are similar to what we have with the `List` module, albeit the way you interface with the API is a little different. If you don't know what LINQ is, don't worry; you won't need it. If you do know what LINQ is, the good news is that you can use it if you want since all F# collection types, including `List`, support `IEnumerable<T>`, the base interface for collections in .NET. Just open the `System.LINQ` namespace and away you go! However, I would recommend against using it in F#: the `List` module is not only a little more powerful, but it's designed to work with F# features like currying and tuples, which weren't around in C# when LINQ was implemented.

7.2.5   Ranges, slices, and indexing

Lists allow you to index into them using standard `list[index]` syntax, even though this can cause run-time errors if you access an index that doesn't exist. F# also supports ranges and slicing for lists, as in the following listing.

Listing 7.4   Creating and consuming a List

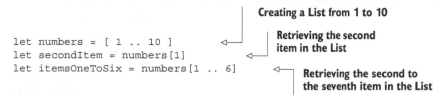

Creating a List from 1 to 10

Retrieving the second item in the List

```
let numbers = [ 1 .. 10 ]
let secondItem = numbers[1]
let itemsOneToSix = numbers[1 .. 6]
```

Retrieving the second to the seventh item in the List

As with most (but not all) languages, F# indexers are zero based. F# ranges are quite powerful: you can use steps to say things like "get every third number from the range 1 to 30." I don't use them much, but they're powerful, and it's worth looking into more in your own time

7.3   Other collection types

In addition to the F# `List`, there are several more collection types, which I will briefly outline in this section. The main thing to note is that they can broadly be split into two categories:

- *.NET collection types*—Types that are part of the core .NET library. These collection types were generally designed with C# in mind (e.g., mutable data structures). Some have F#-specific APIs to make them easier to use from F#. The nice thing with this approach is that you can consume data provided from some C# code in your system but process it in F# using F#-friendly functions.

- *F# collection types*—Types that were developed specifically for F#. They're generally immutable in nature, and their APIs take full advantage of features such as tuples, currying, and pipelining.

Most of these collection types have an associated module of the same name in which you'll find lots of useful functions for working with that data type. Of course, many third-party collections and types are available as packages, but I'm just going to focus on the core ones bundled with .NET for now.

7.3.1   Arrays

The .NET Array type is a mutable, generic array of a fixed size. Just like the `List`, it allows indexing and has a module, `Array`, which contains virtually the exact same functions as the `List` module. Therefore, all the functions you learn with List can be reused on Array. The syntax for creating arrays is also similar to lists, except instead of a square bracket to denote start and stop for a List, it's square brackets and a pipe (see listing 7.5).

Arrays are a high-performance collection, and they're a general-purpose .NET type. Thus, if you interoperate with, for example, C#, they will be familiar to you. However, they don't take advantage of some of the nicer features that the `List` has, such as deep support for pattern matching (which we'll see in the next chapters) and guaranteed immutability.

Listing 7.5   Creating and consuming an Array

```
let numbers = [| 1 .. 10 |]           ← Creates an Array from 1 to 10
let secondElement = numbers[1]        ← Retrieves the second item in the Array
let squares = numbers |> Array.map (fun x -> x * x)   ← Performs a simple map on the Array
```

In FSI, you'll get the following output:

```
val squares: int[] = [|1; 4; 9; 16; 25; 36; 49; 64; 81; 100|]
```

One thing to note is that the type of hints you'll see in editors can be a little confusing. The type of `numbers` in the previous code snippet (which is an array of integers) can be annotated in two ways:

```
let numbers : int array
let numbers : int []
```

This can be confusing: Why are we using list-style syntax `[ ]` instead of array-style `[| |]`? The answer is that this is a legacy .NET thing. It's confusing, and I suspect that one day the latter style will either be removed from or fixed in F#.

7.3.2 *Sequences*

The Sequence type is actually an alias for one of the most common interface types in .NET: `System.Collections.Generic.IEnumerable<T>`, and it's a special kind of collection. This type essentially underpins most collections in .NET, so arrays, lists, etc. all can be treated as a Sequence. The Sequence allows lazy, forward-only navigation of a sequence of items. Rather than representing some fixed set of in-memory data (as with lists and arrays), it's a computation that can generate data on demand.

Sequences are represented in code as `seq { item1; … ; itemN }` (see listing 7.6), and there's a large set of collection functions for them in the `Seq` module. Note that as Sequences aren't contiguous blocks of data in memory but computational generators, they don't support indexers. Instead, use the `Seq.item` function.

Listing 7.6   Creating and consuming a Sequence

Creates a Sequence from 1 to 10

Retrieves the second
item in the Sequence

```
let numbers = seq { 1 .. 10 }
let secondElement = numbers |> Seq.item 1
let squares = numbers |> Seq.map (fun x -> x * x)
```

Performs a simple
map on the Sequence

I've got more to say on Sequences, so we'll come back to it once I've finished giving you an overview of the other collection types.

7.3.3 *ResizeArray*

We've already looked at `ResizeArray`, but just for completeness, I'm including it here. It's full name is actually `System.Collections.Generic.List<T>`. It's essentially a wrapper around the Array type that, as the name suggests, manages the size for you so you can `Add` items to the array. If the array is full, this type will automatically create a new, larger array and copy the items from the old one across. One other drawback of the `ResizeArray` is that it doesn't have a specific module for functions, so you'll need to use the `Seq` module or fall back to LINQ.

7.3.4 *Dictionary*

The `System.Collections.Generic.Dictionary` is a .NET type that provides rapid key/value pair lookups in a mutable value. You can add and remove keys from the collection as well as modify the values within them in place. It's very fast, but its API doesn't necessarily lend itself especially well to F#; it's a mutable collection and isn't designed to take advantage of things like pipeline or curried functions.

You can use this type for situations such as "I have a list of customers and want to be able to look up the customer by their ID." Dictionaries also guarantee uniqueness in the key, so you don't have to worry about de-duplicating based on the key.

There is also a variant of this type called the `IReadOnlyDictionary`, for which F# provides a simple way to work via the built-in `readOnlyDict` function. This takes any tupled collection and converts it into a read-only dictionary, as listing 7.7 illustrates.

Listing 7.7   Creating and consuming a read-only dictionary

```
let data = [                    ⟵⎯⎯  A List of tuples
    "Isaac", "F#"; "Fred", "C#"; "Sam", "F#"; "Jo", "PHP"
]
let lookup = readOnlyDict data          ⟵⎯⎯  Converts the List into a
let isaacsLang = lookup["Isaac"]    ⟵⎯⎯      read-only dictionary
lookup["Isaac"] <- "Python"       ⟵⎯⎯  Retrieves a value by key
```

Trying to modify the read-only dictionary
leads to a compile-time error

This is useful if you want to quickly create a lookup from some existing data, map that data into a tupled List, Array, or Sequence of the form [key, value; key, value], and simply push it into the `readOnlyDict` function.

Note that dictionaries are not guaranteed to be run-time safe. For example, you can make an access to a key that doesn't exist using the previously shown indexer notation. If the key does not exist, you'll get a run-time exception. There are, however, methods on the dictionary, such as `ContainsKeys` and `TryGetValue`, that make it possible to put some safeguards in place.

7.3.5   *Map*

`Map` is an F#-specific version of a dictionary. It has a module associated with it that has useful functions that you can perform on it and is immutable in nature. Thus, when you add a new key/value pair to the map, you are given back a new map with the new value inside it. Like dictionaries, you can make unsafe accesses to keys, and functions are available to check whether it's safe to access a key.

Listing 7.8   Creating and consuming an F# map

```
                        Creates a map based          Adds a new item to
                        on a List of tuples          the map using dot
let lookupMap = Map data          ⟵⎯⎯               notation method
let newLookupMap = lookupMap.Add("Isaac", "Python")   ⟵⎯⎯
let newLookupMap = lookupMap |> Map.add "Isaac" "Python"  ⟵⎯⎯
                        Adds a new item to the map
                        using the Map module
```

As you can see in listing 7.8, the F# `Map` type does have some member methods on it, such as `Add` (in addition to the module functions). One other difference between the Dictionary and the Map is that if you try to add a key to a Dictionary and the key already exists, the Dictionary will throw an exception, while the Map will happily throw away the old value and replace it with the new one.

7.3.6   *Set*

The final collection to look at is the F# set. As the name suggests, Sets allow you to create an unordered bag of unique values. Sets also allow you to easily perform set-based operations on them, such as checking whether one set is a subset of another one or adding two sets together. Since F# records and tuples implement comparison for free, you can use Sets with records out of the box. For example, you could have a set of employees for a specific department and another set of employees that are due bonuses. Sets make it easier to answer questions such as "Are all bonus employees in this department?" and "Which employees in this department will not be getting bonuses?"

Listing 7.9   Working with F# sets

```
type Employee = { Name : string }                                           Creates
let salesEmployees = Set [ { Name = "Isaac" }; { Name =  "Brian" } ]         two sets of
let bonusEmployees = Set [ { Name = "Isaac" }; { Name =  "Tanya" } ]         employees

let allBonusesForSalesStaff =
    salesEmployees |> Set.isSubset bonusEmployees           ⟵────┐   Checks whether
                                                                 │   all sales staff are
                                                                 │   on the list of
let salesWithoutBonsues =                Calculates which        │   bonused staff
    salesEmployees - bonusEmployees  ⟵   sales staff did not
                                         receive bonuses
```

As you can see in listing 7.9, Sets also support operators such as + and -, which are aliases for Set.union and Set.difference, respectively.

Converting between collection types

It's not unusual to need to switch between collection types for specific use cases. Perhaps you're using a List but need to turn it into a Dictionary for a specific use case and then back again. Or you need to convert your List into an Array to call some third-party library code that requires an Array as an input. To make this as easy as possible, the collection modules all have toXXX and ofXXX functions, which convert to or from another collection type, such as List.toSeq and Seq.ofArray.

7.3.7   *More on Sequences*

This extra section explains a little more about the unique nature of Sequences (or IEnumerable). At first glance, they look similar to Lists and Arrays, but the big difference is in how Sequences are executed: if you execute the code in listing 7.6 line by line, when you execute the last line, FSI will show the following:

```
val squares: seq<int>
```

No actual squared numbers are shown, unlike the Array or List examples, because with the Sequence version, F# hasn't actually carried out the operation yet. In other words,

Sequences are lazy. They only carry out a computation when it's required. Sequences are generators, so they may not represent in-memory data. As such, they also recompute themselves every time they are evaluated (just like LINQ in .NET) and can be completely unbounded. So, be careful—if you have a large dataset in which you perform a set of `Seq` operations on it and want to keep the results, make sure to convert the result into an Array or List or call `Seq.cache`. Otherwise, every time you access the final bound symbol, it'll re-execute the entire pipeline, as illustrated in the following listing.

Listing 7.10   Creating a long-running Sequence

```
#time          <--| Turns on
                  | timing in FSI
                                          Creates a large Sequence
let largeComputation =                    of numbers with an
    seq { 1 .. 100000000 }      <--|      arbitrary pipeline
    |> Seq.map (fun x -> x * x)
    |> Seq.rev                            Forces eager
    |> Seq.filter (fun x -> x % 2 = 0)    evaluation into
    |> Seq.toArray             <--        an array
```

Notice the use of the `#time` directive, a command that FSI can accept to time any execution and display metrics on it:

```
Real: 00:00:03.028, CPU: 00:00:02.921, GC gen0: 1, gen1: 1, gen2: 0
val it: int = 50000000
```

On my five-year-old laptop, listing 7.10 takes about 3 seconds to run in FSI. However, if you try to access `largeComputation` again (e.g., `largeComputation |> Array.length`), you'll see that the result is almost instant since the computation results have been stored in memory. In comparison, remove the `Seq.toArray` line and try it again. Now, you'll see that the initial execute happens instantly, but now every subsequent call to, for example, `Seq.length` will take around 3 seconds to run! These characteristics explain why if you send the value `squares` to FSI directly, it'll only show you a subset of the data:

```
val it: seq<int> = seq [1; 4; 9; 16; ...]
```

7.3.8   Comprehensions

Another nice trick with Sequences, Arrays, and Lists is that you can create them programmatically, using conditional logic to derive the collection contents. Listing 7.11 shows us how we can use a comprehension to achieve this.

Listing 7.11   Creating a Sequence comprehension

```
let comp = seq {
    1        <--| Adds 1 and 2 to
    2           | the Sequence                                    Only adds
                                                                  99 to the
    if DateTime.Today.DayOfWeek = DayOfWeek.Tuesday then 99  <--  Sequence if it
    4                                                             is Tuesday
}
```

In effect, we're saying "create a Sequence that contains 1 and 2; if the day is Tuesday, have it also contain 99; and end with 4." You can call any code inside a comprehension; other functions, nested `if/then` clauses, even database calls (although I wouldn't always advise that).

This ability to programmatically create lists of any kind through expressions (remember, in F# `if/then` is an expression with a return value) is extremely powerful and can be used to create domain-specific languages (DSLs) in all sorts of places.

The Yield keyword

There's a keyword in F#, `yield`, that is generally now rendered obsolete. In older versions of F# you would have had to write `yield 99` in listing 7.11, but today, you can simply write `99`. There's another keyword, `yield!`, which is still useful when you want to unwrap a List of Lists as part of a comprehension.

Comprehensions in combination with Sequences allow us to do some interesting things, such as converting imperative-style code into what appears to be a stream of data that you can map over or create infinite Sequences and are worth looking into further.

7.3.9 Comparing the different collection types

Table 7.1 lets you quickly see some key differences between the different core three collection types available to F# (rather than the dictionary/hash set style ones).

Table 7.1 Comparing the three main collection types in F#

Collection	Eagerness	Immutable	Performance	.NET Interop	Indexing?
Seq	Lazy	Yes	Medium	Good	No
List	Eager	Yes	Medium/Fast	Medium	Yes
Array	Eager	No	Fast	Good	Yes

My advice is: start with List. It's more expressive than Array in terms of both syntax and features, and it's more predictable than the Sequence type. However, an Array is a little more performant and easier to consume from C#. Lastly, Sequences are useful both for compatibility purposes and for their unique capabilities in terms of laziness. Note that both the List and Array types implement the IEnumerable interface, meaning that both collections can be consumed by any code that expects a Sequence.

7.4 Aggregations

Aggregations represent a type of operation commonly (but not only) seen when working with collections. They provide a way to collapse data from several values into a single value (see figure 7.7).

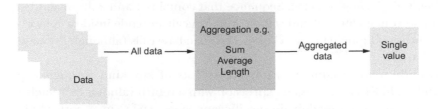

Figure 7.7   Aggregations combine a collection of values into one

Some examples include "I want to total up all debt of a list of customers" or "What's the total price of the user's basket at checkout." You'll typically do this with numerical fields, although not necessarily; for example, concatenating a set of strings into a single string is also an aggregation. The three examples given in figure 7.7 all share a common theme: they take in a collection of items and return a single item. Here are some examples in F# syntax:

```
type Sum        = int seq    -> int
type Average    = float seq  -> float
type Count<'T>  = 'T seq     -> int
```

We perform aggregations all the time—for example, almost any time you use a `while` loop. They all follow a very similar pattern and require the same inputs:

- An input collection
- An accumulator to hold the value of the aggregation
- A default starting value for the accumulator

With these things, you can perform an aggregation following the flow outlined in figure 7.8.

Let's look at how this pattern works in F# in two ways: using imperative loops and a functional fold.

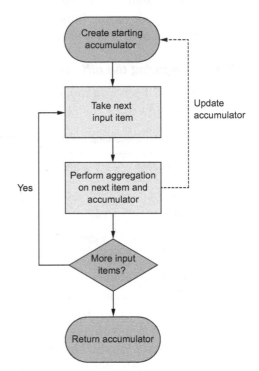

Figure 7.8   Visualizing a typical generic aggregation algorithm

7.4.1 Imperative loops

F# does indeed have support for imperative loops such as for and while. Let's look at them briefly.

```
let numbers = [ 1 .. 10 ] |> List.map string

for n in numbers do
    printfn $"Number {n}"          ←—  A for each–
                                       style loop

for n in 1 .. 10 do
    printfn "Number %i" n          ←———— A for-style loop

let mutable counter = 1
while counter <= 10 do
    printfn $"Number {counter}"    ←———— A while loop
    counter <- counter + 1
```

There is still a place for them in F# but only in a couple of scenarios:

- You're at the end of a functional pipeline chain and want to perform some side-effectful operation (e.g., "Save every customer in this list to the database").
- You're trying to generate a Sequence or similar using a comprehension. I'll give an example of this later in this chapter, as it's a useful technique.

We use them much more in other languages and certainly before the advent of functional collection libraries became mainstream features in C#, Java, JavaScript, etc.

Let's now implement sum using for loops in the algorithm shown in figure 7.7:

```
let inputs = [ 1 .. 10 ]              Creates a mutable
let sum inputs =                      accumulator initialized to 0
    let mutable accumulator = 0   ←
    for input in inputs do        ←———————— A for each loop
        accumulator <- accumulator + input
    accumulator   ←                       Increments the accumulator
                                          on each iteration
                 Returns the total
                 accumulator value
```

Interestingly, F#'s type inference engine correctly calculates the type of inputs to be an int seq. It knows that it's a seq because we use inputs within a for loop and that it's an int because it's added to accumulator.

7.4.2 Functional folds

Let's now look at the typical way to do the same thing in a functional way with fold, which lives in the Seq, Array, and List modules. It's a generalized way of performing aggregations and implements the same aggregation algorithm we saw earlier but takes care of a lot of the boilerplate for you. Again, I'd advise looking at the documentation in your IDE to see whether you can figure this out yourself, but here it's used to achieve the same output as the imperative sum:

```
let sum inputs =
    inputs              ◁———— Input collection
    |> Seq.fold
        (fun accumulator input -> accumulator + input)    ◁┐ Aggregation
        0         ◁┐                                        ┘ function
                   ┘ Starts value
```

If you compare this to the previous code, you'll see that the same three things are there:

- The input dataset (1–10)
- The starting value of the accumulator (0)
- The logic for how to aggregate the next item in the collection to the accumulator (adding them together)

The fold function takes care of the rest of the logic. You don't need to create any mutable data. Instead, your folder function has to calculate the new accumulator value; fold will automatically thread that through to the next call for you. With a bit of printfn logging, you can see this for yourself:

```
let sum inputs =
    inputs
    |> Seq.fold
        (fun accumulator input ->                          ◁┐ Adds logging
            printfn $"Acc {accumulator} + input {input} =>"  ┤ code in the
            accumulator + input)                             │ middle of the
        0                                                    │ aggregation
                                                             ┘ function

sum [ 1 .. 5 ]
```

This now outputs the following log messages to the console:

```
Acc 0 + input 1 =>
Acc 1 + input 2 =>
Acc 3 + input 3 =>
Acc 6 + input 4 =>
Acc 10 + input 5 =>
val it: int = 15
```

You should be able to see from the log output how the result of each log line becomes the accumulator on the next one.

Virtually anytime you feel yourself reaching for a while or for loop (except for the specific scenarios I gave earlier), ask yourself if you could instead use a fold or one of its variants, such as reduce and scan. I also haven't covered (nor will I) recursive functions

(functions that call themselves) in this book, but these can also be used to implement aggregations.

7.4.3 Simulating Sequences

I'm going to round off this chapter with a couple of samples of how you can generate fake Sequences through comprehensions. This is a useful technique when you're working with data sources that don't necessarily lend themselves well to list processing by default.

WORKING WITH DATES

Calculate the dates of all Mondays between February and May 2020 inclusively. By default, this might feel like a highly imperative challenge in .NET, but by using comprehensions, you can treat dates as a near-infinite stream that you can do standard Sequence filtering on:

```
let allDates = seq {              ← Creates a Sequence              A mutable
    let mutable theDate = DateTime.MinValue     ←                   value storing
    while theDate <= DateTime.MaxValue do                          the next date
        theDate                   ←    Yields the date
        theDate <- theDate.AddDays 1.   ←    in the sequence
}                                        Moves to the next date
```

The type of `allDates` is a `DateTime seq` for every possible date. Once we have this, it's now trivial to calculate the dates as required:

```
let mondays =
    allDates
    |> Seq.skipWhile (fun d -> d.Year < 2020 || d.Month < 2)
    |> Seq.filter (fun d -> d.DayOfWeek = DayOfWeek.Monday)
    |> Seq.takeWhile (fun d -> d.Year = 2020 && d.Month < 6)
    |> Seq.toArray
```

TREATING CONSOLE INPUT AS A SEQUENCE

Another data source that can't typically be treated as a Sequence is user input from the console, but with Sequence comprehensions, it's easy to do:

```
let userInput = seq {
    printfn "Enter command (X to exit)"
    while true do
        Console.ReadKey().KeyChar
}
```

Treating user input in this way is very useful since you can start to write code completely decoupled from the actual console that operates on a sequence of characters, meaning you can easily test your code with specific input data. Here's a sample command processor function that can be plugged into any list of characters and can be easily plugged into the previous `userInput` stream:

```
let processInputCommands commands =          ⟵————  Command processor,
    commands                                           decoupled from console input
    |> Seq.takeWhile (fun cmd -> cmd <> 'x')
    |> Seq.iter (fun cmd ->
        printfn ""
        if cmd = 'w' then printfn "Withdrawing money!"
        elif cmd = 'd' then printfn "Depositing money!"          ⟵—  Applies the user
        else printfn $"You executed command {cmd}")                  input stream to
                                                                     the processing
userInput |> processInputCommands                              ⟵
[ 'w'; 'd'; 'z'; 'x'; 'w' ] |> processInputCommands    ⟵      Applies an in-memory
                                                              test stream of
                                                              commands
```

You can even test this out in an FSI script session!

7.5   *Answers to exercises*

EXERCISE 7.1

```
let calculate (operation, name) a b =
    let answer = operation a b
    printfn $"{name} {a} and {b} = {answer}"
    answer

calculate ((fun x y -> x + y), "add") 5 10 // etc.
```

EXERCISE 7.2

```
results
|> List.filter (fun r ->
    r.AwayTeam = "Ronaldo City" || r.HomeTeam = "Ronaldo City")
|> List.length
```

EXERCISE 7.3

```
results
|> List.collect (fun result ->
    [
        {| Team = result.HomeTeam; Goals = result.HomeGoals |}
        {| Team = result.AwayTeam; Goals = result.AwayGoals |}
    ])
|> List.groupBy (fun result -> result.Team)
|> List.map (fun (team, games) ->
    team, games |> List.sumBy (fun game -> game.Goals))
|> List.maxBy snd
```

Summary

- Functions that take other functions as arguments are known as higher-order functions (HOFs).

- F# makes creating and consuming HOFs easy thanks to its powerful type inference.

- F# encourages us to create small data transformation functions that can be reused and composed together into more powerful pipelines.

- F# favors a declarative approach to processing data transformations, even over collections.

- When working in scripts, you can see step by step what a pipeline is doing by executing just a subset of it.

- The language comes with a set of utility collection functions in modules such as `List`, `Array`, `Seq`, and `Set`.

- `Seq` is a special type of collection that supports lazy evaluation.

- There are several other useful collection types that F# has access to, including Map, Dictionary, and Set.

- `Fold` is the functional equivalent of `for each` and `while` loops when it comes to aggregating data.

- Comprehensions allow us to create collections based on imperative logic.

- You can use Sequences to create lists from computations, such as streams of dates or console inputs.

Patterns and unions 8

This chapter covers

- Conditional logic with pattern matching
- Discriminated unions
- Summarizing the F# type system

This chapter finishes our look at the core F# language! It deals with two things: first, how we perform conditional logic, such as `if`/`then` and, second, the final kind of type supported in F#—the discriminated union—which provides a solution to parts of domain modeling that records and tuples can't really address. When you finish this, you'll have a rounded appreciation of the F# type system and understand when to use which component.

8.1 Introducing pattern matching

We've already seen `if`/`then` expressions in F#. As it turns out, in everyday F#, they are used only in a couple of specific scenarios because F# has a much more powerful mechanism for conditional logic: pattern matching.

I've heard pattern matching described as "`switch`/`case` on steroids" by some people. It's basically a way of performing logic over different conditions (known as *patterns*) in a flexible expression-oriented construct.

> **F# uses pattern matching, not if/then**
>
> As a bit of history, pattern matching isn't an F#-specific feature; it's been common in most ML languages for years and is now finding its way into many curly brace languages such as C#, Java, TypeScript, and Python. The challenge I see many of those languages face (along with many other functional programming features) is that if/then and switch/case statements are so commonplace that changing how people write code in a language they've known for years can be challenging. In F#, pattern matching has always been the idiomatic way for conditional logic and is pervasive throughout the language and libraries.

Let's start with an example of pattern matching to show you what it looks like, which takes a ConsoleModifier key press and returns a textual description of that keypress.

Listing 8.1   Basic pattern matching

```
let value = System.ConsoleModifiers.Alt

let description =
    match value with                              Matches over the
      | System.ConsoleModifiers.Alt -> "Alt was pressed."         symbol value.
      | System.ConsoleModifiers.Control -> "You hit control!"     Handlers
      | System.ConsoleModifiers.Shift -> "Shift held down..."     for different
      | _ -> "Some modifier was pressed"           patterns
                                    A wildcard
                                    catch-all handler
```

This code matches over value; for example, if the value is Alt, it returns the string Alt was pressed. At first glance, pattern matching looks like switch/case, which is popular in some languages. However

- Instead of switch, F# uses match with
- Instead of case, F# uses |
- Instead of : for each handler, F# uses ->

As pattern matching is an expression, all branches need to return a value of the same type (in listing 8.1, this is a string), which the entire match returns and is bound to a symbol (in this case, description).

8.1.1   *Exhaustive matching*

If you remove the wildcard match case (the _), you'll see the compiler gives a warning:

```
warning FS0104: Enums may take values outside known cases. For example, the
value 'enum<System.ConsoleModifiers> (0)' may indicate a case not covered
by the pattern(s).
```

The compiler is warning us that we've not handled every possibility that value may have. Unlike statements, expressions must always return a value. So, if a pattern match encounters a value it doesn't have a handler for, the runtime will throw an exception. If you think about it, this is pretty much the only thing it can do. Otherwise, in such a case as in listing 8.1, what would you expect the value of `description` to be?

F# will also tell us if we have two patterns that overlap. You can observe this if you duplicate one of the patterns in listing 8.1; you'll see a compiler warning on the line of the duplicate pattern: `This rule will never be matched`. It's also important to note that patterns are processed in order, so putting the wildcard as the first pattern would mean that no other pattern in your match will ever get hit!

It's quite common in the F# world to treat either of these warnings (if not all warnings) as errors. I certainly wouldn't allow code to pass a review that had unhandled pattern matches. Instead, I would suggest either throwing a specific exception in an explicit wildcard match that could log the value of the match or perhaps return an error value instead (which we'll see in chapter 9).

Wildcards, while sometimes unavoidable, are a bit of a code smell in everyday F#. We'll see later in this chapter how it is possible, and preferable, to avoid using them at all.

> **NOTE** The more eagle-eyed among you will have spotted that there are only three values of `ConsoleModifiers`, so why is there a need for a wildcard handler? Well, in .NET, an enum is more or less a kind of type-safe alias for an integer. The problem here is that you can cast any integer to an enum, even one that doesn't correspond to an enum case; the .NET runtime will happily permit this.

8.1.2 *Tuple matching*

Pattern matching starts to get somewhat more powerful when you match against different patterns. There are many different patterns supported in F#; we'll start with tuples. Tuple matching is great when you want to perform if/then statements with some AND logic inside it.

For example, let's say that you have a request for a loan in a financial application, and you want to determine whether to allow the loan based on both whether the customer's account is currently overdrawn *and* how many years they've been a customer:

- Customers who have not been with us for at least one year can never take out a loan.
- Customers with one year of history can only take a loan if they are not overdrawn.
- Customers with two years of history can always take out a loan.
- All customers with more than two years of history can always take out a loan.

Let's look at this using a simple tabular view in table 8.1. This table can be mapped to an F# pattern matching almost one-to-one, as in listing 8.2.

Table 8.1 Conditional logic laid out as a truth table

Input 1: Years as customer	Input 2: Is overdrawn	Output: Can take a loan
0	True	False
0	False	False
1	True	False
1	False	True
2	False	True
2	True	True
Any other duration	True or False	True

Listing 8.2 Tuple pattern matching

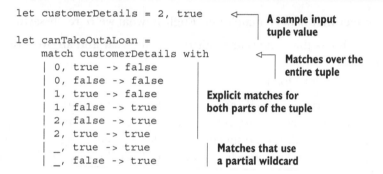

```
let customerDetails = 2, true          ◁──┐  A sample input
                                          │  tuple value
let canTakeOutALoan =
    match customerDetails with      ◁──      Matches over the
    | 0, true -> false                       entire tuple
    | 0, false -> false
    | 1, true -> false            Explicit matches for
    | 1, false -> true           both parts of the tuple
    | 2, false -> true
    | 2, true -> true
    | _, true -> true            Matches that use
    | _, false -> true           a partial wildcard
```

8.1.3 Simplifying pattern matches: A worked example

The entire rule set in table 8.1 is a little verbose, and we can simplify it in several ways:

- Customers with two years or more than two years of history can be combined.
- We don't need to have explicit cases for those customers: both true and false overdrawn cases lead to the same outcome.
- We don't need to have explicit cases for customers with less than one year of history: both true and false overdrawn cases lead to the same outcome.

This allows us to simplify the pattern match as follows:

```
let canTakeOutALoan =
    match customerDetails with
    | 0, _ -> false
    | 1, true -> false
    | 1, false -> true
    | _ -> true
```

We can do even better as F# allows us to combine multiple matches that have the same outcome:

```
let canTakeOutALoanSimpler =
    match customerDetails with
    | 0, _                        Two patterns with
    | 1, true ->                  the same handler
        false           <──┐
    | 1, false             │     Shared handler
    | _ ->
        true
```

Finally, you can now combine both `true` patterns into a single wildcard:

```
let canTakeOutALoanSimplest =
    match customerDetails with
    | 0, _
    | 1, true ->
        false
    | _ ->
        true
```

If we reverse-engineer that pattern match into English, what we're really saying is

- Customers with less than one year of history or one year and an overdraft can't get a loan.
- Everyone else can get a loan.

Compare this with the original specification we outlined at the start. This is a more succinct description than that, but to get to that, we needed to use some pattern matching and refactoring to distill the specification. Pattern matching is great for simplifying what might appear to be somewhat more complex rules with this kind of step-by-step approach.

NOTE One thing that I don't particularly like about this kind of code is that it's hard to know at a glance what, for example, `0, true` represents at a glance. You need to know what the `int * bool` represents. Fear not! There are several features in F# that improve this that you'll see later in this chapter.

8.1.4 Record matching

You can also match on F# records at a field-by-field level. The following listing provides a variant of the match from the previous exercise but using a record type.

Listing 8.3   Record pattern matching

```
type CustomerDetails =                                    Defines a
    { YearsOfHistory : int;  HasOverdraft : bool }  <──┘  customer record
let customerDetailsRecord =
    { YearsOfHistory = 2; HasOverdraft = true }     <──   Creates a sample
                                                          customer
let canTakeOutALoanRecord =
    match customerDetailsRecord with
    | { YearsOfHistory = 0 } -> false               <──   Matches on a
                                                          single record field
```

```
| { YearsOfHistory = 1; HasOverdraft = true } -> false      Matches on multiple
| { YearsOfHistory = 1; HasOverdraft = false } -> true      record fields
| _ -> true
```

Using records can be a little more verbose than tuple matching, but the readability is often better as you can see the names of the fields you're matching on. Additionally, unlike a tuple match, each pattern in a record only needs to match against whichever arbitrary fields you want to. Observe how the first pattern only matches against `Years-OfHistory`, whereas the second and third patterns match against both `YearsOfHistory` and `HasOverdraft`. This can really improve readability compared to tuple matching if you're matching against, for example, five or six values but only ever need one or two in any given pattern.

8.1.5 Type inference

As you might now expect, pattern matching plays nicely with type inference. The following listing provides the code from listing 8.3 but shown as a function.

Listing 8.4   Pattern matching type inference

```
let canTakeOutALoanRecordFn customer =      ◄─┐  Defines a function that has a
    match customer with                        │  customer as an input argument
    | { YearsOfHistory = 0 } -> false       ◄──┘  without a type annotation
    | { YearsOfHistory = 1; HasOverdraft = true } -> false   ┐ Pattern matching
    | { YearsOfHistory = 1; HasOverdraft = false } -> true   ┘ on the customer
    | _ -> true
```

As you can see, the type of customer is never specified, yet the compiler is still able to infer that `customer` is of type `CustomerDetails` through the usage in the pattern match.

8.1.6 When guards

One of the problems with the pattern matching I've shown so far is that it only matches against absolute values—specific numbers, strings, Booleans, etc. What if you wanted to match on something more arbitrary—for example, "When the current time is after 5 pm" or "If `overdraft` is more than a specific amount"—in short, any time that you want to match on some computation, rather than an absolute value? This is where `when` guards come into play.

Let's assume that the record shown in listing 8.3 has an extra field representing the value of the overdraft (assume that customers without an overdraft have this set to `0`). We want to implement code so customers with one year of history should only be refused if their overdraft is over $500. Listing 8.5 shows how we can use a when guard clause to specify this check.

Listing 8.5   Using `When` within Pattern Matches

```
let canTakeOutALoanRecord =
    match customerDetailsRecord with
    | { YearsOfHistory = 0 } -> false
```

```
| { YearsOfHistory = 1; HasOverdraft = true } when
⟹  customerDetailsRecord.Overdraft > 500 -> false        ⟵── Uses a when
| { YearsOfHistory = 1 } -> true                                 guard clause
| _ -> true          ⟵──┐
                        Mandatory
                        wildcard match
```

You can put any code you like in a when clause (e.g., function calls, IO operations, etc.). However, I would advise against this; keeping matches based on data rather than computations generally makes them easier to work with.

There's also one limitation about when guards that you should be aware of: they limit the ability of the compiler to detect whether your pattern matches are exhaustive, so you'll often need to put a wildcard in as a fail-safe. You can work around this by creating values before matching that have all the logic of the when clause in it and then matching on that as, for example, a tuple:

```
let canTakeOutALoanNoGuard (recordWithOverdraft:CustomerDetailsOverdraft) =
⟹   let hasLargeOverdraft = recordWithOverdraft.Overdraft > 500
    match recordWithOverdraft, hasLargeOverdraft with        ⟵──────────┐
    | { YearsOfHistory = 0 }, _ -> false
    | { YearsOfHistory = 1; HasOverdraft = true }, true -> false    ⟵──┐
```

Creates a simple Boolean ahead   **Matches on the Boolean**
of time for large overdrafts   **as part of a tuple**

Active patterns

The idea of creating temporary data to support pattern matching is not uncommon and can be a useful way to simplify more complex matching. F# also has a more powerful feature known as *active patterns* that allow you to apply such logic in a reusable fashion. They're beyond the scope of this book but are worth checking out when you want to level up your F#.

EXERCISE 8.1

Modify the code in listing 8.5 so that the guard calls a function that calculates the maximum overdraft based on the number of years of history the customer has. For every year, add an overdraft limit of $250 and place it on every rejected handler for years 1 and 2.

8.2   *More advanced pattern matching*

With the basics of pattern matching out of the way, let's look at more powerful applications of the feature—things that make pattern matching the go-to option for conditional branching logic.

8.2.1   *Recursive matching*

One of the best things about patterns is that they can be combined or contain multiple patterns. This is known as *recursive* matching. Don't confuse this with recursive functions (functions that call themselves). Recursive patterns are about nesting multiple pattern matches inside of one another. Again, it's best to illustrate it by example, as shown in the following listing.

Listing 8.6   Using when within pattern matches

```
type OverdraftDetails =
    {
        Approved : bool
        MaxAmount : decimal
        CurrentAmount : decimal
    }

type CustomerWithOverdraft =
    {
        YearsOfHistory : int
        Overdraft : OverdraftDetails
    }

let canTakeOutALoanRecursive customer =
    match customer with
    | { YearsOfHistory = 0; Overdraft = { Approved = true } } ->
        true
    | { YearsOfHistory = 0 } ->
        false
    | { YearsOfHistory = 1; Overdraft = { Approved = true } } ->
        true
    | { YearsOfHistory = 1 } ->
        false
    | _ ->
        true
```

Defines two records; the first is the type of a field on the second

Simultaneously matches on fields of the parent record and on a child field

As you can see, we can unwrap the inner field `Overdraft` and match it against the contents of `Approved`. This recursive matching works with every type of pattern, and you can mix and match. So, you could, for example, have a record with a field that's a tuple whose first value is a record and match all the way down within the object. Compare this to the following:

```
let canTakeOutALoanRecursive customer =
    match customer with
    | { YearsOfHistory = 0 } ->
        match customer.Overdraft with
        | { Approved = true } -> true
        | { Approved = false } -> false
    | { YearsOfHistory = 1 } ->
        match customer.Overdraft with
        | { Approved = true } -> true
        | { Approved = false } -> false
    | _ -> true
```

Matches just on the top level fields

Matches on the child fields as a separate, nested match

As you can see, this code is more involved and not as easy to read. At first glance, recursive matching may not sound especially powerful, but trust me when I say it's a complete game changer. You can create extremely elegant solutions for conditional logic.

EXERCISE 8.2

Extend the logic in listing 8.6 so that the CustomerWithOverdraft record also contains a field, Address on it, which is a record containing at least a string field, Country. Now, add as a further requirement to approve a loan that Country must equal "US". Experiment with both recursive matching and nested matches to see the differences between them.

8.2.2 Nested or conditions

Another aspect of pattern matching worth highlighting is that you can create nested or conditions. Look at listing 8.6 again: see how the first and third matches are the same except YearsOfHistory is 0 in one and 1 in another? Well, you can also merge that check:

```
match customer with
| { YearsOfHistory = 0 | 1; Overdraft = { Approved = true } } -> true
| { YearsOfHistory = 0 | 1 } -> false
| _ -> true
```

Pattern matches with a nested or against YearsOfHistory

8.2.3 Binding symbols

Something that is occasionally useful is the ability to use a value within a match on the handler side of a pattern. You can simply bind that value to a symbol instead of (or in addition to) comparing it to some constant value.

Listing 8.7 Binding to symbols during pattern matching

Binds the CurrentAmount value to the symbol amount

References the symbol amount within the handler

```
match customer with
| { Overdraft = { Approved = true; CurrentAmount = amount } } ->
    printfn $"Loan approved; current overdraft is {amount}"
    true
| { Overdraft = { Approved = false } as overdraftDetails } ->
    printfn $"Loan declined; overdraft details are {overdraftDetails}"
    true
| _ ->
    false
```

Binds an entire record to a symbol

8.2.4 Collection matching

One of the biggest benefits that F# Lists have over any other collection type is that they have rich support for pattern matching (Arrays have some limited support). You can do the following with List patterns:

- Check for empty lists.
- Extract the head item of the List (which can then be matched against recursively).
- Check for lists of specific lengths (and extract details of any element):

```
type LoanRequest =
    { YearsOfHistory : int
```

```
                    HasOverdraft : bool
                    LoanRequestAmount : decimal
                    IsLargeRequest : bool }

        let summariseLoanRequests requests =
            match requests with
            | [] ->
                "No requests made!"
            | [ { IsLargeRequest = true } ] ->
                "Single large request!"
            | [ { IsLargeRequest = true }; { IsLargeRequest = true } ] ->
                "Two large requests!"
            | { IsLargeRequest = false } :: remainingItems ->
                $"Several items, the first of which is a small request.
            Remaining items: {remainingItems}."
            | _ :: { HasOverdraft = true } :: _ ->
                "Second item has an overdraft!"
            | _ ->
                "Anything else"
```

Matches against an empty list

Matches against a single list item, recursively

Matches on a List of 2 requests, recursively

Matches on the head of a list of unknown length

Repeatedly uses the head operator in a match

The difference compared to using indexers is that indexers are not type-safe. You need to check the length of the collection first, before accessing it by index. Otherwise, the runtime will raise an exception. Conversely, pattern matching does both checks in one, and importantly, it does it all at compile time.

EXERCISE 8.3

One last point: remember earlier I said that the compiler will warn you when you don't handle all cases? To give you an example of how much it will do to help here, comment out the final wildcard match and observe as it suggests a specific, explicit pattern that hasn't been handled (in this case, a list of three items of which the middle element does not have an overdraft).

I don't use List matching daily in F# code, but when I do need it, it's extremely useful to have it available.

8.2.5 *Match vs. if/then*

There are, at the time of this writing, 17 different types of patterns that F# can match against; I've shown you what I consider the most important ones. However, it's worth looking at the official documentation to see what the others are; they also have their place.

Since pattern matching is the main mechanism you'll use for conditional logic, why do we still have if/then/else in F#? Well, there are a couple of situations where that is a better fit than pattern matching.

The first is when you're directly matching on Boolean values. In such cases, if/then is preferred since it's directly optimized for doing exactly that:

```
let description =
    match x with
    | true -> "Value is true!"
    | false -> "Value is false!"
```

Pattern matching on a boolean

```
let description =
    if x then "Value is true!"          ◁─┐  Using if/then
    else "Value is false!"                └─  on a boolean
```

The `if`/`else` in this case is not only less to write but, more importantly, easier to read and reason about.

The second situation where `if`/`else` might be preferable to pattern matching is if you're working with an expression that returns `unit`—typically some side-effectful operation. Suppose you had an order request; if the order has been modified by the user, it needs to be saved to the database by calling the `DbRepository.save` function, which has a signature of `OrderRequest -> unit`. However, if the request has not been modified, we don't need to do anything. If we were to implement this with pattern matching, things would be a little more verbose than needed, since you always need to handle every possible case, and each branch must return the same type, meaning you'll end up with a dead handler that just returns a unit:

```
                                                             ┌─ Calls the database
                                                             │  save function, which
                                                             │  returns unit
match orderRequest with
| { IsDirty = true } -> DbRepository.save orderRequest  ◁──┘
| { IsDirty = false } -> ()       ◁──┐
                                     └─ Explicitly handles the other case with
                                        a unit value to satisfy the compiler
```

On the other hand, `if`/`else` expressions have a neat trick up their sleeve. If the expression returns `unit`, you can completely omit the catch-all `else ()` branch; the compiler will add it in for you. This means that you can write code like this:

```
if orderRequest.IsDirty then DbRepository.save orderRequest
```

8.3   *Discriminated unions*

Now that we've dealt with pattern matching, we need to move on to the final element of the core F# type system that we've not yet seen: *discriminated unions*. Earlier in this book, when I introduced tuples and records, I touched on AND and OR types. While most languages have very good support for ANDing data together (properties on classes, fields on records or tuples), OR cases—situations where a value can be one of a set of values—are sometimes more difficult to model. Many languages today have a few options, such as enums or inheritance, which in most languages are either too simple or too heavyweight to be especially useful.

Discriminated unions are the answer to this. They form a core part of the type system in F# and are extremely useful. With them added to F#, you can effectively model domains quickly and succinctly for both AND and OR cases.

I can't stress enough how important discriminated unions are to F# as a way of rounding out the type system; having them fills a gap that many languages can't solve easily (if at all). More than that, they're lightweight, flexible, and simple to reason about; they are not a kind of powerful but hard-to-learn feature. Once you learn them, you'll find yourself using them all the time.

Figure 8.1 illustrates where records, tuples, and discriminated unions sit in terms of domain modeling. Use records and tuples to model cases where all of the values exist alongside one another simultaneously; use discriminated unions to model values where only one of the possible values can exist at any time.

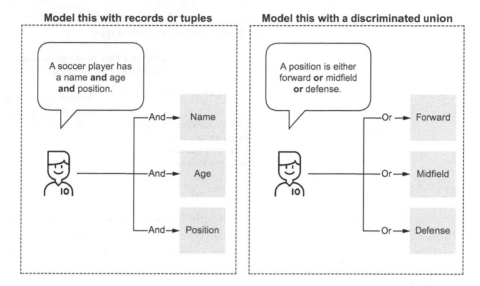

Figure 8.1 Comparing and contrasting AND and OR types in F#

8.3.1 Basics of discriminated unions

Consider the following example (figure 8.2): You're modeling a customer in your application—in particular, how you might contact them. When registering, every customer in your application needs to select one of three contact methods:

- Email address (in which case, they need to provide their email address)
- Telephone number (requiring the country code and telephone number)
- Post (address lines 1 and 2, city, and country)

```
Name : string
Age : int
ContactMethod :
    One of:
    Email
        EmailAddress : string
    Telephone Number
        CountryCode : string
        TelephoneNumber : string
    Post
        Line1 : string
        Line2 : string
        City : string
        Country : string
```

Figure 8.2 Sketching out a customer domain model. This model has a combination of AND and OR values at multiple levels.

The `Name` and `Age` part should be obvious here. Where it gets interesting is when you try to model the `ContactMethod` part because this is an OR relationship and we don't yet know how to model this in F#. The following listing shows what it looks like via a discriminated union.

Listing 8.8   Our first discriminated union

Defines the ContactMethod type

```
type ContactMethod =           ◄───────┐
    | Email of address:string   ◄───────
    | Telephone of country:string * number:string   ◄───
    | Post of
        {|
            Line1 : string
            Line2 : string
            City : string
            Country : string
        |}
```

Defines a case of the contact method (email) along with the data it requires

Defines another case, using a tuple to handle multiple fields

Defines another case, using an anonymous record to handle multiple fields

---

Each case of a discriminated union has a simple format: `<name> of <data>`. The data portion can be any type you want: a simple type, a record, a tuple, an anonymous record, or even another discriminated union (including itself!). Creating an instance of a discriminated union is also extremely lightweight:

Creates an email case of Contact Method

Creates a telephone Contact Method, passing the tuple inline

```
let isaacEmail = Email "isaac@myemailaddress.com"   ◄────
let isaacPhone = Telephone ("UK", "020-8123-4567")   ◄───
let isaacPost = Post {| Line1 = "1 The Street" … |} // etc.
```

Notice that to create an `Email`, we only need to supply the address; for `Telephone`, we need to provide the country and number tuple—only the data that's required for that particular case.

> **NOTE**   The naming of each "element" in the data portion of listing 8.8 e.g. `country:string * number:string` is optional; you can simply use types only (e.g. `string * string`). However, entering names will allow code editors to provide intellisense when creating union values.

It's also important to understand that `isaacEmail`, `isaacPhone`, and `isaacPost` are all `ContactMethod` values; they aren't of `Email` or `Telephone` types. Instead, those are simply *cases* of the `ContactMethod` type and act as factory functions that create an instance of `ContactMethod`. Look at figure 8.2 again and then with the following:

```
type CustomerDu =
    { Name: string
      Age : int
      ContactMethod : ContactMethod }
```

Observe how we're using several different F# types here, but they all boil down to either AND or OR relationships:

- `Customer` has a `Name`, `Age`, AND `ContactMethod` (Record)
- `ContactMethod` is either an `Email`, `Telephone`, OR `Post` (discriminated union)
- `Telephone` has a `Country` AND `Number` (tuple)
- `Post` has `Line1`, `Line2`, `City`, AND `Country` (record)

Notice how closely the code and the sketched-out model align.

8.3.2   Pattern matching

OK, so we know how to model and build discriminated unions, but how do we consume them? You might be tempted to try to dot into the contact method to get at the data, but you'll be left disappointed. There appear to be no fields to access. All the following will result in a compiler error that there is no such member:

```
isaacEmail.Address
isaacEmail.Telephone
isaacEmail.Post.Line1
```

So how do we get to the data? With pattern matching, of course!

Listing 8.9   Pattern matching over a discriminated union

```
let message = "Discriminated Unions FTW!"

match customer.ContactMethod with          ◁──── Matches on the
| Email address -> $"Emailing '{message}' to {address}."   union value
| Telephone (country, number) ->
    $"Calling {country}-{number} with the       Safely unwraps
➥ message '{message}'!"                          each case and
| Post postDetails ->                            binds its contents
    $"Printing a letter with contents '{message}'   to a symbol
➥ to {postDetails.Line1} {postDetails.City}..."
```

What we're seeing here is a regular pattern match, except each branch handles a different case of the union. There are several profound things to note about this that you might not notice immediately though, so let's go through them one by one.

First, it's very safe to work with discriminated unions. We bind the data of each case to a symbol; for example, the email address is bound to the `address` symbol, the telephone data is bound to the tuple `(country, number)`, etc. However, we can only bind to the data for that case and only when pattern matching: it's impossible to access the telephone data if the contact method is an email. So, there's no danger of, for example, accidentally reading some null data from another case.

Second, we have a single function that deals with all three cases together. This might be very surprising if you're coming from an objection oriented background because it's almost the opposite of what you might normally do. You could delegate each handler into its own function; however, fundamentally, with a discriminated union, there's a coupling here that you might not expect. If you're confused by this and trying to mentally compare this with, for example, polymorphism, remember the following:

- Polymorphism makes it easy to add new subtypes but hard to add new behaviors. Every time you add a new method to the base class, you need to modify every subtype; it's a breaking change. But adding a new subtype is easy: you inherit from the base class and ensure that your abstract factory can generate them as needed.
- Discriminated unions make it easy to add new behaviors but harder to add new types. New behaviors are just new functions; there's no breaking changes—just a pattern match over each case in the union. However, adding a new case means fixing up every function that matches over the union (thankfully, the compiler will show us every place that this needs to happen).

Generally, domains tend to have a mostly stable set of cases, but behaviors (e.g., methods, functions) are often added quickly. You can, of course, have situations where you're consistently creating new cases, but it doesn't happen very often. In the contact example, you might have many different behaviors: contact a customer, print out their contact details, update a contact method, validate a contact method, etc. But you probably won't be adding new contact methods quite so frequently.

8.3.3 *Exhaustive matching with discriminated unions*

One of the truly beautiful things about discriminated unions is that the compiler can provide us with what's known as *exhaustive* pattern matching. In other words, the compiler can know in any pattern match whether we've handled all possible cases of the discriminated union and warn us if we've forgotten one. In listing 8.9, notice we don't have a wildcard case. That's because the compiler understands that there are three cases of contact method, and we've handled all of them. If, for example, `Contact-Method` was a string field, the compiler couldn't know that we'd handled all the cases because someone could easily pass a different string instead.

Let's see what happens when we add a fourth case now. In your code, add a new fourth case to the `ContactMethod`: `SMS of number:string`. Now, look at the `sendTo` function that we created and observe the following warning:

```
Incomplete pattern matches on this expression. For example, the value 'Sms
(_)' may indicate a case not covered by the pattern(s)
```

In other words, the compiler is warning us that we added a new case but haven't yet dealt with it. As soon as you add a handler for SMS, the compiler warning will go away, and you won't need a wildcard. This safety net is incredibly powerful: you can make changes to your discriminated unions and immediately get notified by the compiler everywhere that you'll need to update to handle the new case.

8.3.4 *Nested types with discriminated unions*

Discriminated unions don't just have to contain primitives; they can contain records, tuples, and other union types (even themselves!). In listing 8.10, I've created a new union, which represents a mobile number that can be either `Local` or `International`. I've then changed the SMS case to be represented by a new type called `Telephone-Number` (not just a `string`). In other words, a contact method can be `SMS`, which itself can be either `Local` or `International`.

Listing 8.10 Modeling a nested (recursive) relationship with unions

```
type TelephoneNumber =              ◁───┤ Creates a simple
    | Local of number:string             discriminated union
    | International of countryCode:string * number:string

type ContactMethod =                      Nests one discriminated
    | // … other cases omitted            union inside another
    | Sms of TelephoneNumber        ◁──

let smsContact = Sms (Local "123-4567")    ◁──┤ Creates an instance
                                               of an SMS number
```

Note that in listing 8.10, I've created both the `SMS` and `Local` values inline, but you could create them as two separate values, one at a time, if you wanted. Now watch what happens when we only match on one of the `TelephoneNumber` cases under `SMS`:

```
let sendTo customer message =                    Handles Local but not
    match customer.ContactMethod with            International SMS
    | // other contact methods omitted…               numbers
    | Sms (Local number) -> $"Texting local number {number}"   ◁──
```

We now get a compiler warning as follows:

```
Incomplete pattern matches on this expression. For example, the value 'Sms
(International (_, _))' may indicate a case not covered by the pattern(s).
```

As you can see, the compiler has identified the exact case that we've not yet covered—international SMS numbers. You can use this kind of exhaustive matching with discriminated unions to remove many cases where you might otherwise need wildcards.

EXERCISE 8.4

Rewrite the loan decision code from listing 8.2 (or its final, distilled version) using the types defined as follows:

```
type YearsAsCustomer =        ◁──    Replaces an unbounded
    | LessThanAYear                  integer with a union
    | OneYear                        with four cases
    | TwoYears
    | MoreThanTwoYears

type OverdraftStatus =        ◁──    Replaces a boolean with
    | InCredit                       a more readable union
    | Overdrawn
```

```
type LoanDecision =
    | LoanRejected
    | LoanAccepted
```

⟵ Replaces the result boolean with a more readable union

Once done, you should not need any Booleans or integers. There are a couple of benefits:

- Your pattern matching is now more readable (i.e., instead of `1`, `true`, you'll have `OneYear`, `Overdrawn`). This also applies to the function signature, which now represents a contract that makes much more sense from a domain-modeling point of view. Previously it was `int * bool -> bool`; now, it's `YearsAsCustomer * OverdraftStatus -> LoanDecision`.
- Your pattern matching is now what is known as "total." There will be no need for wildcards because your types are bounded to just a few cases each (rather than, for example, integers, which have billions of values). If you miss any case, the compiler will tell you exactly which one it is.

This should also illustrate why wildcards are not a great idea: If you add a new case to your types and have a wildcard match that's too broad, the compiler won't warn you that you've not handled a case; instead, it'll just naturally fall into the wildcard. Sometimes, that may be what you want, but other times, it won't be. I'd recommend, in such situations, being as explicit as you can with pattern matches (as you can see from my suggested solution to this exercise) rather than using wildcards, unless you're very sure you won't be adding new cases to that union ever again.

> **Pattern matching in C#**
>
> C# supports pattern matching but (at the time of this writing) does not support discriminated unions or closed hierarchies. When writing *Get Programming with F#*, it was heavily implied to me that this would come out in C#8, but we're now approaching C#11 or 12, and it's still not there. Without them, you can't get exhaustive pattern-matching checks, which, to me, is a big drawback, as the compiler won't help you identify missing cases as your domain model grows.

8.3.5 *Single-case discriminated unions*

Single-case discriminated unions are a special kind of union that, as the name suggests, only has one case. Why would you want to do this when there's no union, nothing to pattern match over? It turns out that because the syntax for single-case unions is so lightweight, they can easily be used as *wrapper types*. Consider the contact method domain that we created in the previous section. Let's focus on the telephone number:

```
type TelephoneNumber =
    | Local of number:string
    | International of countryCode:string * number:string
```

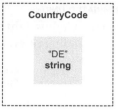

Figure 8.3   Single-case discriminated unions wrap other values to provide richer types. Here, `TelephoneNumber` and `CountryCode` are two types that both wrap strings but have different uses and meanings.

There are three fields across both `Local` and `International` cases (two called `number` and one called `countryCode`). However, all of them are the same type: strings. Two of them (`number`) represent the same thing, while the country code represents something else entirely (figure 8.3). Single-case discriminated unions allow us to not only improve readability in such cases but also to provide more type-safety and enable us to model a domain more richly.

Listing 8.11   Working with single-case discriminated unions

```
type PhoneNumber = PhoneNumber of string        Creates two single case
type CountryCode = CountryCode of string        discriminated unions

type TelephoneNumberRevised =
    | Local of PhoneNumber                       Applies them
    | International of CountryCode * PhoneNumber  in the domain

let localNumber = Local (PhoneNumber "123-456")  ←— Creates a single
let internationalNumber =                           case union inline
    let countryCode = CountryCode "+44"          Creates two single-case
    let phoneNumber = PhoneNumber "208-123-4567" unions and uses their
    International (countryCode, phoneNumber)      values in another value
```

The benefits of working with single-case discriminated unions are not only readability (e.g., I omitted the names of the arguments for `Local` and `International` cases in listing 8.11 since the type names tell us everything we need to know), but they also provide an extra level of type safety, since you can't now mix up country code and phone numbers. Try to switch the `countryCode` and `phoneNumber` values when creating the `International` value. You'll see that we receive a suitable error message such as

```
This expression was expected to have type 'CountryCode' but here has type
'PhoneNumber'
```

This wouldn't have happened if we had used strings for the country code and phone number. At best, we'd have realized when running a unit test and, at worst, when the monthly batch run of the system took place and tried to contact a nonexistent telephone number.

I like to think of this as a kind of trade between myself and the compiler: as I invest the time to create a richer domain with more types in it, the compiler can better support me because I've told it more about what I'm trying to do.

QUICKLY UNWRAPPING SINGLE-CASE DISCRIMINATED UNIONS

Single-case discriminated unions also have a lightweight syntax for unwrapping them to get at their inner values, either using `let` binding or even within a function argument:

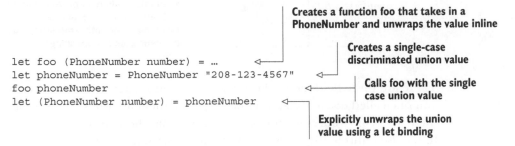

Creates a function foo that takes in a PhoneNumber and unwraps the value inline

Creates a single-case discriminated union value

Calls foo with the single case union value

Explicitly unwraps the union value using a let binding

```
let foo (PhoneNumber number) = ...
let phoneNumber = PhoneNumber "208-123-4567"
foo phoneNumber
let (PhoneNumber number) = phoneNumber
```

USING SINGLE-CASE DISCRIMINATED UNIONS TO ENFORCE INVARIANTS

You can also start to create functions that build on top of single case unions to help enforce business rules. Imagine the case where you have an email address that the user entered on the website but only want to send messages to those email addresses that have been validated. We can model this in the type system directly:

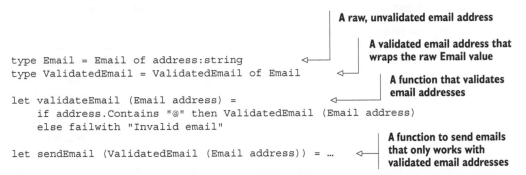

A raw, unvalidated email address

A validated email address that wraps the raw Email value

A function that validates email addresses

A function to send emails that only works with validated email addresses

```
type Email = Email of address:string
type ValidatedEmail = ValidatedEmail of Email

let validateEmail (Email address) =
    if address.Contains "@" then ValidatedEmail (Email address)
    else failwith "Invalid email"

let sendEmail (ValidatedEmail (Email address)) = ...
```

In this sample, we first model our domain with a couple of types. We start with a basic `Email` type—something that represents an email captured from a web application, perhaps; it's unvalidated and could be anything. We then have another type, `Validated-Email`, which wraps `Email`; it represents an email address that has been validated.

The function `validateEmail` is important. It takes in a normal `Email` value and returns a `ValidatedEmail`. If the email isn't valid, it throws an exception! (Don't worry if this doesn't sit well with you; in the next chapter, we'll discuss a good way to deal with this.) Lastly, it's clear from the `sendEmail` function that it doesn't accept just any email address but only those that have been validated, meaning you would need to go through the `validateEmail` function first.

This use of types to enforce rules is extremely useful because anywhere you use, for example, `ValidatedEmail` in your system, you don't have to check whether the email is valid; the type tells us that this has already taken place. This is much better than comments, as the compiler can enforce these rules for you rather than relying on the developer to remember to never call `sendEmail` with an email address that hasn't yet been validated.

> **NOTE** While you can match on many different constructs in F# without a problem, one thing that isn't supported is members such as properties and classes in general. This is another example of how F# has almost two type systems—the objection oriented half and the functional programming half.

8.4   The F# type system

Congratulations! You now know all the core tools you need to model domains in F#. You can represent the two core kinds of relationships between values that you'll ever need—AND and OR—as well as perform conditional logic over them.

8.4.1   ANDing types

ANDing refers to the ability to compose types together. For example, a customer has a name (`String` type) AND an address (`Address` type); from an F# perspective, we're talking about composing a `String` and an `Address` together. AND types in F# are represented by tuples and records. Use them to model values that exist and travel together:

- A customer has a name AND an address.
- An order has a customer AND a list of items AND a price, etc.

8.4.2   ORing types

OR types represent the ability to say a value might be one of several types. OR types in F# are represented by discriminated unions:

- An order is in draft OR active OR completed state.
- A customer can be contacted by phone OR email OR post.

8.4.3   ANDing values

Don't confuse ANDing types with values! For example, if I wanted to model the fact that a customer can have multiple addresses, I would probably use a list:

```
type CustomerWithAddresses =
    {
        Name : string
        Addresses : Address list
    }
```

In this case, as far as F# is concerned, this record is only composed of two types: `string` and `Address list`. The fact that the list may have 1 or 50 entries is irrelevant from a type system point of view.

On the other hand, if you wanted to be more specific—for example, a customer has a billing AND a post address—then you would probably have two explicit fields on the record:

```
type CustomerWithAddresses =
    {
        Name : string
        BillingAddress : Address
        PostalAddress : Address
    }
```

Of course, you can mix and match these two kinds of relationships however you want. A union case's data can be represented by a record (as we saw in listing 8.8), and a record can contain unions as fields. In this way, you can nest both types of usages however you see fit to model essentially anything you like. You can then use single-case discriminated unions to provide an extra layer of richness to distinguish between fields that would otherwise appear the same if only using primitives. Don't worry if it feels a bit much to take in; we'll be revisiting and using these techniques in the coming chapters, so you'll have the opportunity to see and use them in practice.

Summary

- Pattern matching is the de facto way to perform conditional logic in F#.
- Pattern matching is very flexible, working with constants, tuples, records, discriminated unions, lists, and more.
- Pattern matching gives us compiler support to ensure we've dealt with any possible case in a match.
- Discriminated unions allow us to model OR cases in types.
- Discriminated unions are lightweight and both simple to use and reason about.
- Single-case discriminated unions are a powerful tool to add further type safety and enrich your domain.
- The combination of records, tuples, and unions allows you to model the real-world extremely effectively.

Building rich domains

9

This chapter covers

- Working with missing values
- Working with errors
- Computation expressions
- A worked example for modeling domains in F#

In the previous chapter, we more or less finished the language part of the book. There will still be a few new features scattered around, but we'll start to look at applying those techniques in different scenarios now and looking at F# libraries (both out-of-the-box and third-party) that you should know.

This chapter builds on the previous one, which discussed discriminated unions, by focusing on two specific types that come bundled with F#: Option and Result. These are two key types that are bundled with F# and are very important to learn in order to model domains correctly and effectively.

9.1 Working with missing values

Missing data is a natural part of working with not only data from third parties (where we might not be in control of the data and quality may be sketchy) but simply a part of modeling in the real world. We deal with this every day. For example, when registering with an e-commerce website, your account will *always* have an email address, and it *might* have your home address. Maybe you haven't gotten around to providing your home address or perhaps you never intend to because your only purchases will be digital ones.

It's unfortunate, but one of the biggest challenges we face in software development in many programming languages is how to reason about working with data that might not be there. When I say "reason about," I'm referring to how we write code to deal with missing data in an understandable, consistent, and reliable fashion.

9.1.1   *The billion-dollar mistake: Working with nulls*

The most common case we see in many programming languages that were created more than, say, five years ago is the use of `null` as a first-class feature. I say *feature*, but it's turned out to be a massive cost to the industry (the inventor of `null`, Tony Hoare, infamously called it a billion-dollar mistake—most likely a massive underestimate). Depending on the language and environment, nulls have historically worked something like this, for at least some subset of types (e.g., on .NET, all reference type values can be null, but value types cannot):

- Any value in the application can at any time be either null (i.e., not set) or not null (i.e., it has a value). There is no way to determine this in the type system; you can't mark a value as non-nullable.
- If you try to access a member (e.g., a field, property, or method) on a null value, you'll raise a run-time exception or error.
- It's your responsibility to check whether a value is null before accessing it.

In such languages, there are *two* reasons why a value might be null:

- The value is mandatory from a domain point of view (e.g., the email address in the earlier example), but there's no way to enforce this from the type system point of view. You still have to check for nulls, just in case. This is what I call the *implicit null case.*
- The value is genuinely optional from a domain point of view e.g., the home address from the earlier example—You use `null` to represent the case when the user has not yet entered their address (i.e., the *explicit null case*). However, you still need to remember to check this every single time you access the value. If you forget, you run the risk of a null reference exception.

From a type system point of view, you have no way of knowing which one you're referring to because both are represented in the same unsatisfying way: `null`. When you don't want null, it's there whether you like it or not. When you do want it, it's hard to reason about because anything can be null, and the compiler doesn't force you to check values before accessing them.

There are a whole bunch of workarounds that have been developed over the years for this sort of thing outside of fixing the language in question: design patterns, annotations, IDE tricks, third-party libraries and packages, coding practices (also known as "just don't make mistakes"), etc. None are especially satisfying.

Thankfully, some modern languages like Kotlin, Swift, and Rust don't suffer from these issues, and C#8 onward introduced an optional feature known as *non-nullable reference types* to help ameliorate the issue, although it suffers from being a complex feature with many corner cases.

The history of optionality on .NET

In .NET, reference types can be set to null, but value types cannot be (I suspect this inconsistent decision was made for all the wrong reasons). Anyway, when .NET first came out, this was a problem because you couldn't model, for example, a number not being set. This was even more problematic because SQL databases *do* allow this. This led to developers using magic numbers like –1 to represent null for integers. In .NET 2, this was fixed by the introduction of the Nullable<T> generic type.

9.1.2   *Options are the answer*

F# takes the following approach: any values that you create using types defined in F# cannot be null, ever. Instead, F# has a built-in type called `option`, which is used to model, as the name suggests, a value that is optional. Regarding the F# type system, `option` is nothing special; it's just a discriminated union with two cases. Either it has some content, or it has nothing. The easiest way to demonstrate this is with a simple example:

```
let presentNumber : int option = Some 10        Creates an optional
let missingNumber : int option = None           int that has a value
let mandatoryNumber : int = 10
                                                Creates an optional
                                                int that has no value
```

Both `optionalNumber` and `missingNumber` are the same type—an `int option` (`Option<int>` is also valid F# syntax). The important thing to note is that they are a completely different type from a regular `int`: think of it as a wrapper around any value. The `option` type is generic, so it works with any value, including value types. So, Integers and Booleans will work just as well as reference types like String, etc.

The important thing to note is that it's illegal to access the data of an `option` value without first pattern matching on it to check that the value actually exists; there is no implicit casting or converting between options and mandatory data, in either direction, as illustrated in figure 9.1. In addition, because options are explicit opt-ins and the default for F# types is that every value is mandatory, we effectively remove the uncertainty about dealing with missing data:

```
                                           Legal—int compared to another int
mandatoryNumber.CompareTo 55
missingNumber.CompareTo 55                 Error—No such method called
missingNumber + mandatoryNumber            CompareTo exists on Option

                                           Error—Can't add an optional
let description =                           int to a mandatory int
    match optionalNumber with
    | Some number -> $"The number is {number}"      Using pattern matching to
    | None -> "There is no number"                  safely access an optional value
```

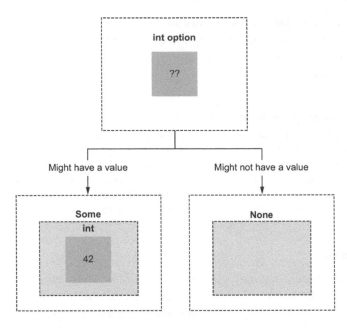

Figure 9.1 Unlike an `int`, an `int` option can have two outcomes: either it wraps a real `int`, or it has nothing in it. You need to pattern match on the value to safely check whether there's data inside it and then proceed accordingly.

Another crucial thing to note is as everything in F# is an expression, you have to handle both the `Some` and `None` cases. In other words, you can't just deal with the "happy path." While this might sound like extra work, think about it: if you've modeled your domain to say that a given value might be absent, why wouldn't you want to handle that?

Getting the value out of an option

There is a `.Value` member of the option type that allows you to get the underlying data without needing to pattern match first. If the value doesn't exist, you'll get a runtime exception. *Don't ever use this in a real application*, no matter how sure you are that the value will never be `None`. You're essentially turning off the type system and losing all the safety of `option`. It is, however, sometimes useful as an escape hatch if you're working in scripts in a data exploration mode and want to quickly get at some data you know is there.

9.1.3 *Option.map*

Working with options does introduce a little bit of extra work for us as you'll very often have times when you're matching on an optional value and want to handle only the `Some` case—for example, you're getting the age of an optional customer to use in a calculation elsewhere. As an example, imagine we've tried to load a customer from the database by ID; this customer may or may not exist. If they exist, get their age, and then describe their age as a text string (see figure 9.2).

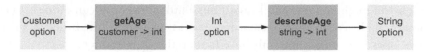

Figure 9.2   A pipeline of operations over optional data

The code for the getAge function might be something as simple as this:

```
let getAge customer : int option =
    match customer with
    | Some c -> Some c.Age          Stay in the
    | None -> None                  option world
```

In other words, we're keeping the optionality, except instead of having a Customer option, we now have an int option (the age). However, there's one problem: if we keep the optionality, we need to do a full pattern match check every time you want to get at the customer (or age or description), unwrapping and then rewrapping values as you go. There are several problems with this:

- Not only is this a pain to do, there's extra code to read and maintain.
- It reduces readability. The actual business logic to get the age is just a single expression (c.Age); the rest is just boilerplate.
- The previous code only works with optional customers. If you have a standard customer, this function wouldn't work unless you explicitly wrapped your customer into an option.

All of these problems are solved with Option.map:

```
let getAge customer : int option =
    customer
    |> Option.map (fun c -> c.Age)
```

Option.map is designed specifically to do the unwrap and rewrap for you; you have to pass in a function that says what to map to if the value is Some. The key thing to recognize is that Option.map makes normal functions work with options, including automatically wrapping the output of the function with Some (this will be important when we look at Option.bind). You can chain multiple calls for Option.map together and use functions rather than lambdas as required:

```
let optionalClassification =
    optionalCustomer
    |> Option.map getAge
    |> Option.map classifyAge
```

The good thing here is that getAge and classifyAge are now much more flexible and simpler to write; they don't need to know about options. Instead, they are adapted to work with options on demand using Option.map.

Although you might need to think about this a little more, you can even short-circuit the previous code by composing `getAge` and `classifyAge` into one function using the compose `>>` operator so that you only have to map the option once:

```
let optionalClassification =
    optionalCustomer
    |> Option.map (getAge >> classifyAge)
```

This kind of short-circuit isn't always the most readable, but it's actually worth seeing this in terms of function signatures: you can plug `getAge` and `classifyAge` together because the output of the first is the same as the input of the second (i.e., `getAge` returns an int; `classifyAge` takes in an int). This gives back a new function, which we then pass into `Option.map`. Doing this means that we only wrap/unwrap the optionality once instead of twice, so this would be a tiny bit more efficient, too. In other words, any time you see calls to maps chained together (whether it's options, collections, results etc.), you can always compress them into a single map.

> **NOTE** Be careful of putting too much into a single map call in terms of logic. It's a good idea to factor out mappers into separate, small, reusable functions and then plug them together later. Your code will be more reusable, and individual functions easier to reason about.

EXERCISE 9.1

Write a function that can read the contents of a text file from disk (see the `System.IO.File` class), returning the contents of the file as a single string. If the file does not exist, it should return `None`. Then, write a second function that can count the words in a single string. Compose the two together in a function, using either pattern matching or `Option.map`. The function signatures should look something like as follows:

- `tryGetFileContents : string -> string option`—Takes in a filename and optionally returns the text
- `countWords : string -> int`—Takes in some text, splits on string, and returns the number of words
- `countWordsInFile : string -> int option`—Takes in a filename and optionally returns the number of words, composing the two other functions together

9.1.4   *Option.bind*

The second function worth knowing about is `Option.bind`, which is a slightly more powerful version of `map`. Just like `map`, it starts with an option of some data, but this time, the function you supply must *also* return an Option. As an example of where `map` isn't sufficient, let's assume that the age of the customer in the previous example was also an optional field:

```
type Customer = { Name : string; Age : int option }    ⟵  Defines a type with
                                                           an optional field, Age
let getAge c = c.Age    ⟵  A function that returns
                           the age of a customer
```

If you run `Option.map` over this, you'll get back an `int option option`:

```
let theCustomer = Some { Name = "Isaac"; Age = Some 42 }
let optionalAge : int option option = theCustomer |> Option.map getAge
```

An optional customer

Getting a double option back from Option.map

What's an `int option option`? Remember what `Option.map` does: it automatically wraps the result of the function you supply with `Some`. But in this case, we don't want that because our function *already* returns an `option` (the age value)! That's where `bind` comes in. It's designed to compress two options into one—only if both the customer and the age are `Some` will it return `Some`. `bind` expects your mapping function to already return an `option`, so you don't end up with the double-wrapped option.

```
let optionalAge : int option = theCustomer |> Option.bind getAge
```

Uses Option.bind to remove the option double wrap

Another good sign that `Option.bind` might be of use is if you are pattern matching and end up with a double-nested pattern match:

```
let optionalAge =
    match theCustomer with
    | Some theCustomer ->
        match theCustomer.Age with
        | Some age ->
            Some age
        | None ->
            None
    | None ->
        None
```

Safely unwraps the top-level customer value

Safely unwraps the Age field

Wraps the Age back up into an option

Handles both None cases

There are a bunch of other functions in the `Option` module, such as `filter` and `toList`. They're good to be aware of and learn, although I would expect that 90% of the time, `map` and `bind` will be all you're using. Learn these two well; they're common patterns you'll see cropping up again and again, and once you learn them, you'll be able to re-apply them in many other situations (as we'll see in the very next section!).

9.1.5   Interop with .NET

Working with .NET poses some challenges when it comes to optional data. `Option<'T>` is an F#-specific thing, but we're running on .NET in which `null` is considered a first-class feature, and to maintain backward compatibility, it will never go away. Therefore, whenever you're working with any .NET reference types, be aware that that data could potentially be null. Also, .NET value types can't be null, but there's the `Nullable<'T>` instead that I mentioned earlier. To cater to this, F# provides a few handy functions in the `Option` module to convert between options and primitives:

```
open System                                    Null is mapped to None

let optionalName : string option = null |> Option.ofObj        Non-null is
let optionalNameTwo = "Isaac" |> Option.ofObj                  mapped to Some
let optionalAge = Nullable() |> Option.ofNullable
let optionalAgeTwo = Nullable 123 |> Option.ofNullable         Empty Nullable is
                                                               mapped to None
        Non-empty Nullable is mapped to Some
```

There are also `toObj` and `toNullable` functions to get back out in the other direction. My advice is to stick with `Option` throughout your code. Don't start mixing and matching `Nullable<T>` or naked nulls alongside options for domain modeling; it's inconsistent and will cause confusion about when to use what. Besides, `Option` is a much better fit than the other two. Instead, at the boundaries of your F# code, convert from the various .NET ways of modeling missing data into `Option`, and on the way back out to other .NET code, unwrap back from `Option` to `Nullable` or naked reference values (figure 9.3).

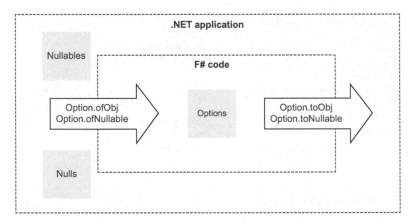

Figure 9.3 When interoperating with non-F# .NET code, using built-in conversion functions in the `Option` module to safely marshal data between options, nulls, and nullables, allowing you to focus solely on using options in your F# code

The only exception to this rule is when you want to model mandatory values that are reference types (e.g., strings). In such a case, it's not worth wrapping these in options if you have good checking at the boundary of your application. Instead, reject data that is null (with exceptions or results, which we'll see shortly) and let the good non-null data in; never check for nulls within your pure F# code.

NOTE F# has a preview feature waiting in the wings, which is a variant of the non-nullability checks that C# introduced in C#8. It's not a supercritical feature that is going to change the guidance I've given (F# already has options, and there are no plans to remove that), but it will make it a little bit nicer to work with mandatory reference types.

9.1.6 Options and collections

There's an affinity between options and collections: you can think of an option as a collection that is either empty or has a single value, and both have similar functions such as map and bind (although in the F# collections world, it's known as collect, and some languages call it SelectMany or FlatMap).

It's also not unusual to mix options and lists—for example, having a collection of optional values. There are also operations on collections that might not always return a value: take List.find. It finds the first item in a collection that matches a predicate you provide. If it doesn't find it, tough luck—now, you've got a runtime exception on your hands. F# therefore also provides a set of sibling try functions such as List.tryFind and List.tryPick. These functions work the same as their non-try versions, except they return options instead of throwing exceptions. You should nearly always prefer these try variants. They're clearer about what they're doing, and they force you to deal with the missing data in code rather than risk throwing a runtime exception.

One other function that's worth looking at in the collection world is choose. It works in a similar way to map, except it's designed to work with a list of options. If you have a function that might return a value and want to apply it to a collection, use choose. It will safely remove the None values and safely unwrap the Some values for you.

9.2 Handling errors

Working with options gives us a great way to handle missing data, but a problem arises when you want to have something along for the ride on the None channel. A common example is data validation: you have a function that takes in some data to validate; it will either pass or fail. If it fails, you want to be able to record what went wrong. F# offers two ways to do this: Results and Exceptions.

9.2.1 Results

Let's imagine you're processing some data that comes in from the outside world of your application. Let's also assume this is a direct mapping to some JSON you've deserialized using .NET's built-in JSON capabilities in the System.Text.Json namespace:

```
type RawCustomer =
    {
        CustomerId : string
        Name : string
        Street : string
        City : string
        Country : string
        AccountBalance : decimal
    }
```

You need to validate this data to ensure certain invariants are held. Perhaps the CustomerId is mandatory and must be in a certain format, while Country shouldn't be a simple string but either Domestic or Foreign.

What should the signature of the validation function look like? We know it should take a `RawCustomer` value, but what is the return type? We might be tempted to say `Boolean`, but I would reject that. I want something that's going to help enforce the use of this validation function. If it's a Boolean, we'll have no way downstream of confirming whether this function was ever called. So, instead, we can use the type system itself to help us by creating a richer, validated `Customer` type; if we use that type in the rest of the system, then the only way to call those functions will be to convert our `RawCustomer` into a full `Customer` value, as shown in the following listing.

Listing 9.1   A rich domain model for a customer

```
type CustomerId = CustomerId of int
type Name = Name of string
type Street = Street of string                          Defines a set of
type City = City of string                              primitive discriminated
type Country = Domestic | Foreign of string             union wrappers
type AccountBalance = AccountBalance of decimal


type Customer =                        ◁─────   Enriches the
    {                                           customer record
        Id : CustomerId                         with wrapper types
        Name : Name
        Address :
            {|
                Street : Street
                City : City
                Country : Country
            |}
        Balance : AccountBalance
    }
```

Now that we've defined what our return type `Customer` will look like, we could have our validation function return a `Customer option` to model the fact that the function might not be successful: If the validation passes, we return `Some` customer, and if it fails, we return `None`. The problem is that we won't be able to say *what* the failure was because there's no way to encode that in an option: we only have `None` for the failure channel. This is where the `Result` type comes in: it allows you to pass data back on both success and failure channels. It's a two-case discriminated union that looks as follows:

```
Result<'TOk, 'TError>
```

Instead of `Some` or `None`, a result has two cases, `Ok` or `Error`, each of which can carry some payload. Both can be different types—for example, the `Ok` channel can return a number, while the error channel could be a string. The following listing provides an example of a validation function that tries to convert a `RawCustomer` to a `Customer`.

Listing 9.2 Using results instead of options for validation

```fsharp
let validateCustomer (rawCustomer:RawCustomer) =
    let customerId =
        if rawCustomer.CustomerId.StartsWith "C" then
            Ok (CustomerId(int rawCustomer.CustomerId[1..]))
        else
            Error $"Invalid Customer Id '{rawCustomer.CustomerId}'."
    let country =
        match rawCustomer.Country with
        | "" -> Error "No country supplied"
        | "USA" -> Ok Domestic
        | other -> Ok (Foreign other)

    match customerId, country with
    | Ok customerId, Ok country ->
        Ok … // body omitted for clarity
    | Error err, _
    | _, Error err ->
        Error err
```

Uses Ok to model the happy path result

Uses Error for the failure path, with specific error details

Pattern matching on both Ok values

Returns the first error we encounter

Notice how the implementation returns an `Error` with specific details for each case (instead of just `None` with the option type), but each value supplied to the `Error` constructor is the same type (string). Also, instead of returning `Some` customer in the happy path scenario, we return an `Ok` customer. Finally, note the signature of the function is `RawCustomer -> Result<Customer, string>`: given a raw customer, we either return a full customer or an error of type string. This could be used in a web API, for example, where the `Error` could be converted into an HTTP 400 error code; in an app with a user interface, it could manifest itself as an error dialog; etc.

> **Mapping results**
>
> The nice thing about F# is that there's a reasonable amount of consistency in terms of the patterns that you see applied across different contexts or types. We've already seen `map` used with List and Option; using it with Result is pretty much the same (except Result also has a `mapError` function!). `bind` also works pretty much the same as it does with Option and collections.

9.2.2 Handling multiple errors

The example in listing 9.2 can only return a single error when performing validation. If multiple errors are returned, we only return the first one. What if we want to return multiple errors? No problem! We can change our Result type from `Result<Customer, string>` to `Result <Customer, string list>`. In other words, in the case of failure, we'll have a list of errors. The *number* of errors is unspecified: it could be 1 or 10. The following listing shows how you might implement such a validation function.

Listing 9.3 **Handling multiple error values in a single return value**

```
let resultValidateCustomer rawCustomer =
    let customerId = // body omitted for clarity
    let country = // body omitted for clarity

    match customerId, country with
    | Ok customerId, Ok country ->
        // body omitted for clarity
    | customerId, country ->
        Error [
            match customerId with Ok _ -> () | Error x -> x
            match country with Ok _ -> () | Error x -> x
        ]
```

Pattern matching against anything but (Ok _, Ok _) means there must be at least one error.

Uses a list comprehension to conditionally return each possible error imperatively

9.2.3 *Strongly typed errors*

A challenge with errors that are stringly typed as I've shown so far is that it's difficult to reason about them:

- You can't easily see from the function's signature what a list of possible errors it could return—they're all strings.
- You can't reason about them afterward. What if you wanted to handle one error differently from another—for example, return different HTTP error codes depending on the error type?

For this reason, you might prefer to create an actual type for your errors—typically a discriminated union:

```
type CustomerValidationError =
    | InvalidCustomerId of string
    | InvalidName of string
    | InvalidCountry of string
```

Our validation code would now be updated something like as follows:

```
let validateCustomerId (cId:string) =
    if cId.StartsWith "C" then
        Ok (int cId[1..])
    else
        Error (InvalidCustomerId $"Invalid Customer Id '{cId}'.")
```

Returns a specific kind of error that allows us to understand what field the error occurred on programmatically

And the result of our validation function would now be

```
RawCustomer -> Result<Customer, CustomerValidationError list>
```

This is now starting to reflect a rich domain; our errors are now starting to be encoded in our types. However, we still can't easily distinguish the *exact* error—just what field it was against. To fix that, we can create specific cases for each type of note, as shown in listing 9.4.

Listing 9.4 Creating a set of error cases for validation

```
type CustomerValidationError =          ◁── ┐  Creates a type
    | EmptyCustomerId                          for all possible
    | InvalidCustomerIdFormat                  errors
    | NoNameSupplied
    | TooManyNameParts
    | NoCountrySupplied
```

Don't be afraid of this kind of type-all-the-things approach! It might not always be appropriate, but when you do need to reason about the exact error, using types like this is the best way to do it. The compiler can help you all the way through, so the more information you put in, the more you'll get back out later on.

There is one final possibility—to create a separate type for each function and then compose them together at the end in a kind of all-errors type.

Listing 9.5 Creating a hierarchy of errors

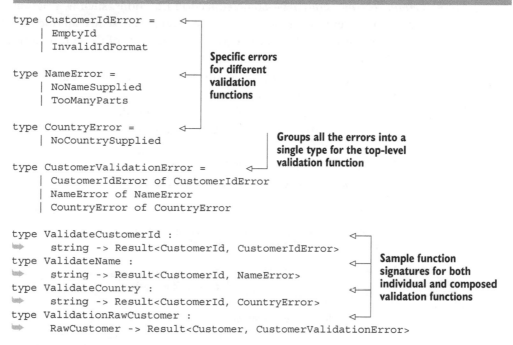

```
type CustomerIdError =          ◁──┐
    | EmptyId
    | InvalidIdFormat
                                      Specific errors
                                      for different
type NameError =                ◁──   validation
    | NoNameSupplied                  functions
    | TooManyParts

type CountryError =             ◁──┘
    | NoCountrySupplied
                                      Groups all the errors into a
                                      single type for the top-level
type CustomerValidationError =  ◁──   validation function
    | CustomerIdError of CustomerIdError
    | NameError of NameError
    | CountryError of CountryError

type ValidateCustomerId :                                    ◁──┐
      string -> Result<CustomerId, CustomerIdError>
type ValidateName :                                          ◁──   Sample function
      string -> Result<CustomerId, NameError>                      signatures for both
type ValidateCountry :                                       ◁──   individual and composed
      string -> Result<CustomerId, CountryError>                   validation functions
type ValidationRawCustomer :                                 ◁──┘
      RawCustomer -> Result<Customer, CustomerValidationError>
```

Why might we want to do this? Well, it's the best way of explicitly defining the errors each function might give, and clearly shows that each validation function (e.g., validate customer ID) has its own set of errors. You can go to the definition on that type and see immediately what the possible errors are, so it serves as a living document—a specification that is always up to date. Have a look at the source code online for a full sample of this.

9.2.4 *Exceptions*

I'm going to touch on exceptions briefly. Although they tend not to be the standard way to model errors, you need to know about them because they're an integral part of .NET. There's a lot of information on exceptions in the official .NET documentation, so this is a high-level view plus some advice from an F# perspective.

When exceptions are thrown in .NET, the application stops and unwinds back up the call stack; you can catch an exception in F# and handle it or leave it to bubble up the call stack until at the very top. If you're in a web application, this will manifest itself as an HTTP 500 to the caller for that request; if you're running a console or desktop application, it'll most likely stop the entire program.

Exceptions don't form part of the type signature of a function, so there's always a hidden channel that a function can use that you won't be able to see. In most code you write yourself, you won't normally need to worry about exceptions, but there are a few places to be aware of:

- *Certain collection functions*—Some collection functions, such as `find` or `reduce`, can throw exceptions under specific conditions. These are all documented on those functions, and there are nearly always variants of those functions that are runtime safe (e.g., `tryFind` or `fold`).
- *Array indexing*—Array indexing is inherently unsafe. For example, `myCollection[4]` will throw an exception if there are only four items in the collection (remember F# indexing is zero-based!). To avoid this, you can either use pattern matching or the runtime-safe `tryItem`, which returns an option (`None` if the index is out of bounds).
- *Certain arithmetic operations*—Like dividing by zero.
- *External libraries/code*—When calling libraries or code you have no control over.

If you are concerned about exceptions, you can handle them using `try with` syntax:

```
try
    Some (1 / 0)
with ex ->
    printfn $"Error: {ex.Message}"
    None
```

Creates a try/with block. Any exceptions thrown inside the try section will be caught by the with handler.

Some code that throws a runtime exception

Returns an acceptable value from the with block

You can also write generic functions to, for example, make any code handle exceptions:

```
let handleException func arg =
    try func arg |> Ok
    with ex -> Error ex
let divide (a, b) = a / b
let divideSafe = handleException divide
let result = divideSafe (2, 0)
```

A helper function that converts any exceptions raised by a function into an Error

An example function that may throw an exception

Converts the function into a safe variant

Tests out the safe variant of divide

Here, `func` is any function that takes in `arg` as input. You can partially apply it to create a safe version of the function, which returns `Ok` if it works or `Error` (with the exception) if it fails.

9.2.5 *When to safely leave options and results*

Your initial instinct might be to get out of the option or result world as quickly as possible, as though there's something wrong with it. Resist that temptation. Instead, keep data inside that container for as long as it's required, which is normally until you can answer the question, "What should I replace `None` or `Error` with?" If you can't answer that, *keep the data inside the container.* Options and Results, like many effects, are somewhat viral in nature in the sense that once you start working with them, they bleed out into your calling code. Don't be surprised or repelled by that!

It's very common to bring in unstructured or weakly typed data (e.g., from a CSV or JSON file, etc.), map it into a rich domain model in F#, and then only unwrap the container at the boundary of the workflow—for example, when you're writing an HTTP response or writing something to disk.

> ### Railway-oriented programming
> If you're more interested in this style of programming, you should check out Scott Wlaschin's wonderful F# For Fun and Profit website (https://fsharpforfunandprofit .com/), as well as his book *Domain Modelling Made Functional.* Among the many detailed and readable posts are a series on working with the Result type. In it, Scott coined the phrase *railway-oriented programming*—the idea of plugging together functions within the context of results, where any error in the pipeline moves onto the "failure track" and immediately exits the program. I highly recommend reading it or watching one of his videos on the subject. However, railway-oriented programming does have its limitations; I describe where I think you should and shouldn't use Results in the real world in the next section.

9.2.6 *When to use options, results, and exceptions*

Before we move onto the last part of this chapter, I think it's a good idea to briefly compare and contrast Options, Results, and Exceptions (figure 9.4). When should you use which?

- *Options*—Use options to model a potential absence of data. Use pattern matching when you want to finally handle the `None` case (or `Option.defaultValue`) and `Option.map` or `bind` when you want to work with the `Some` data without removing it from the `Option` container.
- *Results*—Use results when you need to model something that might pass or fail and need to reason about it afterward—perhaps take a different code path depending on the specific error, etc. If you need to supply information about what went wrong, use the error channel to encode that. Again, consider pattern

matching and `map/bind` to work with them effectively. Consider custom union types to model your error domain tightly rather than, for example, just strings.

- *Exceptions*—Use exceptions for panic situations—situations that are truly exceptional, where there is no way out, and your only choice is to fail fast. If you have a call stack that's 10 functions deep, and you're returning an error from the bottom function that goes all the way to the top and is simply returned as, for example, an HTTP 500 or similar, you're probably better off simply throwing an exception from the bottom all the way to the top: it's less code and fewer types. However, don't use exceptions for regular control flow. Not only are they computationally expensive, but they are difficult to reason about. The compiler won't support you in the same way it does with Options or Results, and you can't easily see what exceptions a function may throw.

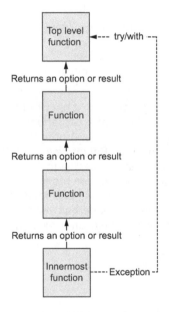

Figure 9.4   **Options and results are normal return values of functions, whereas an exception can implicitly bubble all the way up the call stack until it encounters a `try/with` block.**

9.3   *Computation expressions*

At this point, I will introduce another language feature in F#, called *computation expressions* (CEs). CEs are a way of managing some kind of effect without having to explicitly handle it through code. By *effect*, I mean a container that wraps around your data—for example, Options, Results, or asynchronous code (as we'll see later in the book) that you can wrap around data. For example, imagine being able to write code that deals with options without explicitly using pattern matching or `Option.map` and instead allows you to simply carry on if there's `Some` value or automatically stops if there's `None`. They're especially useful when dealing with more complex logic where using `Option.map/bind` is too difficult to read, and pattern matching too verbose—for example, when you have multiple optional values to deal with and want to combine them all. The easiest way to illustrate this is with a before-and-after example. Here's a simple one: we have a text file that contains three numbers in it:

```
1
345
23
```

We want to perform a simple calculation over those three numbers. I've omitted the step of reading from the file, but as an exercise for you, I'd suggest trying to read that in using the methods on the System.IO.File type if your .NET I/O skills are a little rusty!

Once we've bound the three numbers to symbols, we first need to try to parse the strings into integers—an operation that could realistically fail (e.g., instead of 1, the string had spaces in it or some other nonnumeric character). The function in listing 9.6 shows a function tryParseNumber, which wraps the in-built Int32.TryParse method; it has a signature of string -> int option (it's common practice to place the word try at the front of such functions, even though you can see from the int option return type that the function might not succeed). Armed with this function, we can now parse all three strings; if they're all valid, we can call our calculate function on them; if any fail, we should stop.

> **Listing 9.6   Mapping and binding on multiple options using pattern matching**

```
open System

let calc (a: int) (b: int) (c: int) : int = a + b * c        ⊲──┐ Simple calculation
                                                                 │ function

let tryParseNumber (numberAsString:string) =         ⊲──┐ String-to-number
    match Int32.TryParse numberAsString with              │ parse function
    | true, number -> Some number
    | false, _ -> None

let calcResult : int option =
    match tryParseNumber "1", tryParseNumber "2", tryParseNumber "3" with
    | Some firstNumber, Some secondNumber, Some thirdNumber ->        ⊲──┐
        Some (calc firstNumber secondNumber thirdNumber)                 │
    | _ ->
        None          Matching on all three values as a tuple;         │
                      if all pass, perform the calculation.            │
```

Here's a few things to observe:

- The calc function does not take in options. We've kept this function free of effects (like Option or Result); it's the responsibility of the caller to unwrap those effects and to supply simple values to the function. This also helps us be a little more explicit about this function. It won't even compile if you supply it with optional values.
- The implementation code that unwraps the three options isn't exactly super readable. It's acceptable, but if this was any more complex—for example, if the

values had some dependencies between them, or there were more than just three values—this code would quickly become unreadable. (In the full code samples, you'll see several alternative versions to solve this using pattern matching and `Option.map` / `bind`. All of them suffer from readability challenges.)

Here's the alternative version using the option CE:

```
#r "nuget:FSToolkit.ErrorHandling, 2.13.0"          References and opens the
open FsToolkit.ErrorHandling                        FSToolkit package

let myMaybeData = option {                           Creates an option CE, signified
    let! numberOne = tryParseNumber "1"             by the option { } block
    let! numberTwo = tryParseNumber "2"             Uses the let! keyword to
    let! numberThree = tryParseNumber "3"           safely unwrap options
    return calc numberOne numberTwo numberThree      Implicitly rewraps the
}                                                    answer using return
```

You'll see that the CE version looks almost like the happy path version; there's no unwrapping or checking at all. In fact, it appears as though there are no optional values whatsoever! So where have they gone? This is where the CE comes into play: whenever you see a `let!` (pronounced "let bang"), the compiler effectively does the pattern match for us: if the value is `Some`, it safely unwraps it, binds it to the symbol, and carries on. If it's `None`, it stops the entire CE immediately and returns `None`. It's worth checking the type annotations from your IDE at this point to prove this; figures 9.5 and 9.6 are using VS Code.

```
int
let myMaybeData : int  =
··· let numberOne : int option = tryParseNumber numberAsString = "1"
··· let numberTwo : int option = tryParseNumber numberAsString = "2"
··· let numberThree : int option = tryParseNumber numberAsString = "3"
··· calc numberOne numberTwo numberThree    This expression was expected to have type 'int' but here has type 'int option'
```

Figure 9.5   Attempting to add together three optional values without a CE and no pattern matching. Note that all three values are `int` options and therefore cannot be passed into the `calc` function.

```
option<int>
let myMaybeData : int option = option {
··· let! numberOne : int = tryParseNumber numberAsString = "1"
··· let! numberTwo : int = tryParseNumber numberAsString = "2"
··· let! numberThree : int = tryParseNumber numberAsString = "3"
··· return calc numberOne numberTwo numberThree
}
```

Figure 9.6   Virtually the same code as figure 9.5 inside an option { } block, using `let!` to safely unwrap optional values. Notice the inferred type hints show that the three numbers are correctly unwrapped as `int`s. Also note the use of the `return` keyword, which is only required inside CE blocks.

CEs like this `option { }` block allow us to write code in a much more conventional, and imperative style and let the CE handle the boilerplate of working with the effect for us.

There's one other thing to note about this `option { }` CE: it isn't bundled with the `FSharp.Core` library. Many CEs are not baked into the language but are rather libraries that we can install to add this functionality. This means we can actually extend F# with new CEs to handle other effects (or even write our own). This CE exists in the `FsToolkit.ErrorHandling` package, a free, open source package that contains lots of nice extensions for working with options and results. You'll see more about NuGet and package management in the upcoming chapters.

EXERCISE 9.2
Remodel the customer validation exercise that we built throughout this chapter using the `result { }` computation expression in the `FsToolkit.ErrorHandling` package. It works in a virtually identical manner to the `option { }` block, except the `let!` keyword will automatically unwrap `Ok` and discard `Error` values.

9.4 *Domain modeling: A worked example*

As your knowledge of types has increased throughout this book, here's a more challenging scenario for you to model. Imagine you're a developer meeting a customer for the first workshop. They're looking for you to build an IT system that can manage their train stock and inventory, and the first thing you want to understand is what a *train* is. What information needs to be captured? What kind of carriages does a train have? After talking awhile with your customer, you identify the following requirements. I've highlighted some of the key elements throughout the scenario as hints:

- A *train* is comprised of a *collection* of *carriages*.
- Trains have their own *train identification code*, an *origin* and *destination stop*, plus a *collection* of intermediate *stops* along the route.
- Each stop is comprised of a *station name* and a *time of arrival*. Don't worry about time zones for this exercise—that's a whole other can of worms! Just assume times are local for the stop.
- A train *may* also have a stop allocated where the drivers change over.
- A *carriage* is *either* for *passengers* or a *buffet food car*.
- Each carriage has a *unique identifier* that indicates its position in the train (e.g. 1, 2, 3, etc.).
- Each carriage has a *number of seats*.
- Each carriage (passenger and buffet) may have some of the following *features* in it:
  - A quiet carriage
  - Wifi connectivity
  - A washroom

- Each passenger carriage can be either *first* or *second class*, but not both; there are no split carriages.
- Buffet cars can serve *hot* or *cold food*, or both.

The onboard software also needs to support functionality to tell the driver at any given time:

- The total number of seats the train
- How much time it takes to travel from any given stop to another stop along the route
- Which carriages have a specific feature (e.g., washrooms)

Figure 9.7 shows an example manifest for how a train journey looks.

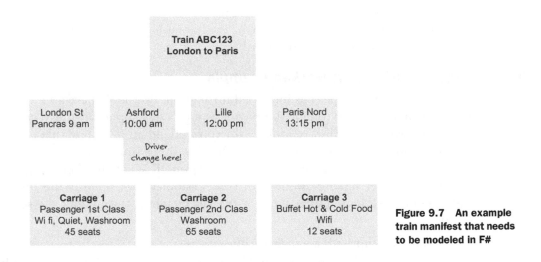

Figure 9.7   An example train manifest that needs to be modeled in F#

EXERCISE 9.3

Model the previous train scenario in F#. Use all the types at your disposal as you see fit: tuples, records (and anonymous records), and discriminated unions; refer to the previous chapter if you need some guidance as to which type to use when. Use collections as needed; be thoughtful about selecting the right collection for the task, such as lists, sequences, maps, or sets!

Don't bother with a console application. Use a script to model the domain as you go, experimenting with sample data that tests the domain as you're building it.

To help you out, here are some sample function signatures that may help you when creating the implementations of the three functions:

```
getTotalNumberOfSeats : Train -> int
calculateTimeBetweenStops :
    Stop * Stop -> Train -> Result<TimeSpan, TimeCalculationError>
findCarriagesWithFeature : Feature -> Train -> Carriage list
```

Observe that I've deliberately put the `Train` argument for the second and third functions as the last input argument so that you can pipe it in (e.g., `train |> findCarriagesWithFeature Wifi`).

You'll find a suggested solution to this exercise in source code, but there's really so many ways to model something like this that there's no one right answer. However, there are certainly wrong things that one might do when modeling it. Focus on asking yourself questions like the following:

- How ergonomic is my solution? Does it fit with the scenario described?
- Implement the train manifest in figure 9.7 in code. How does it look in code? Sometimes, only when plugging in real data will you see issues with your model.
- How easy is it to make "illegal" states, such as duplicate features in the same train carriage? Or the same station stop twice? Some of these rules are simply impossible to model through types in F#, but others are if you're careful about what types you use.

Summary

- `null` is common in many popular programming languages but has several shortcomings.
- F# attempts to solve `null` using the Option type.
- `Option.map` and its sibling `Option.bind` are two common functions you'll use when working with options.
- You can interoperate with C#/VB .NET and F#'s Option type with several combinator functions.
- The Result type builds on top of Option and also allows you to supply data for the "unhappy path" channel.
- It is common to work with lists of results, and there are several standard functions for dealing with them in F# libraries.
- Exceptions are a standard part of .NET; knowing when to use them instead of Options and Results is important for effectively handling errors in F#.
- Computation expressions are custom blocks of code in F# to deal with specific effects more easily.
- You can reference third-party packages in F# scripts using the `#r "nuget:…"` directive.

Working effectively
with data

10

This chapter covers

- Best practices for working with data
- Serialization
- Type providers
- Data visualization
- Tooling

When I first started using F#, coming from a C# background and used to writing database-driven web applications and the like, I was amazed that I could use .NET for analytical workloads, ad hoc data exploration, and even machine learning. This chapter will give you an overview of some of the different tools and techniques you can use to effectively start working with external data sources within F#, both for full-blown applications and for ad hoc analysis.

10.1 Best practices

Working with data in F# is something you'll be doing all the time, regardless of the source (e.g., a SQL database, web service, an event stream, etc.). This section covers some general best practices for working with collections of data in general.

10.1.1 Data is data

One of the things I like about F# is that there is a common set of principles and practices that you can apply across all data, no matter where it comes from—whether it's loading a JSON file with stock price data, data that's come from a SQL database with order information, transient data that represents a different shape of customer information that you're dealing with in a pipeline, or data that is sourced from user input. All of these represent some form of data and can normally be treated in the same way.

If you find yourself in the process of working with data, but you're not writing functions that take in some data and return some other data as a result of some mapping operation, take a step back for a second and check whether there's a way that you can redesign your code to better fit with the idiomatic way of doing this in F#: it works, and it works very well. An example is event streams: you can treat them as standard sequences of data, even though they're *push* rather than *pull* models, using some built-in F# functions as well as third-party libraries.

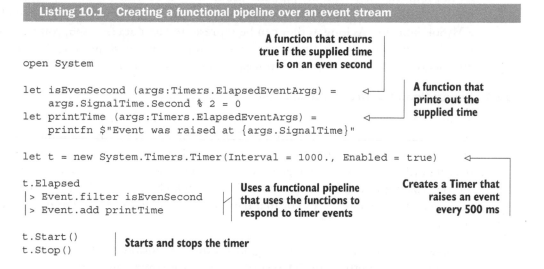

Listing 10.1 Creating a functional pipeline over an event stream

If you try this in a script, after you call the `Start()` method on the timer, you should see output similar to this in the FSI output until you call `Stop()`:

```
Event was raised at 09/10/2022 18:57:14
Event was raised at 09/10/2022 18:57:16
Event was raised at 09/10/2022 18:57:18
```

Again, notice that we're still sticking to the same principles we had earlier: pure functions where possible—simple arguments to simple functions composed together to make more powerful abstractions. We also saw in chapter 7 how you can turn essentially any imperative code into a functional pipeline using sequence comprehensions:

```
let inputs : string seq =
    seq {
        while true do
            Console.Write "Please enter your command: "
            Console.ReadLine()
    }
```

Creates a sequence of strings from an imperative while loop. The sequence can now be used in a pipeline using standard collection functions from the Seq module.

Implicitly yielding back the string from the console to form a sequence

Once you have such a sequence of strings, you can do standard sequence operations over it:

```
inputs
|> Seq.takeWhile isNotExit
|> Seq.choose asCommand
|> Seq.fold (calculateAnswer 0)
```

Of key importance is that the pipeline shown here is completely decoupled from the input coming from the console; the input could just as easily be a text file or data from a MySql database. As long as they can be represented as a `string seq`, you're good to go. Of course, there are times when you can't represent something in a generic abstraction such as this, but when you can, it makes sense to try to do so.

10.1.2 *Separation of data and functionality*

Treat data as data. Don't fall into the trap of looking at it as a class with behavior. If you're coming from an object oriented (OO) background I know it's sometimes difficult to resist this temptation, but you'll be much better off if you do, especially when dealing with data that can change shape over time. Instead, stick to what we know: create records, tuples, and unions to model your data. Create modules that store simple functions that operate on top of that data that can be easily created and removed as required.

> **NOTE** You can create members (and C#-style extension methods and even extension properties) on F# records. There are some cases when it makes sense, such as to take advantage of dot notation and OO-specific features such as overloading, but generally, I would suggest starting with the following simple heuristic: cleanly separate out data and functions. This position shouldn't be too controversial to adopt—even the lead of the C# programming team has publicly stated as much.

Doing so will afford you much more flexibility to create new behaviors as required without worrying about affecting or relying upon the source type. If you couple this with immutability and expressions, you can essentially stop worrying about encapsulation (again, I know this is challenging when coming from an OO background). Instead, you can just focus on the shapes of data, the mappings between them, and how they interact with the outside world (e.g., writing from a database or dealing with web APIs).

10.1.3   Don't treat scripts as programs

You should be doing the bulk of any data exploration in scripts and the REPL. It's often a highly iterative process—trial and error with experimentation. Yet something I see new developers to F# often do, especially those who haven't used a REPL and scripts in the past much, is to treat their script as a program that needs to be executed from the first line to the last in a single execution. I hate seeing this because it loses one of the biggest benefits of the F# REPL (compared to, say, a SQL script or the popular LINQPad tool): the F# REPL is stateful. This means you can load data into the REPL once and then apply multiple operations against it (e.g., data shaping, validation, actions). Instead, take the time to build your script into distinct sections that you can load data into (along with types where required) and then more "scratchpad" areas where you can experiment with that data. This is especially important if you're loading larger datasets or datasets that require some time-intensive operation (e.g., a machine learning operation). Frontload that work and persist the results into a symbol, upon which you can then do any number of operations:

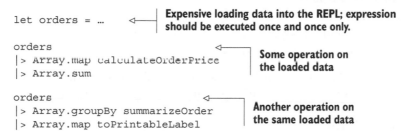

10.1.4   Working with lists of results

It's (obviously) normal when working with data to work with collections of records. Imagine you read in a JSON file containing a set of data, perhaps customers or an inventory of stock, and you want to validate the whole file. Typically, what you'll want is something as follows:

- If *all* the records are correct, the whole collection is OK to continue with.
- If *any* of the records have errors, fail the whole dataset and return all the errors.

This is a very common pattern, so much so that it has a name in functional programming circles: *traverse*. It's not built into F#, but third-party extension libraries to F# contain it (which we'll shortly see). Figure 10.1 is a visualization of what traverse does.

In type system terms, it's as follows:

```
List<Result<'a,'b>> -> Result<'a list, 'b list>
```

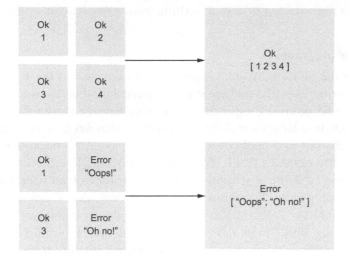

Figure 10.1   Converting a list of result values has two possible outcomes: If *all* values are Ok, the overall result is Ok. But if there are any errors, the overall result is an Error.

If that's confusing, slow down and take it step by step:

- Take in a *list* of results.
- Return *either:*
  - Ok, with a list of all the values
  - Error, with a list of all the errors

The key takeaway is that instead of having a list of results (each of which can be Ok or Error), you end up with a single result with the list of raw values inside it.

10.2   Serialization of data

Serialization (and deserialization) in the context of this chapter refers to the task of going to and from F# values and a format that can be sent "across the wire" (e.g., JSON, XML). This is a common task when working with web applications since (at least at the time of this writing) JSON is the prevalent standard for data transfer on the web. Let's look at this in a little more detail; the key takeaway is to apply the same principles for data manipulation to whichever format and/or library you're using.

10.2.1   Deserializing JSON to F#

Notwithstanding type providers (which we'll cover in the next section), since F# is a statically typed language, you generally need to define some types and an associated mapping that will go from JSON values into F# values. As with SQL, the challenge happens when you try to map from a JSON object into a rich F# domain type with invariants, union types, etc. I've seen a few different approaches people take when working with JSON, but (again, aside from type providers), there's only one approach that I would normally recommend. The following listing shows a simple example domain to get us going, which models a guitar to be used within a music store's inventory system.

Listing 10.2   A sample domain model for a guitar store's inventory

```
type Brand = Brand of string
type Strings = Six | Seven | Eight | Twelve     Domain types to
type Pickup = Single | Humbucker                model a guitar
type Kind =
    | Acoustic
    | Electric of Pickup list

type Guitar =          ◁─────┐  A record that uses the
    {                        types to model a guitar
        Brand : Brand
        Strings : Strings
        Kind: Kind
    }
```

This is a simple model of a guitar; here's some example JSON that maps to it:

```
let ibanezElectric = """     ◁─────┐  Triple quotes denote a multiline string. Such
    { "Brand" : "Ibanez",             strings can use normal quotes within them.
      "Strings" : "6",
      "Pickups" : [ "H", "S", "H" ] }"""
```

How should we deserialize the JSON into our domain type? Well, .NET has a built-in JSON serialization module called `System.Text.Json`, and it has a fairly simple API to get up and running. Let's try it out:

```
JsonSerializer.Deserialize<Guitar> ibanezElectric      ◁─────┐  The type parameter
                                                                indicates to the JSON
                                                                deserializer what the
                                                                target type is.
```

Unfortunately, this code will never work:

```
System.NotSupportedException: F# discriminated union serialization is not
supported. Consider authoring a custom converter for the type.
```

The problem is that `System.Text.Json` does not support discriminated unions. This is fair enough when you think about it; there's no automatic way to know how to map them. For example, in the previous example, how could the library know that `"H"` maps to "Humbucker" and `"S"` to "Single" and so on.

What you can do with `System.Text.Json` is to implement what's known as a *converter*. I'm not going to waste time demonstrating it here (although there is an example of this in the code samples), but suffice it to say that it involves creating a class that knows how to serialize and deserialize a specific type, so you might have a `Pickup-Converter`, a `StringsConverter`, etc. This sounds great in principle, but as with so many frameworks that involve inheritance and overriding methods like this, it's nearly always not worth the hassle involved: you need to work within the confines of a framework, there's magic code that's difficult to debug and reason about, and it's simply not easy to do anything nontrivial unless you invest a lot of time into learning this.

NOTE   There is an extension library known as `FSharp.SystemTextJson`, which comes with a set of common custom converters for F#, such as mapping nullable values to F# options. I would recommend using it, but again, tastefully. Use it for the basics such as `null` to `None`, but don't try to implement domain logic and validation inside it.

I would strongly recommend a much simpler (and perhaps even boring!) approach: create an intermediary model that maps to the JSON very closely and then map that into your rich domain using standard F# code. There are a few options for this intermediary model; the simplest (and one I would recommend) is to use a simple F# data transfer object (DTO) record. The following listing shows such an example.

Listing 10.3   Using raw types to simplify JSON serialization

```
#r "nuget:FsToolkit.ErrorHandling"          ⟵  Imports the
open FsToolkit.ErrorHandling                     FsToolkit.ErrorHandling package


type RawGuitar =          ⟵     Creates a type using only
    {                           primitives that closely
        Brand: string           matches the source JSON
        Strings: string
        Pickups: string list
    }
                                             Uses the result { } block
                                             to simplify validation
let tryAsFullGuitar (raw:RawGuitar) = result {   ⟵
    let! brand =
        if String.IsNullOrWhiteSpace raw.Brand then
            Error "Brand is mandatory"
        else
            Ok (Brand raw.Brand)

    let! strings =                      ⟵        Validates our
        match raw.Strings with                   raw data into
        | "6" -> Ok Six                          domain types
        | "7" -> Ok Seven
        | "8" -> Ok Eight
        | "12" -> Ok Twelve
        | value -> Error $"Invalid value '{value}'"

    let! pickups =                     ⟵
        raw.Pickups
        |> List.traverseResultM (fun pickup ->     ⟵   The traverseResultM
            match pickup with                           function deals with
            | "S" -> Ok Single                          lists of results.
            | "H" -> Ok Humbucker
            | value -> Error $"Invalid value {value}")

    return
        {
            Guitar.Brand = brand
            Guitar.Strings = strings
```

```
        Guitar.Kind =
            match pickups with          Pattern matching
            | [] -> Acoustic            on a list
            | pickups -> Electric pickups
    }
}
```

This sample uses a bunch of techniques that we've seen in isolation earlier in this book, so take the time to read through it step by step and make sure there's nothing that's too intimidating here! The `tryAsFullGuitar` function tries to map from our raw guitar type into our rich domain. If it doesn't work, it returns the first error it receives (if you want to return all errors, the `FsToolkit` package has a type called `Validation`).

We can compose this validation function with the original JSON and `System.Text .Json` as follows:

```
let domainGuitar =
    ibanezElectric
    |> JsonSerializer.Deserialize
    |> tryAsFullGuitar
```

Since the `RawGuitar` maps 1:1 to the source JSON, the risk of getting issues with deserialization is greatly reduced. After we get the data into our raw DTO we pipe the value into the real validation function. One last thing: you might have noticed in this sample the complete absence of a generic type argument for the `Deserialize` call and are wondering where the type argument is (e.g., `JsonSerializer.Deserializer<RawGuitar>`). The answer is simple: F# doesn't need it in this context. It can infer it based on the input of `tryAsFullGuitar`.

10.2.2 *Acceptable alternatives to DTOs*

As mentioned earlier, there are a couple of alternatives that you can use instead of explicit DTOs for this sort of thing (figure 10.2):

- One is to go directly to the serialization API; nearly all serialization libraries allow you to call functions directly against a JSON document programmatically by using something often called a *reader* (e.g., `reader.GetProperty ("Brand").GetStringValue()`).
- Another is to use some kind of key/value pair collection (Dictionary or Map); this can work more efficiently for serialization than deserialization.

I won't go through these options in detail, but to reiterate the main point, do not rely on the serialization library alone to do the magic mapping from the raw JSON to a rich F# domain. It's simply not worth the effort unless you have the simplest of domain models using only primitive values.

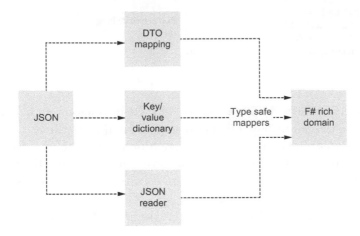

Figure 10.2   Different strategies to safely map from JSON into a rich F# domain model. All utilize some form of intermediate abstraction that allows you to map into F#.

10.2.3 *Serializing F# into JSON*

Serializing data should follow a similar pattern as deserialization, except the process is inverted and does not require validation:

1 Start with your domain type values.
2 Map it into a raw type, which maps 1:1 to the JSON output that you require.
3 Use `System.Text.Json` to serialize it into JSON.

However, one nice trick up F#'s sleeve is that you can use anonymous records to save on a bit of code. Let's imagine we needed to serialize our guitar domain sample to count how many guitars we had by brand and store the result into JSON for transport to a third-party system. Instead of creating an explicit raw output type, we can create an anonymous record whose only purpose is to create the JSON:

```
let createReport (guitars:Guitar list) =
    guitars
    |> List.countBy(fun guitar -> guitar.Brand)
    |> List.map (fun ((Brand brand), count) ->
        {| Brand = brand; Guitars = count |}
    )
    |> JsonSerializer.Serialize

// [ {"Brand":"Ibanez", "Guitars":2}, {"Brand":"Yamaha", "Guitars":1} ]
```

Counts all guitars in the inventory by brand

Unwraps the Brand single case discriminated union to get the inner string value

Creates an anonymous record that has no formal type definition

Serializes the list into JSON

Sample output

I've used this technique to extremely good effect on several projects—you avoid formally defining types that serve no purpose except to output JSON. You can also use this technique on the way in and even supply the type inline with the generic argument, although for anything aside from the simplest types, it makes sense to define a formal record:

```
let test =
    """{ "name" : "value", "age": 10  }"""
    |> JsonSerializer.Deserialize<{|name: string; age :int|}>
```

> **Deserializes a string into an anonymous record using an inline type definition**

10.3   Type providers

Type providers are a lovely feature of F# that, if used tastefully, can dramatically save effort when working with external data sources in F#. Type providers are libraries that hook into the compiler directly and can generate types based on external data. By "generate types," I don't mean to code-generate a file with types in it but to create types as you edit your code. They generally follow the following pattern:

1 Provide a sample dataset representing the schema of the data you're working with, perhaps just a few rows.
2 The type provider will use this sample to create types for you that match the dataset.
3 At runtime, you optionally load in a different dataset, which matches the previously defined schema.

10.3.1   Working with the JSON type provider

As always, an example speaks a thousand words, so let's take the same JSON sample from before and use the `FSharp.Data` library to consume it using the JSON type provider that's included in that package.

Listing 10.4   Working the the JSON type provider

```
#r "nuget:FSharp.Data"
open FSharp.Data

[<Literal>]
let SampleJson = """{
    "Brand": "Ibanez",
    "Strings": "7",
    "Pickups": [ "H", "S", "H" ] }"""
type GuitarJson = JsonProvider<SampleJson>
let sample = GuitarJson.GetSample()
let description = $"{sample.Brand} has {sample.Strings} strings."
```

> **Creates some sample JSON as a literal string. The Literal attribute is required for the type provider.**

> **Creates types using the sample JSON**

> **Reads the sample data**

> **Uses the sample data. Notice that fields like Brand and Strings are valid.**

Just to confirm this: as you enter code into the code editor, the type provider has created a type *based on the string provided*. To prove this, rename the `Brand` field to `Company` in the `SampleJson` value and watch as the compiler immediately flags an error on the final line because the `Brand` field no longer exists.

10.3.2 *Working with external data sources*

Type providers can normally take their schema sample from several sources, such as a literal string value as shown here, and directly inline the angle brackets (for readability, I would only recommend this for small schemas). Most type providers also allow you to connect to external data files directly to create types, such as a local file or even a remote source (e.g., over HTTP). Try the following:

1 Create a new file, `sample-guitars.json`, in the same directory as your script.
2 Copy in the contents of the `SampleJson` string value into that file and save it.
3 Update the type provider definition as follows:

```
type GuitarJson =
    JsonProvider<const(__SOURCE_DIRECTORY__ + "/sample-guitars.json")>
```

4 Rerun the code that gets the sample and prints the description; it should still work.
5 Also observe (by e.g. hovering over) that the `strings` field is inferred by the type provider as an `int`. It does this by analyzing the values in the sample to make an intelligent guess as to the appropriate type.

The somewhat scary-looking line is only necessary because some IDEs (notable, VS Code) don't always play nice with relative paths. `__SOURCE_DIRECTORY__` is a simple macro in F# interactive that returns the current folder that your script file lives in, which we can use to construct a full path to the JSON file; `const` is a shortcut for `[<Literal>]` specifically for type providers.

The JSON type provider can also directly connect to data over HTTP. Here's a sample that connects to a JSON file that contains an array of guitars:

```
type ManyGuitarsOverHttp =
    JsonProvider<"https://raw.githubusercontent.com/        ⟵  Creates a schema based
➡ isaacabraham/fsharp-in-action/main/                          on a remote file
➡ sample-guitars.json">
let inventory = ManyGuitarsOverHttp.GetSamples()      ⟵  Loads the sample data
printfn $"You have {inventory.Length} guitars in stock."  ⟵  from that location
                                                          Gets the length of
                                                          the array of objects
```

At this point, it's worth stressing a key point: to differentiate between schema and data, as shown in figure 10.3. Type providers can blur the lines between them, but they are still two separate things: the initial data sample is used at edit time to create the schema, but the call to `GetSamples()` loads the actual data. A common pattern with type providers is to use one static file that you own to define the schema, perhaps containing just a few rows of data, and, at runtime, load data into that schema from another location, such as a database or a larger, production file. In `FSharp.Data`, this is done using the `Load` method:

```
let inventory =
    ManyGuitarsOverHttp.Load(__SOURCE_DIRECTORY__ + "/full-inventory.json")
```

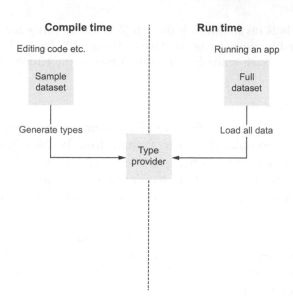

Figure 10.3 Type providers have two distinct phases. At compile time, they are used to create types; at run time, they load in data that meets the previously defined structure.

10.3.3 More data types from FSharp.Data

FSharp.Data also includes both CSV and HTML type providers. The HTML type provider is one that I have a soft spot for because it parses tables and lists from any HTML (and again, that content could be a local source-controlled file or something you're getting from the web). As an example of how powerful this is, almost any table in Wikipedia can be used as a dataset from within F#. In effect, you can use Wikipedia as a programmatic database. The following listing shows an example of retrieving a list of all London boroughs in just a few lines of code (including referencing the appropriate NuGet package).

Listing 10.5　Using the HTML type provider

```
#r "nuget:FSharp.Data"
open FSharp.Data

type LondonBoroughs =
    HtmlProvider<"https://en.wikipedia.org/wiki/
    List_of_London_boroughs">

let boroughs =
    LondonBoroughs.GetSample().Tables.
    ``List of boroughs and local authoritiesEdit``

boroughs.Rows |> Array.map (fun row -> row.Borough)
```

Defines a schema based on a live HTML web page

Accesses a specific table

Uses the data to list all boroughs

Note that this sample is referring to a real, live table. As the HTML may change in months or years (or the page may not exist any longer!), you will find a copy of the HTML in the online source repository to experiment with, which you can use as a local file.

NOTE   Double backtick symbols (as shown in listing 10.5) is another nice feature in F#. Any member or function can be declared with double backticks (e.g., ``List of boroughs``). Such symbols can contain nearly any Unicode character, including spaces.

10.3.4   *Best practices for type providers*

Type providers are an exciting element of F#. I've given many presentations and demos to customers and developers alike where jaws literally drop. People often cannot believe what they see when they witness a type provider in action. Nonetheless, it would be remiss of me to talk about them without tempering that enthusiasm with a taste of reality and some best practices I've learned from working with (and writing my own) type providers.

- *Do shape schemas by hand where required*—Use a sample of data that generates the appropriate types. For example, if a field is sometimes missing in a real JSON dataset, include two rows in your sample, with the first row having the field and the second missing. Good type providers will respond to this appropriately and generate option types or similar.

- *Do separate schema and data*—Keep in mind that the schema file you use for the type argument only needs to be used for the schema; you can normally Load() data from another resource at runtime, which should match the structure of the schema.

- *Consider source-controlling schema files where possible*—Try to avoid going to a live resource for schema definition. Unless it's always on and you control it, you can end up in a situation where your codebase suddenly stops compiling across your whole team because the source of the schema no longer exists (or has changed outside of your control). Of course, this might be a blessing if you're relying on a third party to provide data for your system, and they suddenly change the structure—it's probably a good thing for you to know that as soon as possible.

- *Don't use type provider types in your core domain*—It's tempting to do this, but avoid it unless you are exceedingly confident that you don't require a richer domain type. Provided types have several restrictions. For example, they can't generate discriminated unions, tuples, or records; everything is just classes, enums, and properties. Instead, use them as a quicker and easier way to create your DTO-style types from which you map into your core domain.

- *Do use type providers for scripts*—They're wonderful for the exploration of datasets without needing to build full-blown domain models, use external tools, etc. Once you've familiarized yourself with the data, you can then decide the best way to integrate it with your real application.

10.4   *Data visualization*

Data visualization is another area where F# really shines compared to many languages and platforms. Its lightweight syntax, type provider capabilities, and ability to create DSLs means that you can seamlessly move from data ingestion through to calculations and, ultimately, presentation quickly and easily.

Let's have some fun and use the previous London boroughs dataset to calculate the population density of the different boroughs and then visualize the data in an F# script using another library, `Plotly.NET`. Don't worry: it's much less effort than it sounds. First, create a new script that brings in both `FSharp.Data` and `Plotly.NET`:

```
#r "nuget: Plotly.NET, 3.0.1"
#r "nuget: FSharp.Data, 5.0.2"
open FSharp.Data
open Plotly.NET
```

Now access the same dataset using the HTML type provider as we saw earlier:

```
type LondonBoroughs =
    HtmlProvider<"https://en.wikipedia.org/wiki/
List_of_London_boroughs">
let boroughs =
    LondonBoroughs.GetSample().Tables.
``List of boroughs and local authoritiesEdit``
```

If you look at the dataset in the browser, you'll see several columns, including the borough name, area (square miles), and estimated population. We can calculate the population density by taking the population and dividing by the area:

```
let density =
    boroughs.Rows
    |> Array.map (fun row ->
        row.Borough,
        row.``Population (2019 est)`` / row.``Area (sq mi)``
    )
```

This will return an array of `string * decimal` tuples. For example:

```
("Barnet", 11821.3197969543147208121182741M);
("Bexley", 10619.6321642429426860564585512M);
("Brent", 19746.7664670658682634730538921M);
("Bromley", 5732.8963256856994997412454718M);
```

How do you visualize this? Ironically, this is the easiest part:

```
density
|> Array.sortBy snd
|> Chart.Column
|> Chart.show
```

This will open a browser and display something like figure 10.4.

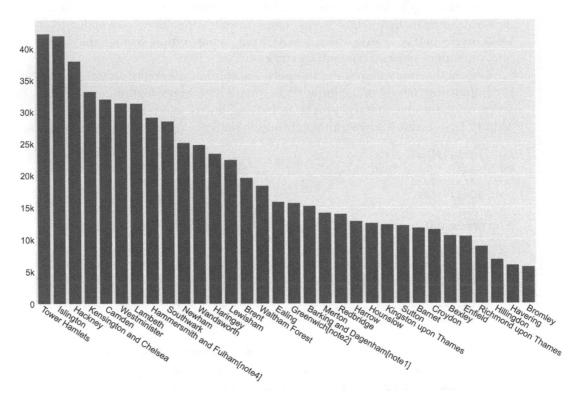

Figure 10.4   Creating a column chart using the `Plotly.NET` library based on data sourced from Wikipedia via the HTML type provider

That's obviously a simple chart, but consider the ease with which we were able to read and shape the data before providing it to another library. Neither of the two libraries (`FSharp.Data` and `Plotly.NET`) require any specific types or interfaces. A basic array of tuples is enough here to act as a data transfer shape. There's no requirement to implement an interface or create classes. Basic data, types, and functions are all we need. Here's the full mapping code as a single expression-oriented pipeline:

```
boroughs.Rows
|> Array.map (fun row ->
    row.Borough,
    row.``Population (2019 est)`` / row.``Area (sq mi)``
)
|> Array.sortByDescending snd
|> Chart.Column
|> Chart.show
```

Again, consider that we're using standard F# fundamentals: collection functions, pipe-lines, and lambdas, plus a couple of libraries for the input/output. This is one of the things I really enjoy about F#: the fundamentals you learn can be applied in many different contexts and manners, often just reusing some basic core types.

10.5 *Working with other data sources*

When working with F# and connecting to the multitude of data sources out there, you will often be dealing with standard .NET libraries, which may or may not have an especially strong F# story. Nonetheless, in general, if the library is a .NET package available on NuGet, it'll work in F#. This section covers a few specific scenarios I've seen that are worth being aware of.

10.5.1 *The CLIMutable attribute*

Some libraries use a .NET feature called *reflection* to dynamically populate data from external data sources. They create an empty object and then imperatively mutate it on a field-by-field basis. However, F# records, as we know, are immutable by default, and some packages will struggle to work with them out of the box. To get around this, you can place the `[<CLIMutable>]` attribute on any record. Behind the scenes, this will create a default (empty) constructor and, at run time, make all fields on the record mutable for these scenarios. However, as far as your F# is concerned, nothing changes; the records will still appear to be immutable.

10.5.2 *Working with SQL*

I only include SQL specifically here because it's such a popular database technology, especially Microsoft SQL Server on .NET. You have multiple options for working with SQL in F#, whether that's low-level .NET SQL code such as the DataReader, popular .NET micro-object-relational mappers, or F#-specific libraries. Whichever option you choose, look for libraries that allow you to map from the source SQL data into a raw type that closely maps to that source. From there, use standard F# (including validation layers, etc.) to act as an anticorruption layer into a trusted, richer domain model (effectively, this is what we looked at with JSON). Within the SQL world, there are popular and high-performance .NET libraries such as Dapper, as well as F#-specific ones such as Facil that will generate the raw types for you from your SQL database. Many of these choices will lead you down the route of separating your reads from your writes, a practice sometimes known as *command query responsibility separation*. This is out of the scope of this book, but it's a pattern that I've seen have very good results from a functional programming point of view.

There is, however, one specific library that I would caution against using in F# (at least at the time of writing), and that's Microsoft's Entity Framework (EF). So-called object-relational mappers (ORMs) are quite popular in some platforms, including .NET, the most popular one being EF. I generally have no problem with the idea of automatically mapping from SQL to .NET types, but there are several shortcomings with this particular approach:

- Many ORMs simply can't cope with F# types. It's not uncommon in other languages to use primitives throughout your domain model, but in F#, we tend to use richer types, such as single-case discriminated unions with invariants that are applied through code. Most ORMs don't know how to deal with these. In fact, EF has particularly poor support for F# types, forcing you (at present, at least) to make types mutable, placing specific attributes and declaring fields in a specific manner (even the `CLIMutable` trick doesn't work). Even mapping from a SQL database to a raw F# record filled with primitive fields is a pain. The last thing you should do is have the implementation of your domain dictated to you because of a concern such as your choice of data access layer. Yes, it may influence the design of your domain, but don't compromise too far.

- It's challenging to support validation of your types within an ORM. You may want to force some invariants or business rules within your types; this can be challenging to integrate with a model populated by an ORM, especially if it uses reflection to set field values.

- Many ORMs, including EF, come with a stateful context object, designed so that you can read data, mutate it however you want in memory, and then simply call a `Save()` method. The context will magically figure out what's changed and generate the appropriate SQL calls for this. This is a poor fit for F#, which encourages immutable data. In addition, the stateless nature of web applications, which is the most popular mechanism for hosting applications, means that you often don't benefit from the stateful magic tracking anyway.

10.6 *Tooling options*

If you're working heavily with data in F#, you have a few options in terms of how best to do it. This section discusses a few different tooling approaches that you might adopt.

The first option is to use whichever IDE you're using right now and scripts—essentially, what we've done so far in the book. You can do everything from F# scripts in terms of data exploration and so on. Rider and Visual Studio both also have, to varying degrees, support for some data exploration outside of F# (e.g., SQL and JSON files). However, if you are sourcing and working with varied datasets that you need to quickly visualize and explore, even before coding, neither compare with the breadth of VS Code's extensions. There are thousands of extensions that allow you to rapidly source and work with data without needing to leave VS Code; for this reason, I always recommend using that as at least one of the tools in your arsenal.

The other option you have is to go for a notebook-like tool. Notebooks like Jupyter and, more recently, .NET Interactive (which is just an extension for VS Code) allow you to create a kind of living document in which you enter snippets of code (which may be in multiple languages), the results of which are shown directly beneath the snippet you entered. You can also enter standard text as markdown, which can function as a form of documentation or report but with real code and results within them (figure 10.5).

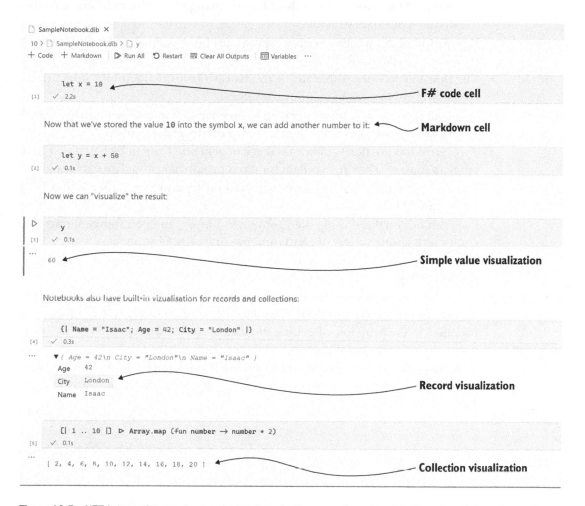

Figure 10.5   NET Interactive notebooks within VS Code. You can mix and match F# and markdown to create a live document, with built-in visualization support for different F# types.

Summary

- Try to use the same common best practices when working with data, regardless of where it comes from, whether an event stream, SQL, JSON, or in-memory list.
- It's important to enforce the separation of data and behavior in functional programming. This gives us more flexibility to change behaviors without affecting the shape of our data structures.
- Be mindful of not treating scripts as programs but as snippets of code that work together in a stateful REPL.
- The best way to work with a list of results is to convert them to a single result containing either a list of `Ok` or `Error` values.
- It is best to serialize and deserialize between JSON and F# using the `System.Text.Json` library and then manually map it into a rich domain type.
- Type providers are flexible libraries that can generate types in F# based on different data sources. They're excellent for rapid prototyping and data exploration.
- The `FSharp.Data` package comes with several type providers, including CSV, JSON, and HTML.
- Data can be visualized using the `Plotly.NET` library, an open source library that comes with a wide variety of charts and has first-class F# support.
- The `CLIMutable` attribute is a useful way to improve interoperability for F# records with many .NET data access libraries.
- There are many options for working with Microsoft SQL Server, such as the DataReader, Dapper, and Facil. Each has pros and cons; whichever option you use, stick to the principle of getting the data in simple types into F# before mapping into a richer domain.
- Tooling options for data-focused F# workloads are standard F# scripts and .NET Interactive notebooks, an approach that merges static markdown text and live F# code into a single format.

11

F# Interop

This chapter covers

- Working with C# code and common .NET constructs
- Consuming NuGet packages
- Mixed-language solutions
- JavaScript and F#

Just to reiterate, F# runs primarily on .NET—and a great deal of .NET, such as the base class library and most NuGet packages, is written in C#. This chapter shows you the techniques for how best to consume such code as well as how to write F# APIs that C# developers can more easily consume.

11.1 Working with other .NET code

You might have already realized this, but you already know how to consume C# from F#: pretty much the entire .NET framework class library is written in C#. This means that virtually all the APIs in the `System` namespace that are available out of the box are written in C#. F# has very good support for consuming such code, as we'll see shortly.

11.1.1 Consuming C# classes

The language designers of F# went to a great deal of effort to try to make consuming C# from F# as easy as possible. You can create instances of classes, call methods on them, and work with mutable, imperative code. This means that F# developers can benefit from the entire .NET library ecosystem while still being able to write functional-first code. Figure 11.1 illustrates some of these features.

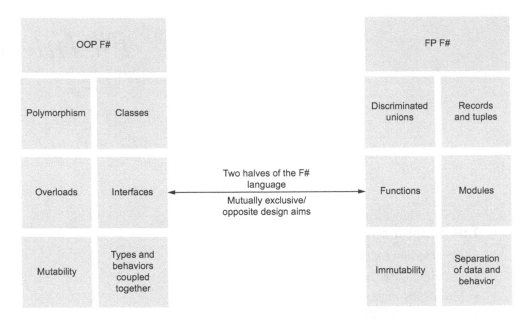

Figure 11.1   Illustrating the clear distinction between the object orientated (OO) and functional programming (FP) halves of F#

It's important to understand that unlike some languages such as Scala (and more recent versions of C#), F# can feel almost like two separate languages. It has a clear distinction between the OO and FP halves of the language and does not try to create a single paradigm using both halves. You can pick and mix features from both halves in an application, but in my experience, most F# folks use the FP feature set 95% of the time and fall back to the OO side for interop purposes and/or specific corner cases—it really doesn't happen very often. The following listing shows some examples of consuming some C# code, with emphasis on the OO features that are exposed in F#.

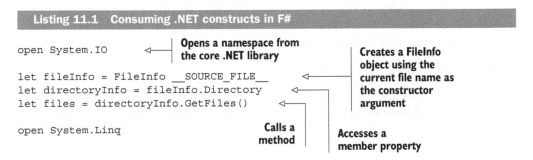

Listing 11.1   Consuming .NET constructs in F#

```
let scriptFiles =
    files
    |> Seq.where (fun f -> Path.GetExtension f.Name = ".fsx")
    |> Seq.map (fun f -> f.Name)

let scriptFilesLinq =
    files
        .Where(fun f -> Path.GetExtension f.Name = ".fsx")
        .Select(fun f -> f.Name)
```

Performs a Seq query pipeline over a .NET array returned by the C# method

Uses the .NET LINQ framework to perform a similar query

Provides an F# lambda to a C# method

> **NOTE** The identifiers __LINE__, __SOURCE_DIRECTORY__, and __SOURCE_ FILE__ are built-in values that enable you to access the source line number, directory, and filename in your code.

There are a few things going on here, but the truth is, you've already done this. There's nothing here that will really be new to you. One thing that is especially nice is how F# lets you treat a class constructor as a function:

```
let fileInfo = FileInfo __SOURCE_FILE__
let fileInfo = new FileInfo(__SOURCE_FILE__)
```

Both are legitimate F# syntax; however, the first is more idiomatic F# to me. It simply says that there's a function called `FileInfo`, which, given a string as input, returns a `FileInfo` object.

EXERCISE 10.1

Let's create a simple console application that demonstrates how to utilize your own C# code from F#:

1 Create a new directory called `MixedCodeApp`.
2 Inside this, create a C# class library: `dotnet new classlib -lang C# -o CsCode`. The `-o` argument specifies the output directory of the project rather than the current directory.
3 Open `Class1.cs` and replace the contents with the following:

   ```
   namespace CsCode;

   public class Person
   {
       public string? Name { get;set;}
       public int? Age { get; set; }

       public Person () {
           Name = "Tamara";
           Age = 21;
       }
   }
   ```

4 Build the C# project to ensure it compiles: `dotnet build ./CsCode`.

5 Now create an F# Console App: `dotnet new console -lang F# -o FsCode`.

6 Let's reference the C# project from our F# project so that we can access the code in it from F#: `dotnet add ./FsCode/ reference ./CsCode/`.

7 If you open `FsCode.fsproj`, you will see XML similar to the following has been added:

```xml
<ItemGroup>
  <ProjectReference Include="..\CsCode\CsCode.csproj" />
</ItemGroup>
```

8 We can now access the C# code from F#. Change `Program.fs` as follows:

```
open CsCode          ◁———  Opens a namespace
let c1 = Person ()          from the C# project    Creates an instance
printfn $"{c1.Name} is {c1.Age} years old!"  ◁———  of the C# class
```

9 Run the F# app: `dotnet run --project ./FsCode`. You should see the following output:

```
Tamara is 21 years old!
```

> **Updating references in mixed-language solutions**
> Some IDEs do a better job than others at automatically updating the referencing project when changing dependent code. For example, Visual Studio and Rider are a little better than VS Code at this. So, if you rename the `Person` class to another name, Visual Studio and Rider automatically refresh the F# type cache. In contrast, VS Code needs an explicit rebuild of the C# project and occasionally a restart to reflect the changes (or the Reload Window shortcut command).

11.1.2 Interfaces

Interfaces are a popular feature in C#. They allow you to specify a contract for a type (such as methods and properties) that multiple classes can implement. You can then reference just the interface without knowing which implementation you're dealing with. Of course, F# lets you consume these as normal, but you can also create your own implementations of existing interfaces. Here, we'll create a class that implements the `IDisposable` interface, an interface in .NET used to signify a handle to a resource (e.g., a file that can be disposed of):

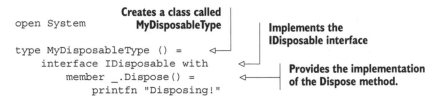

```
open System

type MyDisposableType () =
    interface IDisposable with
        member _.Dispose() =
            printfn "Disposing!"
```

Creates a class called **MyDisposableType**

Implements the **IDisposable interface**

Provides the implementation of the Dispose method.

If you forget any of the members of the interface's contract, the compiler will give you an error message that includes the missing members or those you've included but have the incorrect signature.

You can also create your own interfaces:

```
type MyInterface =
    abstract Capitalize : string -> string      Creates two abstract methods on
    abstract Add : int -> int                   an interface type, MyInterface
```

In F#, we tend to think of interfaces and classes simply as types, hence, there are no specific keywords here (e.g., class or interface). F# infers that this is an interface because all of the members of the type are abstract.

One thing to note is that F# implements interface members explicitly. This means that you won't be able to see the interface's members unless you explicitly annotate the object as that interface.

Listing 11.2 Creating an implementation of an interface in F#

```
type MyImplementation () =          ◄──┤ Implements the          Fails to access the
    interface MyInterface with              MyInterface type        Capitalize method on the
        member this.Capitalize text = text.ToUpper()               implementation object
        member this.Add number = number + 1
                                                                    Annotates a
let implementation = MyImplementation()                             MyImplementation
implementation.Capitalize "test" // compiler error!    ◄──          object as type
                                                                    MyInterface
let implementation : MyInterface = MyImplementation()    ◄──
let text = implementation.Capitalize "test" // works!    ◄──        Successfully calls the
                                                                    Capitalize method
```

Why might you want to create interfaces in a pure F# codebase? There are a few reasons:

- You're writing code that will be consumed by C#; interfaces are an idiomatic construct in that language.
- You need to make a truly open, pluggable API that can be bound at run time.
- You find yourself creating a record with only function signatures as fields. In this case, you've essentially created a functional version of an interface. There's nothing wrong with this per se, but generally, I prefer to think of a contract of functions as an interface and records for transporting data around my application:

```
type MyInterfaceAsRecord =
    {
        Capitalize : string -> string      Defines a record
        Add : int -> int                   of functions
    }
```

OBJECT EXPRESSIONS

F# has a neat trick to simplify the pattern shown in listing 11.2 using what is known as an *object expression*. Object expressions allow you to make instances of interfaces without first creating a concrete implementation type:

```
let implementation =
    { new MyInterface with                              ◄——┤ Creates an instance
        member this.Capitalize text = text.ToUpper()         of an interface
        member _.Add number = number + 1    ◄——┤ Omits the self-
    }                                                binding this with _
let text = implementation.Capitalize "test"   ◄——┤ as it is not used in
                                                     the method body
```

Provides the implementation of   Uses the
each member of the interface   interface directly

Note that the type of `implementation` in this code snippet is `MyInterface`.

INTERFACES ON F# TYPES
You can also apply interfaces to F# records and discriminated unions. You won't find
yourself needing to do this very often at all, but it's good to know that you can. Here's
an example showing how to implement the (more-or-less obsolete) `ICloneable` interface on an F# record:

```
type Person =
    {
        Name : string
        Age : int                                    Implementation
    }                                                 of the interface's
    with                          Interface           members
    interface System.ICloneable with   ◄——┤ declaration
        member this.Clone() = { Name = this.Name; Age = this.Age }   ◄——┤
```

11.1.3 Fluent APIs

When working with C# libraries and APIs, you may find that they don't play quite so
nicely from F#, especially those that follow the so-called fluent style. One of the reasons is that C#, as a primarily statement-oriented language, implicitly ignores the
return value of method calls. This differs from F#, where you must explicitly ignore
the return value of functions that aren't of type `unit`. This can lead to code looking
like the following, for example, where each method on the API mutates itself and
then returns itself, ready for the next method call in a chain:

```
let SetUpWebApp () =
    // some code

    let framework = WebFramework()
                                         Methods that mutate the
    framework                            internal state and return
        .AddAuthentication()             themselves for other
        .AddCors()                       method calls
        .AddCaching()
        |> ignore        ◄——┤ Ignore is required to prevent
                              F# compiler warning.

    // more code in the function here…
```

The use of `ignore` here is the smell. F# APIs typically don't follow this kind of design;
they'll work, but they won't feel especially F# friendly.

11.1.4 Tuples

C# nowadays has support for tuples, similar to F#, although C# tuples are value rather than reference types. We covered value type tuples earlier, but to remind you, you create them with the `struct` keyword:

```
let y = 1,2
let x = struct (1,2)
```

⟵ **A reference tuple**

⟵ **A struct tuple, used by default in C#**

11.1.5 Out parameters

C# didn't always have access to tuples at the language level (although the tuple type has existed in .NET since .NET 4, included at the time when F# was finally included in the box of Visual Studio). In earlier versions (up to C#6), the only sane way to return multiple values from a method was to either create a dedicated class for the two values or to use *out parameters*. A good example of this is the set of `TryParse` methods on many .NET primitive types. Out parameters are awkward to consume and work with in C#, but F# sidesteps the issue nicely by implicitly converting such methods to return standard F# tuples:

```
let parsed, value = System.Int32.TryParse "123"
```

⟵ **A TryParse method returns a tuple of Boolean and the parsed value. The Boolean represents whether the parse operation was successful or not.**

11.1.6 Object-based programming

While F# has good support for consuming classes from C#, it doesn't allow you to implement every OO feature in .NET. For example, you can consume protected members on a class when inheriting, but you cannot create your own protected members. You'll find a few edge cases like this—F# actively discourages you from using and abusing features that don't really fit with the spirit of the language.

It's worth bearing in mind that F# is an opinionated language and leads us down a path of functional programming first; after all, that's what it's optimized for. If you want to use the OO half of F#, as you've seen so far in this chapter, some things will work just fine, but others are somewhat restricted. Figure 11.2 outlines a set of classic OO plus imperative language features and my advice when using them from F#. What you're left with is a set of cut-down OO features that amount to what is known as *object-based programming*—essentially, immutable objects without inheritance, simple interfaces, and extremely limited mutability.

11.1.7 F# wrappers

One common approach to dealing with some of the challenges when working with existing C# libraries that are not necessarily a good fit for idiomatic F# is to create *wrapper* libraries. These libraries are essentially thin veneers over a C# library, and are designed to smooth out any rough edges so that it is easier to consume from F#, as well as to enable you to take advantage of F#-specific features. We'll see some very

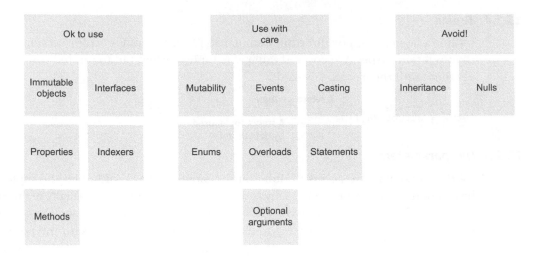

Figure 11.2   Some of the different OO features in F#. Many of these can be happily used in idiomatic F#, but others should be avoided except where necessary.

good examples of this when we get to web programming later, but for now, here are a few examples of how you might do this.

TRYPARSE METHODS

We've already seen how `TryParse` methods are made easier in F#. However, they still don't fully take advantage of F# types. A better (and more type-safe) fit would be to have them return an Option: if the value was successfully parsed as the target type, return Some value; otherwise, return None. You can quickly create a generic function for this:

```
let parseOption parser (value:string) =        ◄─  Defines a generic function
    match parser value with                        that works with any
    | true, v -> Some v                            TryParse method
    | false, _ -> None

                                                    Creates an F#-friendly
                                                    tryParse that returns
                                                    an Option<int>
let parseIntOption = parseOption System.Int32.TryParse   ◄─┘
let maybeANumber = parseIntOption "123"   ◄─┐
                                            │  Tests out the new function
                                               with a number as a string
```

There are other ways to create more succinct solutions with features such as active patterns and statically resolved type parameters (SRTPs). Both are beyond the scope of this book, but I've included an example of both in the online source code for you to look at in your own time.

> **NOTE** The FsToolkit.ErrorHandling package, which we saw in earlier chapters, comes with a number of useful wrapper functions, including one for working with TryParse.

SINGLE-METHOD INTERFACES

You may find yourself needing to provide types to C# libraries, which are essentially nothing more than one-method interfaces. To a functional programmer, these are simply functions, nothing more. Using object expressions, you can map functions into interfaces quickly. Here's a fictional interface, IDisplayTime, which is used by a C# application to print the current time to the user. You're developing several implementations that the user can select based on their preferences:

```
open System

/// The IDisplayTime interface is used to print the time.
type IDisplayTime =
    /// Prints the time to the user.
    abstract Display : DateTime -> string
```

Armed with this interface, we can create a helper function that can quickly create instances of that interface, taking in the implementation as a function. If you come from an OO background, you can think of this as a kind of abstract factory:

```
let makeIDisplayTime implementation =      ←——  Passes in the display
    { new IDisplayTime with                      implementation as an argument
        member _.Display date = implementation date   ←————
    }
```
Creates the interface instance, using the supplied argument as the body

And here's how you might use it:

Two different implementations using only functions

```
let normalPrinter =
    makeIDisplayTime (fun date -> $"The time is now {date}!")   ←——
let shortPrinter =
    makeIDisplayTime (fun date -> $"It's {date.ToShortTimeString()}.")   ←——
```

PARTIAL APPLICATION AND PIPELINES

You can always create wrappers around methods to be partially applied. This can be useful not only so that you can pass in arguments individually but also so that you can pipeline methods together more easily. Here, I create a single wrapper function to make it easier to append text to a file:

```
open System.IO
                                           A wrapper function around the built-in
module File =                              AppendAllText method, which also
    let append path text =      ←——       returns the path of the file appended
        File.AppendAllText(path, text)
        path
                                                     Creates a basic
                                                     text file as input
File.WriteAllText ("text.txt", "test")      ←——

let fileInfo =
    "text.txt"                            Uses the built-in ReadAllText
    |> File.ReadAllText      ←——          method in the pipeline
```

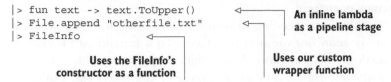

```
|> fun text -> text.ToUpper()
|> File.append "otherfile.txt"
|> FileInfo
```

An inline lambda as a pipeline stage

Uses our custom wrapper function

Uses the FileInfo's constructor as a function

Observe here that we construct a pipeline out of several different elements:

- *A normal .NET C# method*—F# can happily use C# methods in a pipeline if the method signature matches what's expected. Typically, single-argument methods work best.
- *An inline lambda*—I don't use these often as readability can suffer if they do too much, but they are fine for short functions like this. There's also a feature due in F#8 to make lambda syntax shorter in F#, that would allow you to rewrite the lambda simply as `.ToUpper()`.
- *A custom F# wrapper function around some C# code.*
- *A constructor*—Again, F# looks at constructors as just functions, and we can therefore pipeline them just like anything else.

Be careful not to abuse the use of pipelines though; there's nothing wrong with dot notation and normal method calls. Use pipelines and partial application when it makes sense as a logical flow of data transformations, as we discussed earlier in the book.

11.2 Exposing F# to C#

This section briefly covers how F# types look if you try to reference them from a C# project. The general answer is "surprisingly good," although there are some caveats.

11.2.1 Core F# concepts

Following is a list of core F# features and how they will render when consumed from C#:

- *Namespaces*—Namespaces are just .NET namespaces. They're exactly the same as C# ones and behave the same way.
- *Modules*—These appear as static classes in C#; functions or types you've defined in them will appear as members on the class.
- *Functions*—These appear as methods in C#. Partially applied functions automatically are rewritten as normal C# method arguments.
- *Types*—
  - *Records*—These are exposed as normal C# classes. Each field is exposed as a public getter-only property. A nondefault constructor is included, with one argument for each field you define.
  - *Tuples*—These are exposed as a `System.Tuple` or `System.ValueTuple` depending on whether or not you use the `struct` keyword on the F# side.
  - *Discriminated unions*—These are exposed as a class hierarchy; the type of the discriminated union is the base class, with each case as a subclass. You'll also be given static builder methods on the base class from which to create the

appropriate subclasses. Therefore, you can also use C#'s pattern matching on them, although C# doesn't (as yet) support exhaustive matching, so you won't get the same level of type safety as F#.

- *Type providers*—These are not supported in C# and will appear as just objects, with no magic properties on them.

11.2.2 Tips and tricks

The following list provides some tips and tricks to more smoothly work between F# and C#. You won't need them all very often, but it's good to know them for the edge cases that inevitably appear:

- If you apply the `CLIMutable` attribute, record properties will also include a public setter, and the default constructor will be exposed. This can be useful for a more idiomatic C# experience.
- The `CompiledName` attribute can be a useful tool. It allows you to expose a type or function from F# to C# with a different name. Just place the attribute above the symbol. In F#, it'll retain its original name, but in C#, it will be exposed as the name in the attribute:

```
[<CompiledName "SaveCustomer">]
let saveCustomer customer = …
```

- Avoid allowing the F# list in an API to be consumed by C#. Instead, use the standard Array or Sequence types (don't forget Sequence is just an alias for IEnumerable). Although all three work fine with LINQ, the last two are commonly used in C#, and developers will be very familiar with them.
- Attributes like these may only get you some of the way to making the API appear native to C# developers. Consider a façade layer between the C# code and F# to make the API especially nice to consume from C#.

11.2.3 Introducing F# into existing codebases

This section discusses some challenges you'll face when introducing F# into an existing predominantly C# codebase, and some gotchas to watch out for.

COMMON MISTAKES

I regularly speak with people who try to introduce F# into an existing C# .NET application, with their initial intention being to introduce F# piece-by-piece (e.g., so-called "hard" or "numerical" calculations) or by writing unit tests or building scripts in F#. As you've seen earlier in this section, they will most likely work without too much effort. However, in my experience, these strategies will generally all be limited in their success, usually because of one of the following reasons:

1 You'll come to only see F# as a language for very specific use cases, such as writing tests or "difficult" logic. Not only is this missing out on using F# for all general-purpose coding, but it'll also not show F# at its best—it's not especially easy

to jump between two (or more!) development paradigms, and it can lead to just one or two developers ending up as the "F# devs" who write all the tests while the others stay in the C# world.

2 You'll find it frustrating moving back and forth between F# and C#-styles, and you'll miss all the nice features of F#. Slowly, your F# will start to bleed out into the bigger codebase, doing more and more and ending up with an inconsistent set of patterns and practices as to when to use F# or C#.

3 The more F# you write, the more you risk writing C# in an F# style, which risks other team members finding the C# code you're writing somehow atypical. I've personally run into this in the past.

Another common mistake I see when working with mixed solutions is to deliberately write your F# in the style of a C# app to make it easier for other developers to understand F#. Trust me—it won't work. You'll avoid addressing the hard truth that F# is not C# with a different syntax, but an entirely different way of structuring and designing code. Instead, all you'll end up with is an F# codebase that not only doesn't make full use of F# (in fact, it will probably show F# in a poor light) but will also leave your colleagues rightly asking, "Why not just do this in C#?" Remember that F# is great at writing expression-oriented, immutable, typed code with separation of functions and data; C# is great at writing mostly statement-oriented, mutable, typed code that combines data and behavior through classes. The more you push either language in the other direction, the more they'll push back against you.

LAYERED ARCHITECTURES

I recommend being a little more ambitious: focus on either the horizontal tiers of an app or, better yet, the vertical slices of an application. In a horizontal tiers approach (figure 11.3), you focus on either so-called cross-cutting concerns (e.g., caching, error handling, validation, etc.) or specific tiers of the application (e.g., data access, business logic, UI, etc.), which are used across the whole application. With this approach, every part of the system will use the new F# layer you've written. And, depending on how you've organized your team (e.g., full-stack developers), everyone can get involved in doing some F#. However, one potential drawback to this approach is that you will still need to deal with interoperability between C# and F#.

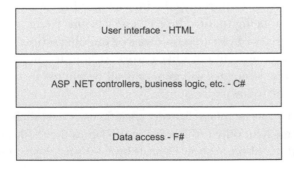

Figure 11.3   A horizontal tiers approach to introducing F# into a mixed-language application. Here, F# is used for all data access operations but is called from a C# layer on top.

In a vertical slices approach (figure 11.4), you take an entire vertical area of your system (e.g., the Order module, the Data Input module, etc.) and implement it entirely from start to finish in F#. There's no C# for the F# tier to interact with because everything is in F#. You don't have to compromise on your F# coding patterns or worry about how it will be consumed from C#. This approach is more ambitious since you'll need to implement all the tiers in F# to deliver a feature, although the flipside is that you're only affecting one vertical tier of the system; the rest can carry on unaffected.

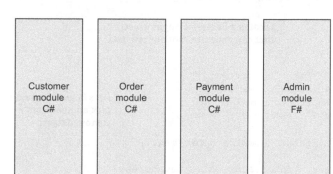

Figure 11.4   A vertical slice approach to a mixed-language application. Each slice contains all tiers, such as UI, logic, and web and data access.

I prefer the vertical slices approach. You'll immediately start to look upon F# as a proper general-purpose language and can experience its benefits across your technical stack rather than seeing it as a niche language for very specific areas.

11.3   Consuming NuGet packages

We've already started using NuGet packages in scripts in the last few chapters, using libraries such as `FSharp.Data` for data access and `Plotly.NET` for charting and the `#r "nuget:..."` syntax. In this section, we'll take a step back and review how to use NuGet packages within the context of a standalone application, as well as a little more about the .NET package ecosystem in general.

11.3.1   Working with NuGet package dependencies

This section will show you how to add and work with NuGet packages that you can use from within F# applications. We're going to create a new console application that uses the free, open source package Bogus, a simple fake data generator for .NET:

1 Create a new F# console application in an empty directory `NuGetSample` using the usual dotnet command-line interface syntax `dotnet new console -lang F#`.

2 Add the Bogus package: `dotnet add package Bogus -v 34.0.2`. In this case, I've specified a version number, but you don't have to; dotnet will, by default, download the latest version.

3 Open the `NuGetSample.fsproj` file. You should notice that a new element has been added:

```
<ItemGroup>
  <PackageReference Include="Bogus" Version="34.0.2" />
</ItemGroup>
```

4 Open the `Program.fs` file and add the code in the following listing.

Listing 11.3   Using the Bogus library to create fake employees

```
open Bogus          ◁——|  Opens the Bogus namespace

let faker = Faker ()        ◁——|  Creates a Faker—a Bogus object
                                    that can generate randomized data
let customers = [
    for i in 1..100 do
        {| EmployeeId = faker.Random.Guid()
           Name = faker.Name.FullName()
           Role = faker.PickRandom [              Uses Bogus to randomly
               "Manager"; "Team Lead"; "Member"   pick an item from a
           ]                                       custom dataset
           Department = faker.Commerce.Department()
           Address =
               {| Street = faker.Address.StreetAddress()
                  State = faker.Address.State() |}
        |}
]

for customer in customers do          Prints out all
    printfn "%A" customer   ◁——       employees
```

Uses Bogus to generate random data

Paket

There's an alternative open source, community-led project known as Paket. Paket is compatible with all NuGet packages but provides a different command line and project-level experience. It provides several benefits over NuGet, such as out-of-the-box lock files and repository-wide package versions (features that NuGet has finally started to support as well but are still not commonplace or actively being developed).

11.3.2 Working with NuGet tools

In addition to standard NuGet packages which act as dependencies in your projects, you can also create a special kind of NuGet package known as a *tool*. NuGet tools are actual programs you can add to your repository; they typically function as supporting tools used during the development process (e.g., code generators, build tools, etc.). Let's look at one such tool, Fantomas, a code formatter for F#:

1 Enter the command `dotnet new tool-manifest`. This will create a file `.config/dotnet-tools.json`, which is a JSON file that contains the list of all dotnet tools in your repository.

2 Enter the command `dotnet tool install fantomas --version 5.1.3`.

3 Observe that the configuration file now has the details of the new tool in it.

4 Run `dotnet tool restore`. This will download Fantomas onto your machine. Like all NuGet packages, dotnet is smart enough to download it machine-wide, so that the next time you use this tool, it won't need to download it.

5 Open the `Program.fs` file in VS Code.

6 Run the following command: `dotnet fantomas Program.fs`.

7 Observe that Fantomas has reformatted the F# into a consistent style.

Fantomas is a tool that has been more or less adopted by Microsoft internally for F# code. Indeed, the compiler codebase itself uses Fantomas to ensure consistent formatting. It's quite configurable (you can find out more on the Fantomas homepage; https://fsprojects.github.io/fantomas/) and has built-in support in the main IDEs so that you can have your code automatically formatted whenever you save a file. I'd recommend looking at it, especially in the early days of your F# journey as you try to find a formatting style that fits. Let's finish this section by trying out Fantomas support within VS Code:

1 Add some extra spaces between `State` and `=`.

2 Save the file.

3 From the VS Code Command Palette, select Format Document (SHIFT + ALT + F on Windows or SHIFT + OPTION + F on Mac).

4 Observe the extra spaces have been removed by Fantomas.

NOTE You can have VS Code format documents automatically on saving by setting the `editor.formatOnSave` setting to `true`. Refer to the VS Code documentation for more details on configuration.

> ### Global and local NuGet tools
> NuGet tools can be installed machine-wide (global tool), which you can run from anywhere on your machine, or at the repository level (local tool). I recommend the latter: it's much cleaner as you can have multiple versions of the same tool on your machine siside-by-side, which prevents issues with incompatibilities with other team members or clashing repositories.

11.4 The Fable project: F# and JavaScript

This final section discusses F#'s interop capabilities with the JavaScript language and runtime. If you didn't know about this, strap yourselves in!

11.4.1 JavaScript to F#: A brief history

JS has grown from small beginnings to become probably the most used programming language, period. It has a large, diverse, and vibrant ecosystem (and all the problems that come with that) and is supported by many vendors. The growth of the web browser as an application platform, the increasing complexity of applications, and the fact that JS is the de facto language for application development in the browser have led to it become the dominant language and runtime for application development, whether that's web apps or server-side backend services or even mobile applications using frameworks such as React Native. Google and others have invested time and money into developing browser engines like V8, which optimize JS code to be reasonably performant—not to the extent of, for example, .NET and the Java virtual machine but nonetheless acceptable for most purposes.

But despite all this success, there are real problems with the programming language itself that will probably never go away. For starters, it's very dynamically typed. There is no compile-time static type checking; even at run time, it'll happily let you add a string to a number. It's inconsistent. It's hard to debug and doesn't scale well for even medium-sized teams.

Around the start of this explosion in the popularity of JS, several languages started to crop up that were designed solely to be transpiled into JavaScript (rather than compiled into, for example, a binary executable format), such as CoffeeScript. Some were more successful than others, but wasn't until TypeScript—a superset of JS—came along that people really started to sit up and take notice. The JS tooling ecosystem also continued to evolve, with tools developed that rewrote your handwritten JS into a highly optimized and minified form, which, while also technically JS, is unreadable to the human eye.

Earlier, I said that JS had evolved to become not only the dominant language, but also *runtime*. This was intentional because I (and others) now see the JS platform not only as a programming language but also as a web runtime layer, thanks to these transpilers and JS optimizers, as illustrated in Figure 11.5.

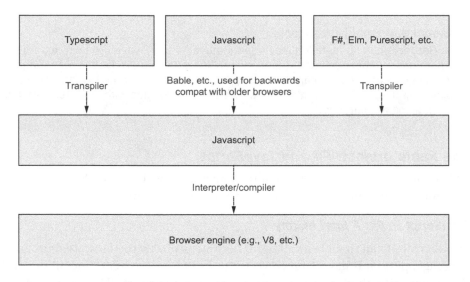

Figure 11.5   The JavaScript language has evolved into a form of an intermediary language that other languages now transpile into to run within the web browser.

11.4.2 *Introducing Fable*

This is where Fable comes in. Fable is a compiler that brings F# into the JS ecosystem, allowing you to write standard F# that can run in the browser. And, unlike some other wall-garden technologies that require proprietary extensions or can only work with handwritten tools or components, Fable allows you to interop with JS in both directions: you can write F# that calls other JS modules, and you can call Fable-compiled F# from JS.

Fable is a .NET tool (the same kind of dotnet tool that we learned about earlier) and can be installed and run relatively easily. Let's try it out:

1 In a clean folder, create a tool manifest file with `dotnet new tool-manifest`.
2 Install Fable with `dotnet tool install Fable --version 3.7.22`.

That's it. You now have the Fable compiler in your repository. Let's continue and write some basic F# in a script file, `sample.fsx`, that we can use to demonstrate Fable:

```
let myFirstVariable = 1
let secondValue = 2
let theAnswer = myFirstVariable + secondValue

printf "%d" theAnswer
```

Let's now compile that code into JS:

1 Enter `dotnet fable sample.fsx` at the command prompt.
2 Observe that you now have a new file, `sample.fs.js`, which contains the transpiled JS:

```
import { printf, toConsole } from
➡ "./fable_modules/fable-library.3.7.20/String.js";

export const myFirstVariable = 1;
export const secondValue = 2;
export const theAnswer = myFirstVariable + secondValue;

toConsole(printf("%d"))(theAnswer);
```

Notice that the transpiled JS has retained the variable names, etc. Fable tries to generate normal JS that is as human-readable and as close to the source F# as possible, although this isn't always easily possible since F# has features that don't exist in JS.

There are a few options to run the transpiled JS. The most complex, but ultimately the way you would do this in a real application, is to use standard JS tooling such as WebPack or Parcel to minify the generated JS, including the required Fable modules from NPM, etc. That's beyond the scope of this section (there are entire books dedicated to the JS build toolchain!), so I will opt for a simpler option—the Fable REPL (figure 11.6):

1 Navigate to the website https://fable.io/repl/, which contains a live running instance of the Fable F#-to-JS compiler running in the browser. On the left-hand side, paste in the F# that you developed and click the Play button on the left.

2 Observe on the right the transpiled JS has been emitted.

3 Observe on the bottom-right console the answer 3 has been printed.

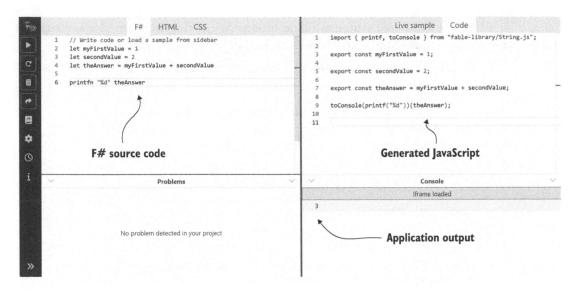

Figure 11.6 The Fable REPL in action. F# entered on the upper-left pane is converted into JS and then run. The output in the bottom-right pane shows any console output.

This last part is important to see: Fable has rewritten the F# `printf` function into the JS equivalent, such as `console.log`. This illustrates that Fable does more than just pure F#-to-JS transpilation; it also rewrites core F# and .NET library functions into their JS equivalents.

> **NodeJS**
> You can also run JS files locally using the NodeJS application. After you've installed NodeJS, rename any generated `.fs.js` to `.mjs` and run it using `node` (e.g., `node ./sample.mjs`).

The following listing provides another, more complex example that illustrates that you can use all the everyday F# features with Fable.

Listing 11.4 A more complex F# domain

```
open System          ←——— Opens namespaces

type ShippingStatus =            ———| Creates a discriminated union
    | Fulfilled of {| FulfilledOn : DateTime; PaidOn : DateTime option |}
    | Outstanding of {| DueOn : DateTime |}      ←
                                                     | Uses anonymous
                                                       records
type Order =          ←
    {                   | Defines records using
        Id : int          tuples, lists, primitives,
        PlacedOn : DateTime   and unions
        Status : ShippingStatus
        Items : (string * decimal) list
    }

let order =           ←| Creates an instance
    {                    | of a record
        Id = 123
        PlacedOn = DateTime(2022, 10, 1)
        Status = Outstanding {| DueOn = DateTime(2022, 10, 3) |}
        Items = [ "F# In Action book", 40M; "New Laptop", 500M ]
    }

let totalValue order = order.Items |> List.sumBy snd      ←| Creates a
                                                             | function

printfn $"Order {order.Id} has a value of {totalValue order}
⇒ and was placed on {order.PlacedOn}"      ←| String interpolation
```

This sample only scratches the surface. You can use features such as partial application, generics, collection functions, etc. As you can see, even .NET types such as `DateTime` are permitted (Fable is smart enough to redirect them to the equivalent JS library function).

We'll see more about Fable and web programming in F# in general later in the book, but hopefully, this section has shown you that F# can bridge the gap into the browser world, which in turn allows full-stack web apps to be developed entirely in F#.

Summary

- F# can easily consume C# libraries and packages. However, sometimes, it is useful to create bespoke F# wrappers around C# libraries to ensure a high-fidelity experience.
- F# can create values that might typically be associated with the OO world, such as interfaces.
- *Object-based programming* is the term used for working with a subset of OO features that are considered safe to use within the F# world.
- The majority of F# constructs can be consumed from C#, and attributes such as `CLIMutable` make it even easier to do so.

- NuGet packages can be consumed from F# applications just like from C#.
- NuGet Tools are packages that can be used to distribute tools that typically support the development process, such as Fantomas, an F# code formatter.
- Fable is a NuGet tool that transpiles F# into JS.
- Fable is very powerful and can work with everyday F# constructs without a problem.

Asynchronous
programming

Asynchronous (async) programming has become commonplace in the world of software development in the last few years. If you want to do any form of web development or distributed programming, you need to understand what it is and how to take advantage of it (luckily, F# has you covered here and has excellent support).

Bear in mind, though: asynchronous programming can be a very complicated subject. It's not just the programming model but the idea of reasoning about multiple things working in parallel, or the idea of long-running background processes, or the fact that the topic of distributed programming often gets interwoven with background async workloads. It can be *really* difficult. I won't try to unravel all its mysteries in this chapter; entire books are dedicated to it. Instead, I want to focus on practical usability in F# and some patterns to get you started.

12.1   *What is asynchronous programming?*

Despite what I've just said, this section will give you a basic overview of what asynchronous means and help you identify when it is useful (or necessary!). Feel free to skip this next section if you're already confident with the idea of asynchronous programming, such as working with `async`/`await` or promises.

12.1.1 *Async and sync programming*

Imagine you're at the office and want to ask someone a question about the project you're working on. You can send them a message by one of several different communication mediums. For example, you could send them an email, message them in Slack, send an SMS, call them in Microsoft Teams, or give them a good old-fashioned phone call on your mobile phone. Each of these examples is a different technology, and we use different tools to work with them. They can also be grouped into two distinct categories: async and synchronous (sync) communication (table 12.1).

Table 12.1   Different communication mediums grouped into async and sync categories

Asynchronous communication	Synchronous communication
Email	Skype call
Slack/Teams message	Mobile phone
SMS	Walk over to their desk for a chat

What's the difference between these two groups? Think about how we get a response from our coworker to our question. In the asynchronous group, we post a message and then wait. We hope we'll get an answer, but we don't know when; in the meantime, we can carry on doing something else. Eventually, we'll get notified that there's an answer waiting for us. We'll probably finish whatever we're doing and then read the reply and act on it. Compare that to the synchronous variety, in which we call our colleague, get connected, and (hopefully!) have their full attention for the duration of the conversation. Neither party can do anything else, and we expect an instant reply to our question. It would be awfully rude of them to leave us hanging on the phone or waiting by their desk while they did something else! We probably also only use synchronous communication for questions that can be answered quickly and easily, not something that would involve hours of delay.

There are also times when you need to ask someone a question, but they're already busy answering someone else. In this case, even if it's a quick question, rather than standing around waiting for them to answer, you might choose an asynchronous form of communication. When your colleague is finished, they'll start work on your request next.

As you can see, synchronous and asynchronous forms of communication are useful and appropriate under different circumstances. This entire analogy works very well when talking about programming: components in a system communicate with one another all the time. Let's look at a few examples:

- Function A calls function B to test whether an email address is correctly formatted.
- An application calls a database to look up the logged-in user's profile.
- A web application sends a JSON message over HTTP to another web application.
- We run a long-running task to process yesterday's orders to calculate the end-of-day financial position.
- We try to make a ticket booking for a high-demand concert that has just gone on sale, where demand for tickets outstrips the web server's capacity to handle every request immediately, and we encounter wait times.

Which do you think might be best modeled as sync or async communication and why? Think about factors such as the time taken to handle a request, the importance of getting an immediate response, and the scalability challenges associated with the task at hand. In general, these are some good candidates for adopting an asynchronous programming model:

- Efficiently working with external I/O such as HTTP and database calls
- Kicking off a fire-and-forget task in the background of your application
- Dividing work into smaller jobs and executing them in parallel to improve performance

12.1.2   A brief history of async on .NET

It's worth giving a tiny bit of history on async in .NET to understand how we've arrived at where we are today, as there's a reasonable amount of legacy on the platform in this area.

.NET, right from .NET 1, has always had support for async communication. However, it was very difficult to implement correctly, requiring the use of things such as callbacks, the Async Programming Model (APM), and event handlers. Take it from me that in those days, it was such a pain to do that almost no one did it unless they absolutely had to. The challenge with asynchronous programming was that you had to split your program into two sections: the part that initiated the async call and then another part of code that would handle the result. Orchestrating these two halves into one was very difficult. Add error handling into the mix and it became a nightmare; instead, we all stuck with synchronous programming, which was much simpler. The problem was that you ended up with desktop applications that froze when you made a call to a database that took a second or so to return: the entire application would be blocked, waiting for the database to return. The benefit of this was that code could be written as you've seen so far in this book: a sequential execution of commands with functions that return results (apparently) immediately. Figure 12.1 illustrates the difference between sync and async models for a simple call to a database that returns a logged-in user's profile. As you can see, there's a split in the async version.

We essentially fire and forget on the first part and then have a handler pick up the response and somehow coordinate this with the first path. This coordination was the bit that we had to do by hand.

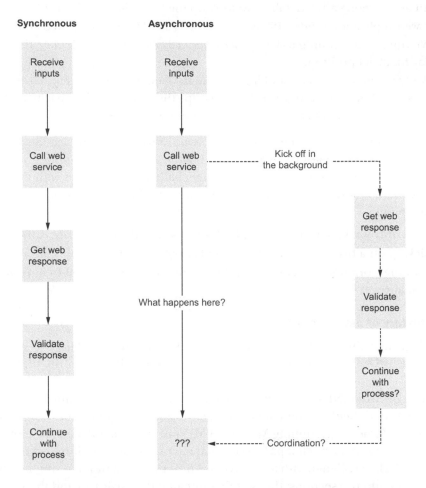

Figure 12.1   Comparing synchronous and asynchronous flows. The synchronous flow follows a single, sequential flow. The asynchronous flow branches into two streams, which requires the ability to coordinate the two streams back into one at some point in the future.

Things in the .NET world became further complicated with *multithreading*. It was designed for a slightly different purpose, but people used it to simulate async communication models. This delivered not only all the same problems that async gave us but a whole bunch of others, such as thread starvation and high memory usage. Basically, .NET wasn't a good place to be for this kind of programming, but then again, this was the situation in basically all mainstream programming languages at the time.

Eventually, things started to improve: When .NET 4 came out in 2010, it introduced the Task type, a flexible abstraction that allowed background work to be carried out much more easily than previously, although composing asynchronous code was still very difficult to do effectively via what is known as *Continuation Passing Style* (CPS). It is essentially the callback model of writing a function that would get called once the asynchronous process completed. It all changed in 2012 when C#5 launched with the introduction of what has now become the popularized `async`/`await` keyword pairing. This feature allowed you to write code with all the benefits of hand-written asynchronous code, such as not blocking the UI when a long-running process started, yet read like normal synchronous code. This `async`/`await` pattern has now found its way into many modern programming languages such as Python, JS, Swift, Rust, and even C++.

12.2 Asynchronous support in F#

F#'s approach to asynchronous programming is a little different from `async`/`await` but achieves the same goal (in fact, `async`/`await` is a cut-down version of F#'s approach, which was introduced a few years previously, in F#2). We'll start by looking in more detail at the type that .NET uses for asynchronous programming, Task, before looking at how to consume it from an F# perspective.

> ### Async and Task
> Because F#'s implementation for asynchronous programming was invented before the .NET Task type existed, F# now has two similar, but ultimately different, abstractions for async-style programming: Async and Task. Async was created first in F#2, whereas F#'s Task wrapper was introduced in F#6. We'll see what the differences are later in this chapter.

12.2.1 Tasks in .NET

In .NET, the standard type today is `System.Threading.Tasks.Task`, a high-performance and flexible abstraction that is used to reflect some operation that may complete at some point in the future. It can represent both CPU-bound background work that runs on the machine (such as a long-running financial calculation) which is executed on low-level threads, or I/O bound operations that occur on an external machine such as waiting for a response from a database or web server. A key distinction between those two workloads is that unlike CPU-bound workloads, I/O bound operations execute remotely (i.e., on another machine) and so don't take up threads on the local machine. Thus, they can be executed very efficiently and scale up very effectively. This is important to know because there are typically only a limited number of threads in a .NET application, so it's critical, especially in applications that need to execute as many requests in parallel as possible (such as web servers), that threads are never "blocked" waiting for external I/O.

Typically, your own business logic code will be *synchronous* in nature—working with data, validating it, reshaping it, etc.—and it's normally only at the boundaries of your application that you'll start needing to get involved with asynchronous Tasks (see figure 12.2).

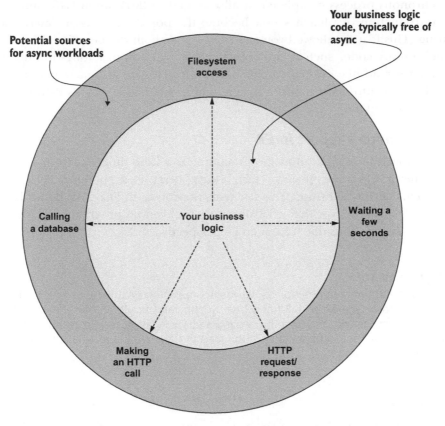

Figure 12.2   Most I/O operations will have asynchronous APIs; your business logic will typically be synchronous in nature, but the boundaries of your application will introduce asynchronous operations, which you can compose together using task { } **blocks.**

Let's look at an example of this with the application of some real-world .NET technologies. Assume you have a long-running database call, such as a complex query that takes a few seconds to run; this represents some external I/O. At the point of calling the database, you would typically use a library/package to do the low-level interop, such as ADO .NET, Dapper, or Entity Framework. Nowadays, in .NET, most libraries contain two versions of I/O methods: a synchronous and an asynchronous variant (by convention, the async version is postfixed with the word Async)—for example, ExecuteSql and ExecuteSqlAsync. The sync version normally returns your data and blocks the executing thread, whereas the latter is a nonblocking optimized asynchronous version. This means that while your application is waiting for the external resource to return with data, it will free up any resources (including the thread itself) back to the application to be utilized by another request; when the request completes, the OS signals to the application, which allocates a new thread to pick up the work where it left off.

This is particularly useful in a high-throughput web application, where you may be receiving hundreds of requests a second: since a .NET application only has a finite number of threads, being able to reuse them while waiting for external I/O responses can greatly improve the throughput of your application. What do I mean by *throughput?* Simply put, each individual web request you receive won't magically become faster just by making it asynchronous. Instead, by using low-level asynchronous libraries, your application will be able to handle more requests at once because the threads, which would otherwise be blocked waiting for external I/O operations, can be repurposed to carry out work on other requests. This is illustrated in figure 12.3, in which we have a web server handling three requests in parallel. Request 1 needs to make a call to the database; while the database call happens, the thread in which the request was running (thread 1) is freed up, meaning request 3 can make use of it. Once the database call has returned, the OS allocates thread 2 to continue the work of request 1.

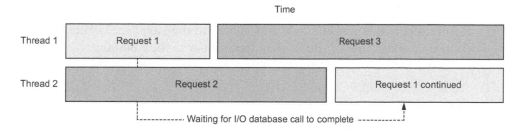

Figure 12.3   Asynchronous operations on .NET allow your application to make more efficient use of threads, which is the low-level primitive that your code ultimately runs on. In this example, request 1 performs a database call; while waiting for the database to return, the thread is freed up for another request to make use of it.

This is really important to grok: don't make the mistake people did when `async/await` first came out, which was to simply wrap regular synchronous workloads into Tasks, await them, and hope that they would magically go faster. Tasks aren't magic, and they won't make your CPU cycle any faster.

12.2.2   Consuming Tasks

Let's first look at a basic call to an async method that returns a Task in F#, and what a Task actually looks like. If you look in the `System.IO.File` class, you'll see a bunch of methods that have two versions, where one has that `Async` postfix that I mentioned earlier. Let's focus on one of them, `ReadAllText`, which reads all text from a file as a string:

```
open System.IO
open System.Threading.Tasks

File.WriteAllText("foo.txt", "Hello, world")
let text : string = File.ReadAllText "foo.txt"
let textAsync : Task<string> = File.ReadAllTextAsync "foo.txt"
```

Creates a file with some text in it

Calls the synchronous version of File.ReadAllText

Calls the asynchronous version of File.ReadAllTextAsync

`ReadAllTextAsync` returns a `Task<string>`. As shown in figure 12.4, `Task<'T>` can be thought of as a wrapper around a value that may not actually exist yet!

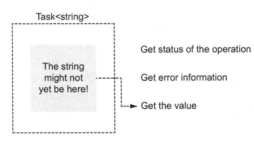

Task<string>

The string might not yet be here!

Get status of the operation

Get error information

Get the value

Figure 12.4   A Task represents a value that will be available at some point in the future. You can retrieve information about the Task to understand the current state of its execution.

If you execute the previous code and then send the `textAsync` symbol to FSI (by executing just that symbol), you'll see output similar to the following:

```
{Exception = null;
 Id = 3;
 IsCanceled = false;
 IsCompleted = true;
 IsCompletedSuccessfully = true;
 IsFaulted = false;
 Status = RanToCompletion}
```

A Task can report on its own status, whether it's completed or not, whether it failed, etc. But how do we get to the *value* of the Task—in our case, the string contents of the file? The easiest way is to access the `Result` property on the Task, which unwraps the Task and gives you the inner content:

```
let theText : string = textAsync.Result
```

Tasks return immediately

It's worth stressing that because a Task represents something that will complete in the future, calling a function that returns a Task will return immediately. That is, if you call a function that returns a Task that takes an hour to complete, the actual function will return that Task *immediately*, but the Task itself will still take an hour until its value is ready to be accessed!

EXERCISE 12.1

Change the file path that both versions try to access (e.g. `"bar.txt"`) to a file that doesn't exist. What happens when you execute both of them? Remember to check the properties on the Task version that is returned, such as `IsFaulted`, `Status` and `Exception`.

EXERCISE 12.2

Accessing the filesystem will return almost immediately. Instead, try using the `Task.Delay` method, which returns a Task that completes after the supplied duration. What happens if you create a Task with a delay of 10,000 ms. Why does the Task return immediately? What is the status of the Task while the delay occurs? What happens if you call the `Wait()` method on the Task before the 10 seconds have expired?

> **NOTE** There's also a base class of `Task<'T>`, simply called `Task`. It's used for Tasks that don't return any value, such as fire-and-forget operations or those that simply don't have a result (e.g., writing to a text file in which failure manifests as an exception). In F#, you can represent all Tasks with the generic variant since you can use `Task<unit>` to represent Tasks that have no value. Indeed, you will see some popular C# packages nowadays with their own definition of `Unit` to model exactly this.

12.2.3 The task { } block: F#'s async/await

The `Result` and `Wait()` members are fine to use in a script, but it's not appropriate to use in a production application. If the Task has not yet completed, the `Result` property will simply block the current thread until the Task has finished, which might be a second, a minute, or even an hour. In effect, it turns off the benefits of asynchronous programming and forces things back into synchronous mode; it can even cause deadlocks in your applications. This is where F#'s task block comes in, which allows you to await an asynchronous operation in a normal code style without blocking the current thread.

Let's look at writing and reading from the filesystem in F#, first with the synchronous version and then the asynchronous version using Tasks:

```
let writeToFile fileName data =
    System.IO.File.AppendAllText(fileName, data)       Calls blocking
    let data = System.IO.File.ReadAllText fileName      I/O functions
    data.Length
let total = writeToFile "sample.txt" "foo"
```

This code appends some text to a file on the local file system and then reads it back and returns the total number of characters in the file. Here's the async version in the following listing, in which we call the async, Task-returning versions of `AppendAllText` and `ReadAllText`.

Listing 12.1   Using the Task block for async programming in F#

**Wraps the operation
in a task { } block**

**Awaits a
Task that
returns unit**

```
let writeToFileAsync fileName data = task {
    do! System.IO.File.AppendAllTextAsync(fileName, data)
    let! data = System.IO.File.ReadAllTextAsync fileName
    return data.Length
}
```

**Returns a value
out of the block**

**Awaits a Task that returns
something other than unit
that is bound to a symbol**

Let's review the differences one by one:

- First, we called the `Async` variants of the two I/O methods (`AppendAllText-Async` and `ReadAllTextAsync`). These both return `Task<string>`, rather than the raw data directly.
- Second, we wrapped the body of the function inside a `task {}` block. This block is another computation expression (CE) much like the `result {}` and `option {}` ones we saw earlier. This CE safely unwraps the value of Tasks without blocking the thread but doesn't force us into rewriting our code using shenanigans like the APM or CPS patterns I touched on earlier.

Inside a `task {}` block, we can also compose multiple tasks together seamlessly.

Listing 12.2   Composing multiple tasks together

```
task {
    let! file1 = System.IO.File.ReadAllTextAsync "file1.txt"
    let! file2 = System.IO.File.ReadAllTextAsync "file2.txt"
    let! file3 = System.IO.File.ReadAllTextAsync "file3.txt"
    return $"{file1} {file2} {file3}"
}
```

**Executes
three tasks
sequentially**

**Composes the values together into a
larger string and returning as a new Task**

12.2.4 *Executing multiple Tasks in parallel*

Looking at listing 12.2, we execute three tasks to read files one after the other (i.e., sequentially). However, we can also execute them *in parallel* and have .NET compose the results together in an array for us, somewhat similarly to how we used `traverse` for Results. For Tasks, we use `WhenAll` (i.e., when all these tasks complete). It has a signature of `Task<'T> array -> Task<'T array>` (i.e., give me an Array of Tasks all of which have the same result type, and I'll give you back a single task which composes the results of all of them into an array).

Listing 12.3   Composing multiple tasks together in parallel

```
task {
    let! allFiles =
        [ "file1.txt"
```

```
                   "file2.txt"
Builds a list      "file3.txt" ]
of filenames    |> List.map File.ReadAllTextAsync
                |> Task.WhenAll

        return
            allFiles
            |> Array.reduce (sprintf "%s %s")
}
```

- Maps those filenames into Task<string>
- Composes them into a single task in parallel
- Combines the results in a single string

At this point, it's worth taking a step back and observing how we're mixing several completely different language and library features together in this small code sample:

- Using |> to create a data pipeline
- task { } CE and let!
- Mapping a collection of data using List.map
- .NET's Task.WhenAll library method
- Array.Reduce to merge together several strings into one

All of these are things you've learned separately and in isolation, yet we bring all of them together here to perform this activity in a consistent manner succinctly.

12.2.5 *Benefits of Tasks' computation expressions*

There are some things about this approach to working with tasks that I find especially appealing in comparison to the async/await approach. First, the CE approach is the same in principle as both the result and option CEs, except each effect is handled differently by the "magic" keywords that live inside a CE (illustrated in table 12.2); async and await are two keywords used in a specific place, whereas F#'s generalized approach is much more consistent across any kind of effect.

Table 12.2 How CEs share a common pattern across different effects

CE	Behavior with let!	Behavior with do!	Behavior with return
Result	Unwrap OK, exit if Error	Like let! but for Result<unit,_>	Wraps output in Ok
Option	Unwrap Some, exit if None	Like let! but for Option<unit>	Wraps output in Some
Task	Await the task's result	Like let! but for Task<unit>	Wraps output in Task

Second, you can clearly see where a task begins and finishes. Look at the following listing.

Listing 12.4 Embedding a task block within a larger expression

```
let writeToFileAsyncMix fileName data : Task<int> =
    printfn "1. This is happening synchronously!"
    Task.Delay(1000).Wait()
    printfn "2. Kicking off the background work!"
```

- Executes code synchronously

```
let result = task {                              ←─────  Creates a task
    do! System.IO.File.AppendAllTextAsync(fileName, data)      to perform some
    do! Task.Delay(1000)                                       work in the
    printfn "4. This is happening asychronously!"             background
    let! data = System.IO.File.ReadAllTextAsync fileName
    return data.Length
}

printfn "3. Doing something more, now let's return the task"   ←──────
result                                                        Continues with
                                                              synchronous code after
Uses Task.Delay to wait in the                                creating the Task value
background task for 1 second
```

In this variant of `writeToAsync`, rather than starting the task block immediately, we only do it part way through the function. Code outside of the task block is executed immediately in the foreground. Unlike `async/await`, you can see exactly where background work starts and stops. If you run this code, you'll see something like the following:

```
1. This is happening synchronously!
2. Kicking off the background work!
3. Doing something more, now let's return the task
4. This is happening asychronously!
```

12.2.6 *The async block*

As mentioned earlier, there's another CE known as the `async { }` block, which predates Task. You still see it in lots of F# code today, even code that is not considered legacy code. There are several reasons for this, but the main one is that although they are similar, Async and Task are not like-for-like replacements. The following listing is the equivalent of listing 12.1 but using the `async {}` block.

Listing 12.5   Using the `async {}` block with interop for tasks

```
let writeToFileAsync fileName data = async {
    do!
        System.IO.File.AppendAllTextAsync(fileName, data)
        |> Async.AwaitTask                            ←──── Converts from
    let! data =                                             a Task<'T> into
        System.IO.File.ReadAllTextAsync fileName            an Async<'T>
        |> Async.AwaitTask                            ←────
    return data.Length
}
```

Creates
an async
block

At first glance `async {}` and `task {}` look very similar: you use `let!` and `do!` to await asynchronous work. However, the async block cannot deal with Tasks natively, so we must use helper methods such as `Async.AwaitTask` and `Async.StartAsTask` to convert between the two types.

That's not the biggest difference between the two, though, which is that unlike `task { }` blocks, `async { }` blocks are true computations: code that is wrapped in an async block is "cold"—it does not immediately start by itself. Instead, you must explicitly start it either via `let!` in an async block or using library functions such as `Async.Start` or `Async.RunSynchronously`. With a `task { }` block (which is considered "hot"), as soon as it is created, it immediately starts execution.

An async computation can also essentially be treated as a function; you can run the computation multiple times, and each time, the entire workflow will be executed. With a Task, once the value is computed, you cannot restart it natively; it will simply immediately return with the cached result on subsequent accesses.

Lastly, one nice benefit of the async block is that task cancellation (the ability for an external block of code to signal to the background work that it should stop processing) happens implicitly. In a Task, you must manually thread a cancellation token down through the call stack. Table 12.3 summarizes some of the key differences between the two abstractions.

Table 12.3 Comparing and contrasting Task and Async

	`task { }`	`async { }`
Starts automatically	Yes (hot)	No (cold)
Execution mode	Executes once	Executes from start each time
Performance	Very high	High
.NET and C# support	Yes	F#-only + converter functions
Traceability	Built-in properties	None
Parallelism	`Task.WhenAll`	`Async.Parallel`
Synchronous execution	`.Result`	`Async.RunSynchronously`
Cancellation token passing	Manual	Automatic

So, which one should you use? The answer, as always, is "It depends." Task is much more popular in the .NET world in general (whereas Async is exclusively an F#-only thing), and indeed, you'll see more and more people in the F# world using Task now that it has first-class support in the language (the `task { }` block was only introduced in F#6, although it had been available as a third-party NuGet package for some years earlier). This means that if you're using any of the standard .NET I/O packages out there for, for example, SQL, HTTP, or cloud vendors such as AWS, Azure, etc., they will all provide their async API variants as Task, not Async. This is not necessarily a blocker for use in the async block; you just need to use a simple converter function at the point where you consume the Task, after which everything works as normal.

Tasks are also a little easier to reason about. You can ask a task what its state is using properties on the value, which aren't present on `Async<'T>` values.

Tasks are also more efficient than async blocks, so for heavy-duty workloads with thousands of tasks, it will most likely consume less memory. I should stress here, though, that in all the years I've used `async` workflows, I've probably only once run into any kind of issue like this, as an extreme corner case. For everyday line of business applications, you almost certainly won't run into this.

Async workflows have some benefits, too. They allow you to pass computations around from one part of the application to another without executing them yet, and if you want to create cold-style workflows, they are a natural fit. They also make it much easier to work with cancellation tokens.

My advice would be to start with Tasks, especially if you know them already from C#, as they are more popular across the .NET world and work very well. However, you still should investigate Async workflows and get some hands-on experience, if for no other reason than to appreciate first-hand the differences between the two and to give you the flexibility to choose which one is appropriate based on the behavior you want.

12.3 *Final thoughts on asynchronous workloads*

This final section wraps up asynchronous programming with a couple of discussion points that you may only appreciate after working with asynchronous programming in F# for some time. Hopefully this saves you a bit of time!

12.3.1 *The importance of immutable data*

At the very start of the book (and when we looked at immutability in general), I mentioned how immutability is a useful attribute for any form of asynchronous programming, multithreading, or parallelism. You'll often hear that the challenge with multithreading is working with shared state across those threads. But this isn't quite true—the challenge comes when dealing with shared *mutable* state across threads. One of the biggest challenges with these workloads is the synchronization of operations. In figure 12.1, we saw how async workloads split a process into two; the challenge is how to join the two threads back safely. This can manifest itself in any number of ways, but imagine having a mutable reference to a customer that doesn't exist yet. At some point in the future, the customer will be set when your database call completes. How do you know when it's completed? What happens if you're accessing that reference to a customer and a second call initiates and overwrites the customer while you're working with it?

Conversely, because no data can be changed in the immutable world, you can literally never have a situation where you're reading data on one thread that gets modified (mutated) in another thread. Instead, just as we've seen throughout this book, we have pipelines of operations that take in some data, perform some operation (even if that operation is asynchronous), and return a new value, which represents the outcome of that operation. Taking this approach can (and will) drastically reduce the number of potential bugs that crop up from sharing mutable state across threads.

If you absolutely must have some shared mutable state in F#—for example, you need to build a cache in your web app that stores customers so that you don't need to hit the database repeatedly—don't just create a global mutable variable. Instead, consider a built-in type in .NET such as the `ConcurrentDictionary`, a third-party library such as Polly, or F#'s built-in `MailboxProcessor` abstraction. This handy type allows you to store and modify mutable data in a way guaranteed to be thread-safe by forcing all operations to be throttled to only permit a single operation to occur at any one time.

12.3.2 *The viral nature of asynchronous workloads*

Something that may already be apparent to you is that handling Task or Async values is what is sometimes known as a *viral* operation. That is, once you start working with some async data, you force callers to themselves become async, too. Take the following call stack of three functions that call each other in order.

Listing 12.6   A standard synchronous call chain

```
open System.Text.Json

let loadCustomerFromDb customerId =
    {| Name = "Isaac"; Balance = 0 |}

let tryGetCustomer customerId =
    let customer = loadCustomerFromDb customerId
    if customer.Balance <= 0 then Error "Customer is in debt!"
    else Ok customer

let handleRequest (json:string) =
    let request : {| CustomerId : int |} = JsonSerializer.Deserialize json
    let response = tryGetCustomer request.CustomerId
    match response with
    | Ok c -> {| CustomerName = c.Name.ToUpper() |}
    | Error msg -> failwith $"Bad request: {msg}"
```

Data access function stack returning a customer value

Service function; calls the data access function

Top-level handler; calls the service function

You can visualize the flow of data as follows:

```
loadCustomerFromDb : customerId -> Customer
tryGetCustomer: customerId -> Result<Customer, string>
handleRequest : string -> GetCustomerResponse
```

Observe in the following listing that if we make `loadCustomerFromDb` asynchronous, the requirement to return some `Task` bleeds all the way out to the very top of the call stack (assume in a real implementation we call the database using an async overload, just as we did earlier with the file system example).

Listing 12.7   An asynchronous call chain

```
open System.Text.Json

let loadCustomerFromDb customerId = task {
    return {| Name = "Isaac"; Balance = 0 |}
}

let tryGetCustomer customerId = task {
    let! customer = loadCustomerFromDb customerId
```

Makes the inner function asynchronous, simulating some async I/O operation

The service function is now forced to become asynchronous to await data access function.

```
        return
            if customer.Balance <= 0 then Error "Customer is in debt!"
            else Ok customer
}

let handleRequest (json:string) = task {
    let request : {| CustomerId : int |} = JsonSerializer.Deserialize json
    let! response = tryGetCustomer request.CustomerId        <──┐  The top-level
    return                                                      │  handler is now
        match response with                                     │  forced to become
        | Ok c -> {| CustomerName = c.Name.ToUpper() |}         │  asynchronous to
        | Error msg -> failwith $"Bad request: {msg}"           │  await service
}                                                               │  function.
```

Here are the updated type signatures:

```
loadCustomerFromDb : customerId -> Task<Customer>
tryGetCustomer: customerId -> Task<Result<Customer, string>>
handleRequest : string -> Task<GetCustomerResponse>
```

As you can see, despite the actual only real asynchronous call taking place at the very bottom of the stack, as we needed to `let!` in each function, the entire call chain has become "infected" with Tasks. This is quite normal with Tasks (or, indeed, with any such effect; Results and Options also have this same characteristic). There are ways to design your code around this so that you minimize the amount of code that is affected in such a way (which we'll see in a later chapter), but unless you try really hard, avoiding this virality of an effect like this bleeding up the call stack is not doable. Indeed, it's considered a feature in some crowds as a way of using the type system to illustrate, even at the top level of your call stack, that some side-effectful or I/O operation is potentially going to take place when you call it.

Summary

- Asynchronous programming is a commonplace technique today and is important to understand for many types of applications, including most forms of web programming.
- Async programming is a technique used for dealing with long-running, I/O, or CPU-heavy workloads in an efficient manner to improve throughput of your application.
- .NET has supported asynchronous programming since the very beginning, and there are multiple ways to achieve it. However, the Task type has become the standard abstraction to achieve it.
- While in many languages we use the `async`/`await` keyword pairing, in F# we use `task { }` and `async { }` blocks.
- Within these blocks, we use the `let!` and `do!` keywords to await `Task` and `Async` values asynchronously.

- Tasks and Async workloads can be executed in parallel using `Task.WhenAll` or `Async.Parallel`.
- The `Task` and `Async` types are similar abstractions in F#, but each has specific costs and benefits.
- You probably want to start using `task {}` as a good general-purpose way of doing async programming but should still gain familiarity with `async { }` as well.
- Immutable data, which is a key default in F#, makes asynchronous programming much safer by removing the main risk of shared mutable state from your application.
- It's not unusual for asynchronous data to bleed throughout an application, known as a *viral* effect. There are techniques to reduce this, but it takes a lot of effort to achieve.

Web programming

This chapter covers

- The web and its relationship with functional programming
- Web programming on .NET and F#
- Server-side web development in F#
- Client-side web development with Elmish
- The SAFE Stack

This chapter will tie together even more of what we've seen so far, bringing both the functional paradigm and core abstractions, such as Task-based asynchronous programming and Options to enable web programming that naturally fits with F#.

13.1 The web and functional programming

This section briefly summarizes HTTP and explains why (although this may surprise you) FP is a natural fit for web programming. One of the fundamental underpinnings of the web today was the invention of the Hypertext Transfer Protocol (HTTP), which provided a standard messaging format for web traffic. These days we see many frameworks use OOP patterns as a way of modelling web applications such as Controllers. In such frameworks, you often create classes that have methods decorated in some way such that web requests are correctly routed to a method; you'll often have to inherit from "base classes" which give extra functionality. All of this is especially unfortunate because it's just hiding what HTTP really is (figure 13.1).

Figure 13.1 An HTTP call closely matches a function call, a request payload followed by a response from the server.

In essence, you can think of HTTP as a function call executed remotely on another machine: you call a specific function, and it returns a response at some point in time. An HTTP request can effectively be thought of as the details required to make that function call. It contains data to uniquely identify what function to call, such as the verb and URL path (e.g., GET /mysite/api/customer/1). It has input arguments that can be encoded in the query string, the route itself, the body of the message, or even cookies. And, it can contain optional metadata about both the caller and the expected response in HTTP headers, such as the browser that made the request, authentication information, the time zone, and what format the response should be delivered (e.g., JSON or XML).

Similarly, an HTTP response can be mapped to the result of a function. A response message typically contains some value encoded in the message's body (e.g., a JSON representation of Customer 1). It will also include a response code, such as 200 for OK or 500 for an error. And, just like the request, the response can also include headers, which provide more metadata about the response. You can map many of these concepts directly into functions in general and, as you might already have guessed, F#.

13.1.1 Web programming on .NET and F#

At the time of writing, the most popular web framework for .NET is Microsoft's own ASP.NET. Its popularity is unsurprising since it is essentially bundled with .NET—not that that's a problem since it is performant, reliable, and flexible. There was a large-scale rewrite of ASP.NET a few years ago, and the stack nowadays looks something like what's shown in figure 13.2.

ASP.NET also comes with a whole bunch of different developer-level abstractions that you need to wrap your head around to carry out many common tasks, as shown in figure 13.3. Unfortunately, when you think about handling HTTP requests (which is really all any server-side web application is), very few of the ASP.NET abstractions map directly to it. Some of these abstractions are legacy features that have carried on into today's ASP.NET. Others are attempts to extract features from HTTP into an OO-styled world. That's why, although it's certainly possible to use ASP.NET out of the box in F# (and I've worked with teams that have done this), the experience is not a natural

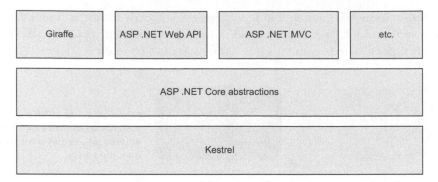

Figure 13.2   The ASP.NET Core stack contains a low-level, high-performance web server called Kestrel, upon which core abstractions exist. Finally, developer-level frameworks exist, such as MVC and Giraffe.

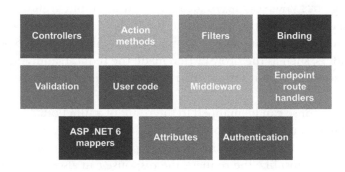

Figure 13.3   ASP.NET Core contains a wide variety of abstractions and types used for different use cases when creating web applications.

fit for the typical F# ethos that we've seen so far in this book—lightweight, generalized, and reusable abstractions that are safe and simple to reason about.

Luckily, we won't be bothering with any of these abstractions. Instead, we will focus on an F# "extension" to ASP.NET called Giraffe, which comes with essentially a single abstraction that will be all you need.

13.1.2 *The HTTP Context*

In ASP.NET, one key type to be aware of is the HttpContext. This type is essentially a value that represents all the information about both the request and response of a single HTTP call. So, it includes the route that was requested, the verb used, query string information, etc., as well as a way to write out content for the response efficiently and set the response content type (figure 13.4). This type is essentially all you need in ASP.NET to develop web applications.

It's worth pointing out that the HTTP Context is a mutable data structure. For example, when you write to the response stream, you don't create a new version of the context but simply mutate the current context with the data you wish to return to the caller.

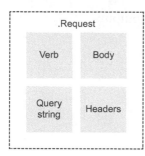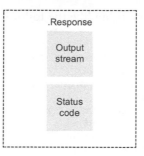

Figure 13.4   The HTTP Context contains properties such as `.Request` and `.Response`, in which you can access data that directly represents the incoming and outgoing HTTP messages.

13.2   Server-side web development in F#

Web server technologies come and go. Indeed, by the time you read this book, it's possible that Giraffe (or even ASP.NET Core) won't be in use anymore (although both are mature and have existed for many years now). So, while this section is certainly about learning how to use Giraffe, it's more about seeing how you can both model the HTTP request/response pipeline in a functional style and how a highly functional library can happily sit on top of one that is much more object-oriented.

> **Functional web frameworks for F#**
>
> There are several web frameworks that can be used with a functional-first approach. For starters, there's ASP.NET Core's own relatively new "Minimal API". This takes a somewhat similar approach to Giraffe, although it's not especially F# friendly and is not truly composable in the same way that Giraffe is. There's also the Falco framework, an F#-friendly package worth looking at. Like Giraffe, it runs on top of ASP.NET Core, so you benefit from all the reliability and performance optimizations that come with ASP.NET.

13.2.1   Creating our first ASP.NET application

Let's start by creating a simple ASP.NET Core 6 web application:

1 Create a new console application in an empty directory (e.g., `MyGiraffeApp`).
2 Add the Giraffe NuGet package to it (`dotnet add package Giraffe -v 6.2.0`).
3 Modify `myGiraffeApp.fsproj` so that the Project SDK is `Microsoft.NET.Sdk.Web`.
4 Remove the code from `Program.fs` and replace it with the code in the following listing.

> **Listing 13.1   Creating a basic ASP.NET application**

```
open Microsoft.AspNetCore.Builder

let builder = WebApplication.CreateBuilder()      ⟩ Creates an
let app = builder.Build()              ⟵──────────┘ ASP.NET web app
app.Run()                      ⟵─── Starts the web host
```

5 Run the application with `dotnet run`.

On Windows, you will see something like the following output:

```
info: Microsoft.Hosting.Lifetime[14]
      Now listening on: http://localhost:5000
info: Microsoft.Hosting.Lifetime[14]
      Now listening on: https://localhost:5001
info: Microsoft.Hosting.Lifetime[0]
      Application started. Press Ctrl+C to shut down.
info: Microsoft.Hosting.Lifetime[0]
      Hosting environment: Production
info: Microsoft.Hosting.Lifetime[0]
      Content root path: C:\Users\IsaacAbraham\code\myGiraffeApp
```

This is a fully featured backend ASP.NET Core web application using the standard out-of-the-box ASP.NET core library; you can think of this as the boilerplate required to create a web app. The change to the SDK in the project file is required in order to add a special type of package reference, known as a *framework reference*. A framework reference is a set of NuGet packages that are built in to the .NET SDK. We could have manually added the specific framework reference, but it's quicker and easier to simply change the SDK. To be honest, it's not strictly necessary: the Giraffe package (which we will shortly be using) automatically adds that framework reference for us.

Currently this web app doesn't do a great deal—if you open a browser and go to `http://localhost:5000` you'll see that it simply returns a 404 Not Found for every request. Let's improve upon it and add support for Giraffe into the mix.

6   Modify the `Program.fs` as in the following listing.

Listing 13.2   Creating a basic Giraffe application

```
open Microsoft.AspNetCore.Builder          Opens the Giraffe
open Giraffe                                namespace

let giraffeApp = text "Hello, world!"       Creates a simple Giraffe
                                            web application
let builder = WebApplication.CreateBuilder()
builder.Services.AddGiraffe() |> ignore
let app = builder.Build()                   Integrates the Giraffe
app.UseGiraffe giraffeApp                    application into ASP.NET
app.Run()
```

Run the application using the standard `dotnet run` and navigate to `http://local-host:5000` in your browser; you'll see the response `Hello, world!`.

The latter code we've added provides support for Giraffe to ASP.NET via a piece of middleware—a component that is plugged into ASP.NET. However, the key part in this sample, which we'll come back to later, is the `giraffeApp` line. That's the F# code that we're interested in; it represents our actual web application, which will contain all routes, business logic, etc.

13.2.2 *The HTTP Handler*

Before we go further, we need to understand the core Giraffe abstraction (which itself is based on an earlier F# web library, Suave), known as the HTTP Handler. To explain it, we'll take a slightly roundabout way with a fictional web app that provides an API to control a machine in a factory responsible for building the gearbox in a car. It should respond to HTTP GET requests on the path /device/status and return the status of the machine, such as Device is operating correctly. We can also think of this in terms of this process having three separate components, as shown in figure 13.5.

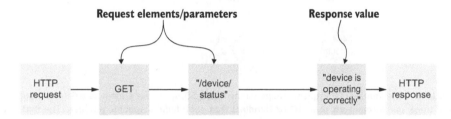

Figure 13.5 Modeling an HTTP request and response in terms of different activities, such as verb, route, and response body. There are, of course, others that would make up such a process, such as setting the status code.

Each of these components does a single thing, such as checking a verb, checking a path, or generating a response. None of them on their own is especially useful, but composing them together can give us something much more powerful. Each of these components in Giraffe is known as an HTTPHandler. An HttpHandler is a component that takes an HttpContext as input and exists as part of a pipeline. Each handler can choose how to continue within the context of the pipeline:

- To end immediately with no response
- To end immediately using whatever is in the response of the HTTP context as the output
- To pass on control to the next handler

I like to think of handlers as falling into one of two categories:

- *Filters*—These check the HTTP request for some parameter (e.g., verb = GET or path = /device/status). If the check fails, the pipeline ends immediately (Giraffe will, by default, return a 404 – Not Found response in such a situation).
- *Writers*—These populate the HTTP response (e.g., set the status code to 202, body as JSON, HTTP headers, etc.).

For example, you may have an HTTP handler that checks if the request verb is GET. If it is, the handler simply passes control over to the next handler in the pipeline. If it isn't, the handler immediately ends the pipeline. Or you may have a handler that knows how to write text to the response stream. Figure 13.6 illustrates a typical Giraffe pipeline made up of three Http Handlers.

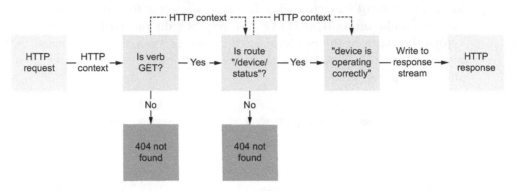

Figure 13.6 The same HTTP request/response as figure 13.5, except shown as a Giraffe pipeline. The central three cards represent three HTTP Handlers that each fulfill a specific purpose. The first two act as filters; the last one writes to the response stream.

The HttpHandler type is a composable and flexible type that essentially replaces many of the abstractions mentioned in figure 13.3. Figure 13.7 shows what it looks like both in code and graphically:

```
HttpFunc -> HttpContext -> Task<HttpContext option>
```

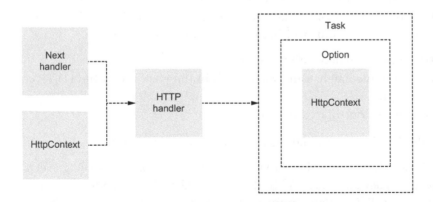

Figure 13.7 The HTTP Handler signature represented graphically. The two inputs are the next handler in the pipeline (called the HttpFunc) and the HTTP Context. The Handler must asynchronously return either nothing or Some context. This can be done itself or by delegating the result to the next handler.

The HTTP Handler is just a *function signature*—it's not even a real type like an interface or class. It represents any function that, as the name suggests, can handle an HTTP request. It takes in two arguments:

- `HttpContext`—This contains all the request information and allows you to write out the response as needed.
- *The* next *handler*—This represents the next component in the pipeline; it's up to you to decide whether you want to call it or not. Consider figure 13.6 again: the GET handler can check the verb of the incoming request and choose—if the verb is correct, pass on the context to the next handler (in our case, one that checks the route). If the verb is incorrect, it can simply return None or explicitly write an error to the response stream itself and not call the next handler.

Let's look at a simple implementation of the GET handler.

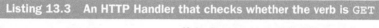

Listing 13.3   An HTTP Handler that checks whether the verb is GET

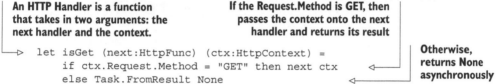

An HTTP Handler is a function that takes in two arguments: the next handler and the context.

If the Request.Method is GET, then passes the context onto the next handler and returns its result

Otherwise, returns None asynchronously

```
let isGet (next:HttpFunc) (ctx:HttpContext) =
    if ctx.Request.Method = "GET" then next ctx
    else Task.FromResult None
```

As you can see, despite the somewhat intimidating type signature we saw in figure 13.7, an HTTP Handler can be very small and quite simple to reason about; this one is just two lines long. Also, notice that this handler has no knowledge of what the next handler is doing; it doesn't matter. We're simply given another handler as next; our only decision is whether we call it or not.

13.2.3   *Composing HTTP Handlers together*

Of course, you can't write an entire application with single handlers. Giraffe's real strength is the ability, which, as you know by now, is common in F# and FP, to rapidly compose smaller components into more powerful ones. In listing 13.2, we saw a simple HTTP Handler that returns the text `"Hello, world!"` (repeated in the following listing).

Listing 13.4   Creating a basic Giraffe application

```
open Microsoft.AspNetCore.Builder
open Giraffe

let giraffeApp = text "Hello, world!"

let builder = WebApplication.CreateBuilder()
builder.Services.AddGiraffe() |> ignore
let app = builder.Build()
app.UseGiraffe giraffeApp
app.Run()
```

A Giraffe application that always returns the text "Hello, world!"

text is an HTTP Handler built into Giraffe, which writes the supplied text to the response stream (and sets the Content Type header to text/plain). What if we wanted to implement the handler shown in figure 13.6 i.e. a request using the HTTP GET method sent to the route /device/status returns the text device is operating correctly? Here's that exact pipeline in F# using Giraffe's custom >=> compose operator:

```
GET >=> route "/device/status" >=> text "device is operating correctly"
```

Try replacing the text "Hello, World!" from listing 13.4 with this code and then navigate to http://localhost:5000/device/status in a browser; you should see the appropriate response. In figure 13.8, I have visualized the results using an alternative tool—the REST Client for VS Code. You could equally use one of the many other HTTP tools out there, such as Fiddler.

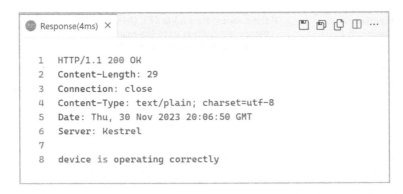

```
1    HTTP/1.1 200 OK
2    Content-Length: 29
3    Connection: close
4    Content-Type: text/plain; charset=utf-8
5    Date: Thu, 30 Nov 2023 20:06:50 GMT
6    Server: Kestrel
7
8    device is operating correctly
```

Figure 13.8   The response to a web request handled by Giraffe by composing together three simple HTTP Handlers, shown directly in VS Code using the REST Client extension

> **NOTE** In figure 13.8, I've used the excellent REST Client extension for VS Code, which allows you to quickly send HTTP requests directly from within the code editor by highlighting a URI and executing it using the Rest Client: Send Request command; results are shown in their own tab. This is extremely useful to test a web application quickly and easily.

What's the >=> operator? It's just an alias for a Giraffe function called compose. As the name suggests (and the operator visually shows), it takes two HttpHandlers and composes them together, so GET >=> route "/device/status" returns a new HttpHandler that will pass the route handler to GET as the next argument. In this way, you can chain together as many handlers as you need.

> ## Custom operators in F#
> F# allows you to define your own custom operators! There's nothing magical about them; mostly, they are just aliases for specific functions, as in the case of Giraffe's compose. Operators can be very useful in specific domains, such as visual pipelines, but be careful not to abuse this feature. It's all too easy to end up creating a whole host of operators that look great and exciting at first, but months down the line are a nightmare to document and understand. Use with care!

13.2.4 Composing multiple routes

Your web applications naturally will want to handle multiple endpoints—for example, GET device/status and POST device/execute to send a command to the device. The way Giraffe handles multiple routes I find to be delightful, as shown in listing 13.5.

Listing 13.5 Composing multiple routes together using `choose`

```
let giraffeApp = choose [          ◁──┤ The choose function is an HTTP handler that
    GET                                 takes a list of handlers to choose from.
        >=> route "/device/status"
        >=> text "device is operating correctly"  ◁─┐
    POST                                             │ Multiple handlers
        >=> route "/device/execute"                  │ composed
        >=> text "executed a command!"  ◁────────────┘ together
]
```

The `choose` handler is an HttpHandler that takes as an argument a list of other Handlers. It executes each of these Handlers in turn until it finds one that returns some Context, at which point it breaks and returns that value immediately. And because `choose` is itself an HttpHandler, you can compose that with other Handlers, too!

To me, this is a beautiful example of FP design—a single abstraction that can be composed together in a flexible manner and can essentially perform any number of different behaviors, simply based on how you compose them together. There's no reflection or inheritance hierarchies, etc.—just a single function signature that can be built on top of into more powerful values.

Giraffe comes with a wide variety of built-in handlers. Here's a brief list of some common ones that you might use:

- `route`—Checks that the request's route matches the route specified. Several variants exist, including `routef` that allows `printf`-style parameterization (e.g., `/device/%i/status` to match on routes in a type-safe manner) as well as regex-supporting routers.
- `GET`, `POST`, `PUT`, `etc.`—Handlers that filter based on the verb specified.
- `setHttpHeader`—Sets an HTTP Header on the response.
- `setStatusCode`—Sets the status code of the response. Giraffe also has a set of built-in handlers for well-known response codes (e.g., `Successful.OK` returns a `200 OK`).

13.2.5 *Writing our own HTTP Handlers*

A typical route in a web app consists of something a little more exciting than simply returning hard-coded text you've seen so far. What about when you need to do something real, such as going to a database, getting some data, shaping it differently, and returning a response as JSON? For example, rather than hard-code the response for the device status, what if we wanted to go off to a database to retrieve that status?

Essentially, this isn't that hard; you've already seen a basic handler in listing 13.5. A simple implementation would probably look something like the code in the following listing.

Listing 13.6   Writing a custom HTTP handler

```
open Giraffe
open Microsoft.AspNetCore.Http

module Db =
    let tryFindDeviceStatus (deviceId:int) = task {
        if deviceId < 50 then return Some "ACTIVE"
        elif deviceId < 100 then return Some "IDLE"
        else return None
    }

let getDeviceStatus next (ctx:HttpContext) = task {
    let deviceId =
        ctx.TryGetQueryStringValue "deviceId"
        |> Option.defaultWith (fun _ -> failwith "Missing device id")
        |> int

    let! deviceStatus = Db.tryFindDeviceStatus deviceId

    match deviceStatus with
    | None ->
        return! RequestErrors.NOT_FOUND
            "No device id found" next ctx
    | Some status ->
        return! json
            {| DeviceId = deviceId; Status = status |} next ctx
}

let myFunctionalWebApp =
    GET >=> route "/device/status" >=> getDeviceStatus
...

app.UseGiraffe myFunctionalWebApp
```

A sample function that simulates reading data from a database

Our custom HTTP Handler which reads from the query string, calls the "database" and creates a suitable response.

If no database record is found, returns a 404 with a suitable error message

If a record is found, creates a response value and serialize it into JSON

Plugs our HTTP Handler into a Giraffe pipeline

Passes the composed Handler to our application

You should be able to get the gist of what we're doing here:

1 We read the input from the HTTP request using the `TryGetQueryStringValue` function; the parsing code in this example is deliberately simplified; the query

string, for example, will cause an exception if there is nothing there or it isn't a valid integer.

2 We call our fake database function—replace with any I/O here e.g., web server, SQL database, cloud storage, etc.

3 We adapt the result of the call to a suitable HTTP response: None maps to 404—not found (NOT_FOUND is an HttpHandler that returns a 404 with the body set to the supplied string); Some status maps to an anonymous record that is serialized into JSON using the json HTTP Handler.

4 We finally compose it with the rest of the pipeline. Again, there's no interface or class structure to inherit from: as long as the type signature of the function we define matches the HttpHandler signature, we're good to go.

Try this code out yourself: put in a few random values in a URL and observe that the code really does work:

- `http://localhost:5000/device/status?deviceId=12` returns JSON with ACTIVE status.
- `http://localhost:5000/device/status?deviceId=52` returns JSON with IDLE status.
- `http://localhost:5000/device/status?deviceId=152` returns an HTTP 404 with content No device id found.
- `http://localhost:5000/device/status` returns an HTTP 500 Internal Server Error

13.2.6 Reading inputs

We've already seen how to read inputs from the query string using the TryGetQueryStringValue method, but there are a couple of other ways to form HTTP requests. One common way is to use the route itself to store parameterized information, such as `http://localhost:5000/device/status/12` (with 12 representing the device ID). Giraffe has an elegant way of modeling this, using the routef Handler:

Adds deviceId as a specific parameter to the handler function

```
let getDeviceStatus (deviceId:int) next (ctx:HttpContext) = …

let myFunctionalWebApp =
    GET >=> routef "/device/status/%i" getDeviceStatus
```

Uses routef to specify a parameterized route

The routef handler function allows us to parameterize routes with type safety; the %i represents an integer, the same as printf or sprintf. Similarly, our Handler function now takes an integer as its first argument; the query string code can be completely removed now. An alternative way to receive inputs is to read from the body of the request, typically as part of a POST or PUT verb. Here's an example POST HTTP message that you can use with, for example, VS Code's REST Client:

```
POST http://localhost:5000/device/status
content-type: application/json

{ "deviceId" : 13 }
```

Here's the updated code snippets:

Uses **BindModelAsync**
to deserialize the body
into an F# anonymous
record

```
let getDeviceStatus next (ctx:HttpContext) = task {
    let! request  = ctx.BindModelAsync<{| DeviceId : int |}>()      ◁─────┐
    ….
}
let myFunctionalWebApp =
    POST >=> route "/device/status" >=> getDeviceStatus      ◁──
```

Changes our
pipeline to check
for **POST**, not **GET**
HTTP messages

Note that `request` now binds to a record with `DeviceId` as a field rather than a simple value. If you make the appropriate code changes to the downstream code to refer to `request.DeviceId` and rerun the app, you should see that your application once again runs.

13.2.7   *Validation*

Validation is something that in ASP.NET there's a whole framework around, known as Data Annotations. These can initially appear quite appealing—you put attributes on your type, and the framework does all the work for you. The problem comes once you have more complex types and rules. You end up either making compromises or having to write your own data annotation attributes. In my opinion, it's simpler and more flexible to use (yes, you've guessed it!) simple values and functions, just as as we saw in earlier chapters when looking at JSON serialization:

- Start with an F# record (or anonymous record) that maps 1:1 to your raw JSON type using simple primitives.
- Create a function that tries to map from this primitive record to your rich domain type, returning a Result with validation messages in the error channel.
- Ultimately, map the error channel back out to an HTTP 4xx code.
- Map the success to whatever handling you need (e.g., calculation/writing to a database and ultimately back out as a 200).

You don't need a huge framework for validation. Often, just some reusable, composable functions will be sufficient to get you most of the way, and there are libraries out there in the F# space that provide you with a healthy set of these for common validation tasks such as the Validus library (e.g., to check whether a string is within a certain length), or you can build your own.

13.3 Functional patterns in a web application

Web Applications are a good example of an application that often has a kind of impure/pure sandwich, as shown in figure 13.9.

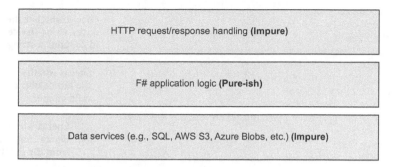

Figure 13.9 Visualizing a web application through the prism of pure/impure layers. F# code should favor purity where it's possible and not overly complicated to achieve.

Normally, I recommend, where possible, trying to decouple your core domain logic from the outer shell of HTTP abstractions and possibly services that provide you with data (e.g., SQL, filesystem, network, etc.). I say "pure-ish" code because F# is not a strict FP language and will happily let you call an impure function or service without wrapping it in things like an "I/O monad" as in Haskell. So, you might bend the rules a little here! Nonetheless, let me show you in listing 13.7 an expanded example from earlier in this chapter that has a clean separation between HTTP abstractions and application logic. It gets the device ID from the query string but does more validation logic to check whether there's a value in the query string and a valid integer, along with a proper domain type for modeling errors. Note the use of the `taskResult { }` block from the `FsToolkit.ErrorHandling` package, which allows you to `let!` on both Task and Result within the same block. That is, `let!` will await a Task (just like a `task { }` block) but will also "fail fast" on an Error—and do both for a `Task<Result>`.

Listing 13.7   A web application as an impure/ pure sandwich

```
type DeviceStatusError =
    | NoDeviceIdSupplied
    | InvalidDeviceId of string
    | NoSuchDeviceId of int
    member this.Description =
        match this with
        | NoDeviceIdSupplied ->
            "No device Id was provided."
        | InvalidDeviceId text ->
            $"'{text}' is not a valid Device Id"
```

◁— **Defines an error domain type with a member to create a human-readable string**

```
                | NoSuchDeviceId deviceId ->
                    $"Device Id {deviceId} does not exist."
    type DeviceStatusResponse =
        { DeviceId: int; DeviceStatus: string }

    let tryGetDeviceStatus maybeDeviceId = taskResult {
        let! (rawDeviceId: string) =
            maybeDeviceId
            |> Result.requireSome NoDeviceIdSupplied
        let! deviceId =
            Option.tryParse rawDeviceId
            |> Result.requireSome
    (InvalidDeviceId rawDeviceId)
        let! deviceStatus = Db.tryFindDeviceStatus deviceId
        let! deviceStatus =
            deviceStatus
            |> Result.requireSome (NoSuchDeviceId deviceId)

        return { DeviceId = deviceId; DeviceStatus = deviceStatus }
    }

    let warehouseApi next (ctx: HttpContext) = task {
        let maybeDeviceId =
            ctx.TryGetQueryStringValue "deviceId"
        let! deviceStatus = tryGetDeviceStatus maybeDeviceId

        match deviceStatus with
        | Error errorCode ->
            return!
                RequestErrors.BAD_REQUEST
    errorCode.Description next ctx
        | Ok deviceInfo ->
            return! json deviceInfo next ctx
    }
```

Annotations:
- Defines a record that represents the response type
- Checks whether the query string Device Id contains a string
- Checks whether the device Id is a valid integer
- Reads the device status from the database
- Checks whether the device contains a status from the database
- Extracts the device Id out of the query string
- If something goes wrong, returns a 400 bad request with the message as the payload
- If the status is successfully accessed, returns a JSON message with the valid status

This code has a clean separation in terms of HTTP and application logic: `warehouse-Api` represents the impure outer layer, with knowledge of the HTTP Context, the query string, response codes, etc. On the other hand, `tryGetDeviceStatus` has no knowledge of those concepts whatsoever. Instead, it is purely concerned with validating that an optional string supplied as input exists, is a valid integer, and that this integer can retrieve a device status from the database. It returns an F# Result type, not an HTTP handler or similar; that's the responsibility of `warehouseApi`, which adapts the F# record into an HTTP response as appropriate—either a 400 or a 202 with JSON serialization.

In this example, I could have gone further by, for example, making a separate type between the response for the pure F# code and the HTTP message. In this case, it wasn't necessary, but in a more complex application, you might have to map between a rich F# record and a raw record that contains primitives which can be easily represented in JSON.

However, you'll notice that the `tryGetDeviceStatus` is not pure, nor is it easily testable: it has a direct call to `Db.tryFindDeviceStatus`. It's relatively easy to solve this from a testability point of view: simply promote the function to the top level as a higher-order function. However, that won't ensure that the function is pure. This is what I meant when I said "pure-ish": you can make the code entirely pure, but it would involve breaking it into two functions—one before the database call and one after and then trampolining back up to `warehouseApi` to orchestrate everything. If that all sounds complicated, it's because it is and certainly for fairly simple applications like this, really not worth the extra effort.

13.4   Creating HTML views

So far, we've looked at data-centric HTTP applications, returning JSON or text and the like. Giraffe also has an extension package that supports generating HTML views (i.e., visual content that can be served up in a web browser) called Giraffe.ViewEngine. It fits nicely within the context of the overall Giraffe framework, using the same basic HTTP Handler abstraction.

13.4.1   Creating views through code

There are a multitude of ways to create user interfaces in .NET, but generally, they follow either a pure declarative model (such as XAML, an XML-based markup language used for Windows-based desktop applications, as well as mobile applications) or a hybrid model where you can inject C# code into "holes" of a markup. This is the approach taken by ASP.NET's Razor HTML view engine. Giraffe takes a different approach and simply uses F# to model your entire view. As you'll see shortly, this is remarkably succinct and close to HTML, except it's just using standard F# code. There are also several benefits of this approach, one being that you can use conditionals and for loops directly when building your view; there's no need for things like XAML Converters or the like because everything is just written in F#.

13.4.2   The ViewEngine DSL

Let's create a view in the following listing that builds on top of the code we've already created in this chapter to make an endpoint that, rather than returning JSON with the status of a device, returns as HTML that can be rendered directly in the browser:

1 Add the NuGet package `Giraffe.ViewEngine` 1.4.0 to your application.
2 open the `Giraffe.ViewEngine` namespace in your program file.
3 Create the function in the following listing above the final part of code that wires up your Giraffe handler to ASP.NET.

> **Listing 13.8   Our first Giraffe HTML view**

```
let simpleView next (ctx: HttpContext) = task {
    let maybeDeviceId = ctx.TryGetQueryStringValue "deviceId"
    let! deviceStatus = tryGetDeviceStatus maybeDeviceId
```

```
    let view =
        html [] [
            body [] [
                h1 [] [ str "Device report" ]
                match deviceStatus with
                | Error errorCode ->
                    str $"Error: {errorCode.Description}"
                | Ok deviceInfo ->
                    str $"Success:
{deviceInfo.DeviceId} has status
{deviceInfo.DeviceStatus.Description}"
                ]
            ]
        return! htmlView view next ctx
}
```

Creates HTML
nodes in a tree
with F# functions

Converts the
tree into an
HTTP Handler

This function is also an HTTP Handler. However, instead of creating a record and returning that as JSON or a string as text, we're building a tree of XML nodes that represents the HTML structure. The ViewEngine library comes with a set of functions for HTML elements such as html, body, h1, etc. Most functions have exactly the same signature:

```
XmlAttribute list -> XmlNode list -> XmlNode
```

In other words, given a list of HTML attributes and a set of child elements (represented as XmlAttribute and XmlNode here), it returns a new element. A simple example that we can take directly from listing 13.8 is h1 [] [str "Device report"]. The h1 function has no attributes, so the first argument is the empty list [], and a single child element, the string "Device Report". The body in this example also has no attributes but has two children: the h1 node we just saw and a string that represents either the success or error. Here's an example of a node that does have some attributes in it:

```
div [ _class "notification is-danger" ] [ str "Something is wrong" ]
```

This F# would eventually be converted into standard HTML as

```
<div class="notification is-danger">"Something is wrong"</div>
```

Again, ViewEngine comes with a bunch of built-in functions for standard HTML attributes, which are prefixed with _ for convention (e.g. _class, _id, _onclick, etc.).

Once you've built up your tree, you can pass it into the htmlView function. This function is just a normal HTTP Handler except, unlike, for example, the text handler (which takes in a string), this takes in an XmlNode and converts it into an HTTP response (setting the Content-Type header to text/html etc.). This means that once you've created a handler to return HTML, you can compose it as normal with any other handler (e.g., route, get, etc.). You should be able to plug this new function within the existing application, replacing just the call to, for example, getDeviceStatus or warehouseApi with `simpleView`, and the app should continue to work except now it will return HTML rather than JSON.

13.4.3 Benefits of an F# DSL for HTML

Why use F# for writing out HTML? If you were just returning static HTML (i.e., the same response every single time), then I would suggest doing just that. But we're dynamically creating HTML content based on the specific Device that is returned and its status. Once you get into this kind of scenario, using F# throughout has many benefits, primarily the fact that you can do anything you want in terms of F# to build the tree. Pattern matching? No problem. For loops within a list comprehension? This is also totally fine. You can call functions or make reusable helpers to quickly create commonly used HTML fragments and splice them together because it's all just F#. Look at this snippet taken from listing 13.8:

```
match deviceStatus with
| Error errorCode -> str $"Error: {errorCode.Description}"
| Ok deviceInfo -> str $"Success: {deviceInfo.DeviceId} has status
```

We're using a standard F# pattern match here to choose what HTML node to return. There's no need for any fancy libraries or code because we're working in standard F# here—it's just functions and data. You can quickly use types such as discriminated unions throughout your view code and decide what CSS class or elements to emit based on the kind of data. Working with collections is simple, too. Let's assume we had a list of devices and wanted to present them in a table as in listing 13.9.

Listing 13.9 Using a list comprehension to create rows from a collection of items

```
let devices = …          ◁──┤ A list of devices
                              (omitted here)

table [] [
      thead [] [            ◁──┤ Creates a single
         tr [] [                table header
            th [] [ str "Device Id"]
            th [] [ str "Device Status" ]
         ]
      ]
      tbody [] [                          ┤ Creaties a table
         for device in devices do   ◁──    row for each device
            tr [] [                        in the list
               td [] [ str $"{device.DeviceId}" ]
               td [] [ str device.DeviceStatus ]
            ]
      ]
]
```

Creates an HTML table

Here, we're using standard F# list comprehensions to yield back a `tr` node for each device in the `devices` collection. We've done this many times throughout this book, except now we're using it in the context of building a UI rather than just working with orders or customers. Of course, F# doesn't care either way—it's just lists of data.

You can, of course, apply stylesheets as required, just like you would when writing a raw HTML application, so without too much effort, you can employ design libraries like Bootstrap or Bulma (figure 13.10).

Device List

Device Id	Device Status
1	Active
2	Idle
3	Active

Figure 13.10   An HTML table styled using the Bulma UI framework

The code to achieve the style in figure 13.10 is directly taken from the Bulma site:

```
table [ _class "table is-bordered is-striped" ] [

]                                    Child tr nodes etc. go here
```

That can also be applied to the main application view we made earlier, as in figure 13.11.

Found device!

Device ID 13 has status of Active

Figure 13.11   Using a Bulma Notification panel with the is-success class to display it, which will appear in green onscreen

In short, it's possible to integrate with any standard CSS library to quickly style up your applications however you want.

This chapter is perhaps one of the more challenging but exciting ones. It brings together lots of the language fundamentals we've worked on in the book to illustrate how to work with a real-world, massively popular area of software development (i.e., web programming). It illustrates how a functional approach allows you to neatly handle the different use cases for web applications in a single function signature. Giraffe is a popular web library within the F# world, but it's not the only one; the main thing I want you to get from this chapter is to see that it's not only possible but eminently recommended to use F# for web applications.

There's a fuller example of the device status application in the source code repository that provides both a JSON and HTML API in a single web application (https://github.com/isaacabraham/fsharp-in-action).

13.5 Full-stack F# apps with SAFE Stack

As I started to use F# more and more, I naturally grew more confident in it and began using it for more and more parts of the stack of a typical web application. Where things fell down in the early days was when you needed to write something that ran inside the browser—this was the remit of JavaScript (TypeScript wasn't really established then). A few years later, the F#-to-JavaScript compiler Fable appeared (covered briefly in chapter 11), which opened the door to all sorts of extra possibilities. Eventually, both the web and F# ecosystem evolved enough that it was theoretically possible to create applications that were written entirely in F#. This was the genesis of the SAFE Stack (https://safe-stack.github.io/), a bundled list of libraries and technologies that allows you to write both the back- and front-end of a web application without the need to compromise on your use of F#. This section will elaborate a little on that and focus in particular on the frontend side of it, showing how you can write dynamic and responsive web applications while still writing code in an idiomatic F# style using immutable data and expression-oriented code.

13.5.1 Overview of SAFE Stack

The SAFE Stack is a collection of F#-first libraries and tools that runs on top of both the .NET and JavaScript ecosystems to allow you to develop standards-compliant applications while benefiting from being able to use a single language to develop an entire application. Figure 13.12 illustrates the different components of the stack at the time of writing.

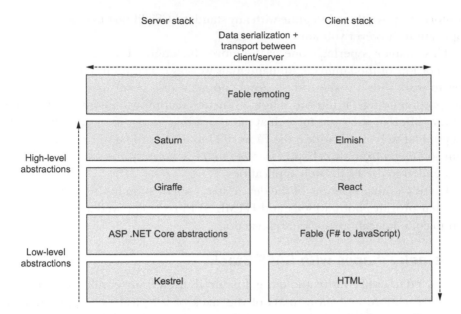

Figure 13.12   The SAFE Stack is a collection of different technologies bundled together to allow writing standards-compliant, rich web applications entirely in F#. The left-hand side of this figure represents the server side of the stack; the right-hand side represents the client side, which typically runs in the browser as a so-called single-page application.

You'll be familiar with some of these technologies; others will be new. We're not going to talk through all of them in depth, but I'll outline the main ones here:

- *Saturn*—A set of extensions that runs on top of Giraffe. It makes common tasks a little quicker and easier to do and provides a set of abstractions that optimize for specific scenarios.
- *Fable Remoting*—A communications library that allows you to create type-safe F# remote procedure call (RPC)-style APIs between browser and server on top of HTTP. It's illustrated as a box that straddles both client and server since there are two components for this library—one that runs in the browser and the other on the server within Giraffe.
- *Elmish*—A library to facilitate a UI pattern sometimes known as TEE, popularized in the Elm programming language, in F#. In the F# world, this pattern has become known as Model-View-Update (MVU).
- *React*—A JavaScript library for building user interfaces. It's very popular, performant, powerful and is well suited to being used in F#.

13.5.2 Installing the SAFE Stack template

The SAFE Stack comes with a dotnet template, so you can quickly get up and running with full-stack F# web applications without having to do all the boilerplate yourself. Being a web app framework, SAFE Stack has a few extra dependencies that are required:

- node.js v16
- npm v8

Once you've installed them, you can install the template:

```
dotnet new install SAFE.Template::4.2.0
```

At this point you will see the following output (slightly simplified in this example):

```
Success: SAFE.Template::4.2.0 installed the following templates:

Template Name           Short Name  Language
----------------------  ----------  --------
SAFE-Stack Web App v4.2.0  SAFE      F#
```

Now that you have the template installed, you can start to create new SAFE Stack applications:

1 Create a new directory for your application: `hellosafe`.
2 Enter the directory: `cd hellosafe`.
3 Create the application: `dotnet new SAFE` (template names are case sensitive!).
4 As a one-off task, run `dotnet tool restore`.
5 Run the application: `dotnet run`.
6 After a short delay, the first time for packages to be downloaded from NPM, NuGet etc., you'll see that both client and server have started:

   ```
   server: Now listening on: http://localhost:5000
   …
   client: webpack 5.65.0 compiled successfully in 1673 ms
   ```

You should now be able to navigate to http://localhost:8080 and will see a to-do style application has been created, as shown in figure 13.13. If you want to stop the entire application, you can simply press CTRL + C or close the terminal, just like you would with any other application.

> **SAFE Stack Template options**
>
> Earlier versions of the SAFE Stack template had all sorts of configuration options. However, these days, the template is fairly simple, with just a single switch. If you create a SAFE application using the `-minimal` flag, it will create a much lighter-weight folder without many of the bells and whistles that the full template comes with.

Figure 13.13   A brand-new SAFE Stack application

You can add new items by entering the to-do and clicking the Add button. Notice also that there is real-time validation in the browser. If the textbox is empty, the Add button will be disabled. If you refresh the browser, the items will remain, but if you stop and start the entire application, the list will be reset; the backing store is just an in-memory list.

Now that we've seen what we've created from an end-result point of view, let's take a brief look at what we have behind the scenes. If you browse through the directory (either manually or through, for example, VS Code) you'll see a whole host of folders. Many of them we can ignore for right now. Here are some of the key elements:

- `src/Server`—Contains the ASP.NET server-side application.
- `src/Client`—Contains the Fable / React / Elmish client-side application.
- `src/Shared`—Contains assets shared across both the client and server, such as API contracts, types, and business rules that need to be applied on both client and server.
- `Build.fsproj`—SAFE comes with an application that is used as a bootstrapper to launch both the client and server at the same time and is what you ran when calling `dotnet run`.

The shared project is especially interesting: one of the benefits of a single-language application is that you can share types and even functions across the client and server. There are some limits to this, but essentially, you can create the full spectrum of F# types, write functions that operate on those types, and have it all compiled to both

.NET on the server and JavaScript on the client. So you could write a validation function for some input data and have it execute on the client but also use that same F# on the server.

13.5.3   *The MVU pattern*

I want to focus on the UI side of the application and the MVU pattern used for creating user interfaces in a functional style. There are two reasons for this:

- It's another example of a functional API; learning this will help you understand how APIs can be designed to take advantage of the benefits of FP.
- You can see how to create frontend web applications in F#, which is useful (and fun!) in its own right.

As the name suggests, the MVU pattern contains three components (figure 13.14):

- *The Model*—Essentially, a type that represents the data of your application. For an e-commerce site, this type might store the basket, logged-in user details, account balance, etc. In F#, this is normally modeled as a record.
- *The View*—A data structure that represents all the controls being displayed. This is quite similar to what we saw earlier with Giraffe's ViewEngine, except in this case we're creating React rather than HTML elements. The View also captures UI actions such as button clicks and other user activities and sends them to the Update function as a command.
- *The Update function*—Understands how to modify the current model given a specific command. For example, an EmptyBasket command in the e-commerce application would probably take the current model and replace the list of items in the current basket with an empty list. The AddItemToBasket command might contain the SKU of the item to add; this would take the basket in the current model and add the item to the existing basket. In F#, we typically model commands via a discriminated union.

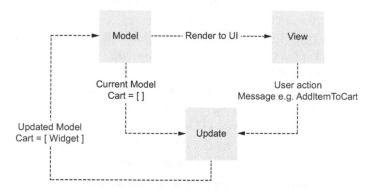

Figure 13.14   The MVU pattern is a pattern that allows you to manage UI changes to a data model in a pure functional style.

This pattern has several advantages:

- It is fairly simple to reason about, with only one place where business logic takes place: the `update` function.
- The pattern is unidirectional. This means that data only flows in one direction rather than allowing components to talk to each other. This again contributes to the simplicity of the pattern.
- The pattern supports asynchronous messaging and concurrency out of the box. If there are multiple UI actions pressed at the same time, the Elmish library will automatically queue them up, calling the `update` function one at a time for each new action.
- The Update function is a pure function; there is no mutation of data.

Let's explore the starter ToDo application created as part of the SAFE Stack template to look at this pattern in action before making some changes ourselves to add a new feature to the application:

1 Navigate to the `Index.fs` file. This file contains the entire frontend application and the three different MVU components.
2 Examine the Model type: `{ Todos: Todo list; Input: string }`. The `Todos` field represents the list of to-dos; the `Input` field stores the data currently in the input textbox.
3 The Msg type is a discriminated union that stores the different possible actions, or messages, that the application can manage. These are typically initiated by UI actions (e.g., text being typed or button clicks) but can also be initiated by the system itself as a result of another message being processed, events on a timer, or an asynchronous callback from a web request.
4 Next, look at the `update` function. Observe that the type signature of the function maps closely to figure 13.14. It takes both the current Model and a Msg as input and returns a new Model as output (for now, you can ignore the `Cmd<Msg>` that is also returned).
5 The `update` function is simply a pattern match; depending on the message that was supplied, it carries out a different action.
6 The `view` function takes in a Model and a function called `dispatch`. The view simply renders the supplied model; it has no knowledge of how that model was created and does not modify it.
7 The `view` function uses a similar (but not identical) dialect to the Giraffe ViewEngine approach for rendering out presentation data, although in this case, it's a React tree rather than raw HTML.
8 The `dispatch` function is used to send a message back into the loop—so when the Add button is clicked, an `AddTodo` message is dispatched.

This is the essence of the entire MVU pattern: you define a model and the messages that can occur in the system; an update function knows how to modify the model based on any given message; the view function renders out the view.

13.5.4 *Removing all ToDo items: A worked exercise*

Let's finish this chapter by adding a new feature to the application—the ability to clear out all to-dos from the application:

1 Ensure that the application is running.
2 Configure your display so that your code editor and the browser with the running app are running side by side. This is because changes you make in code will show up immediately in your running application; there is no need to stop and start every time you make a change!
3 Add a new case to the `Msg` type, `ClearTodos`.
4 Start by duplicating the code for the `Add` button directly below it, starting from line 77 to 84 (these line numbers match from *before* the new case is added!)
5 Save the file. You should see a second button has now appeared in the browser.
6 Change the text of the button to `"Clear"`.
7 Change the color of the button to `isWarning`.
8 Change the value of the `disabled` prop to only be `true` if the to-do list in the model is empty (in other words, the button should be enabled if there is at least one todo).
9 Change the `onClick` handler to dispatch the new `ClearTodos` message.

The view code is now complete, but we must now change the `update` function to handle the new message.

10 Add a new entry to the pattern match of the `update` function for the `ClearTodos` case. Have it return the model with an empty list for the `Todos` field, along with a `Cmd.none`.

You should now be able to press the `Clear` button; this will remove all to-dos in the browser. Note that this code does not remove the ToDo data from the in-memory list on the server. If you refresh the browser, which causes the app to pull fresh data from the server, you'll get all the items back again.

To get server-supported round trips, you'll need to modify the Fable.Remoting API contract that exists to add a new endpoint, call it from the frontend, and then add a server implementation of the endpoint. Here's a brief step-by-step guide, but you'll want to read up more fully on the SAFE Stack website to learn more about this.

1 Modify the `ITodosApi` in `Shared.fs` to add a new endpoint:

```
clearTodos: unit -> Async<Todo list>
```

2 Add the implementation in `Server.fs`:

```
clearTodos = fun () -> async { Storage.todos.Clear();return [] }
```

3 Change the handler of the `ClearTodos` message in the update function to call the new API endpoint instead:

```
| ClearTodos ->
    model, Cmd.OfAsync.perform todosApi.clearTodos () GotTodos
```

That's all that's required to add a new client/server API endpoint—completely type-safe, with serialization carried out automatically. Pretty neat!

Summary

- At its most basic, HTTP represents a simple function call. There's no need to abstract this away with OO representations.
- ASP.NET Core is the de facto standard framework for web programming on .NET.
- While you can use ASP.NET directly in F#, there are options on top of ASP.NET Core, such as Giraffe and Falco, which take full advantage of F#'s features and play to its strengths as an FP language.
- Giraffe introduces a single functional abstraction known as the HTTP Handler, which represents a request-response for an HTTP call.
- HTTP Handlers can be composed together using the `>=>` custom operator.
- You can conceptually divide handlers up into filters, such as checking the request verb, and writers, which modify the response, such as the content.
- It's generally recommended to try to separate HTTP concepts from your internal domain logic and adapt between the two. This makes your code not only more testable but usually also easier to reason about.
- Giraffe also has an extension package to allow you to create HTML in a type-safe manner, using only F# code.
- F# is also fully capable of writing full-stack applications that run in the browser using industry-standard technologies such as React.
- The SAFE Stack is an F#-first package that comes with a template to rapidly get up and running with F# web applications.
- The MVU pattern allows us to write frontend applications using a pure functional style.
- The MVU pattern is relatively simple, with just a few components to learn, and handles much of the complexity of asynchronous web apps for us.

14

Testing F# code

This chapter focuses on writing automated tests of your F# code. There are entire books dedicated to unit testing, and I'm not going to try to cover everything in this chapter. Many (but not all) of the things you'll read in those books still apply to F#, so as with other areas of the book, I'll instead focus more on testing from an F#, FP-first perspective.

14.1 Automated tests: The value proposition

This section is a broad overview of the idea behind automated tests and how automated testing generally fits within the context of F#. Although I briefly covered the idea of unit tests and a process for writing them known as test-driven development (TDD) earlier in the book, if you've never written any automated tests before, you'll want to know what they are and why you should bother with them. Automated tests are simply code you write (so-called test code) that tests the actual ("production") application code of your system. Typically, they'll set up some initial state of the application with some predefined input data, then call some production code, and then test the state of the application again to ensure that the production code has had the expected effect. Tests like this are typically short lived, fine grained and should be highly consistent and reliable.

The benefit of writing tests like this is that once you've written them, they stay forever and can repeatedly be run—even on every check-in of code to source control or build. Thus, they can be thought of as assets whose value increases over time. They give you more confidence that your code is indeed behaving as expected, especially when you make changes to old code.

There are also lots of ways to write bad tests, though—for example, tests that are inconsistent (and therefore untrustworthy), tests that are brittle (and therefore expensive to maintain), or tests that are too slow (and therefore costly to run). So if you want to go down the route of building unit tests pervasively throughout your codebase (generally considered a good thing to do), invest the time in reading a good book or two on high-quality unit tests: if you get them wrong, you'll often only find out months down the line when you realize that you don't trust your tests and that the cost of them nears (or even outweighs) the benefits. My advice when starting is to target the areas that would benefit from automated tests the most and go from there. Typically, this includes complex algorithmic code, areas that are of high risk to the user (e.g., a bug might lead to accidentally deleting all customers from the database), code that is reused in many places throughout your codebase, and code that may not change often (and therefore the cost of maintaining tests will be low).

14.1.1 *F#: Types over tests*

Despite the claim from some that in F#, "if it compiles, it works," the truth is somewhat more nuanced: within the world of F#, there is still a place for automated tests. However, I would suggest that this is less than what you might expect in other languages, certainly less so than dynamic languages like JavaScript or Clojure and still less than "weaker" statically typed languages such as C#, which don't commonly use types in the same way that F# does and make it easy to use mutations and statements. This section shows some examples of how we can simply use the compiler and types to make tests redundant or at least code that is very unlikely to fail. From here, you'll hopefully start to get a feel for the sorts of features you'll want to take advantage of to minimize the need for low-level tests.

USING TYPES TO ENFORCE INVARIANTS AND PREREQUISITES

Consider the following code:

```
let sendEmail message customer =
    if customer.Email.IsValid then
        ….
```

An explicit logic check for the "happy path"

```
...
...

        Ok "Sent message"
    else
        Error InvalidEmail
```

| Handles the "unhappy path"

You might want to test that, given a customer with an invalid email, the system does not send an email, that it returns the correct error code, etc. Also, consider everywhere else in the system that needs to check for valid email addresses; you'd possibly want to test that part of code as well. We can eliminate the need for such tests almost completely by instead simply having this code focus on the "happy path"—the path of code that handles the intended path, where everything works as designed—and enforcing rules through a type:

A single point of entry to safely try to create a ValidatedEmail

A private constructor for the single case discriminated union

A member to easily access the unwrapped "raw" string value

```
type ValidatedEmail =
    private | ValidatedEmail of string
    member this.Value = match this with (ValidatedEmail e) -> e
    static member Create (unvalidatedEmail:string) =
        if unvalidatedEmail.Contains "@" then
            Ok (ValidatedEmail unvalidatedEmail)
        else
            Error "Invalid email!"

let sendEmailSafe message (email:ValidatedEmail) =
    ...
    ...
    ...
    Ok "Sent message"

let sendResult =
    ValidatedEmail.Create "isaac@email.com"
    |> Result.bind (sendEmailSafe "Welcome!")
```

A function that only accepts values of the safe ValidatedEmail type as input

Composes the two functions together

The key thing here is that we've now separated the logic of creating a validated email address and the sending of an email. You can't call `sendEmailSafe` unless you have gone through the validation process, and there's no need to write a test to validate the correctness of `sendEmailSafe`. Instead, you might test out the `Create` method of `ValidatedEmail`, but that's the only place that you would do it. We've successfully not only made our code safer but also enforced testing for something in a single, isolated place.

PATTERN MATCHING AGAINST A DISCRIMINATED UNION

We've already seen how discriminated unions give us a great deal of protection in many ways. One of them is the exhaustive/completeness checking from the compiler to ensure that all possible cases are handled. Something I don't normally write tests for is to ensure that we're handling all possible cases of a union when matching. See the example in listing 14.1.

Listing 14.1   A simply discriminated union and function

```
type Instrument =                    ◁──── A simple
    | Guitar                               discriminated
    | Drums                                union
    | Bass

let play instrument =                ◁──── A function that
    match instrument with                  operates on the
    | Guitar -> "Wah wah"                   union type
    | Drums -> "Ba dam tss"
    | Bass -> "Ba ba bom"
```

The chance of you forgetting to handle a case is so small (assuming you read compiler warnings and/or elect to treat warnings as errors) that I almost never write tests that the match has happened correctly and certainly not in advance of writing code in a TDD fashion. The fact that the code is expression-oriented also means it's impossible to handle one case but not return a string value; the code wouldn't compile. The only thing that realistically can go wrong is if you mix up the text for the instruments. In such a case, a test (whether manual or automated) would be the only way to provide more confidence that the code is doing the right thing.

One extra tip: avoid the temptation to use the wildcard _ to group together the final case (or cases) instead of explicitly writing them out. The benefit of being more explicit here is that if you decide at some point to add a new union case, the compiler will instantly warn you wherever you match against values of that type, forcing you to handle the new case. If you use a wildcard, it'll silently get swallowed into the same handler as the other two cases, which may not be what you want:

```
let play instrument =
    match instrument with
    | Guitar -> "Wah wah"                 Uses a wildcard
    | Drums -> "Ba dam tss"               instead of explicitly
    | _ -> "Ba ba bom"       ◁────        watching on Bass
```

In this example, I've saved a few keystrokes by not matching on `Bass` explicitly. Not only is this less readable, but if I were to add a new instrument to the union type itself (e.g., `Saxophone`), the compiler wouldn't be able to help me here—it will also use the text `"Ba ba bom"` for that, which almost certainly isn't what we want.

USING IMMUTABLE DATA AND EXPRESSIONS WHEREVER POSSIBLE

Just following these two basic suggestions—immutable data and expressions—will immediately have a largely positive effect on the correctness of your code. I know it sounds like a bland suggestion to do, but simply avoiding using mutable data (which will go hand in hand with writing expression-oriented code), and you will immediately cut out a large swathe of things you'll need to test for, and what you do end up testing will be much easier to do (as we'll see shortly).

14.2 Basic unit testing in F#

I'm going to start with an F#-first approach to automated testing of code. We'll start with just creating some basic tests without using a framework and then illustrate how to move to a full test runner that can integrate with IDEs such as Visual Studio.

14.2.1 Tests as functions

Since automated tests are themselves written in F#, we can think of these as test functions that call production functions. I prefer a style of writing tests that follow the so-called Arrange, Act, Assert (AAA) methodology:

- *Arrange*—Set up anything required for the test, such as test data and starting state.
- *Act*—Put the test data into the function you are testing.
- *Assert*—Check that the result meets your expectations.

Listing 14.2 provides an example test I've written as a console application, which would run against my production application code from listing 14.1.

Listing 14.2   Writing some example unit tests

```
module Assert =                         A test helper function to assert
    let equal a b =                     that two values equal each other
        if a <> b then failwith $"Value '{a}' does not equal '{b}'."

let myGuitarGentlyWeeps () =
    // Arrange
    let input = Guitar
                                        Test functions
    // Act                              that follow the
    let output = play input             basic AAA test
                                        setup pattern
    // Assert
    Assert.equal "Wah wah" output

let drumsGoBang () =
    // Arrange
    let input = Drums

    // Act
    let output = play input

    // Assert                           Composes both
    Assert.equal "Ba dumm tss" output   tests together
                                        into a list
let tests = [ myGuitarGentlyWeeps; drumsGoBang ]

printfn $"Running {tests.Length} tests..."    Runs all tests and prints
for test in tests do test ()                  the results to the console
printfn "All tests passed!"
```

If you run this code, you'll see that the first test passes but the second fails and throws an exception. Of course, the tests are deliberately simple here, which is normally a good thing; if your tests get too complex, it's usually a sign that you're either testing too much in one go or that your production code is not easily testable. The tests are also quite verbose in terms of commenting, but you can see that the test code (plus helper functions) already outweighs the size of the production code.

EXERCISE 14.1

1 Create a new console application.
2 Import the code from listings 14.1 and 14.2. The application should execute the two tests when run.
3 Write a further test for testing the bass instrument.
4 Create a new instrument; fix the compiler errors. Do you think writing a test now is adding much value? Why (or why not)?

14.2.2 Expecto

The code just seen all works, but there's clearly some boilerplate that could be reused across tests:

- The test runner that runs each function and outputs the results
- The assertions that take place, such as checking whether a value is equal to another one

This is what a test framework and runner do for us. There are many testing packages out there for .NET; the one that I currently recommend is Expecto. It's an open source test library that is particularly well suited to F#. This isn't because it's F#-only (it works fine with C#) but because it fits very well with the F# ethos of not having lots of "magic" in a framework, works with functions and data, and is highly composable.

14.2.3 Plugging Expecto into our code

Let's modify our existing tests to use Expecto:

1 Add the v9.0.4 of Expecto: `dotnet add package Expecto -v 9.0.4`.
2 Remove the `Assert` module and all code below the unit tests (from `let tests = ... onward`).
3 Amend your test code as in the listing 14.3.

Listing 14.3   Unit tests written with Expecto

```
open Expecto                                        Creates a named
                                                    list of tests
let musicTests = testList "Music tests" [
    test "My guitar gently weeps" {
        let input = Guitar
        let output = play input
        Expect.equal output "Wah wah" "Guitar sound is incorrect"
    }

    test "Drums go bang" {
        let input = Drums
        let output = play input
        Expect.equal output "Ba dum tss" "Drums are wrong"
```

Creates individual named tests

Uses Expecto's Expect module to assert two values equal one another

```
    }
]

[<EntryPoint>]
let main args =
    runTestsWithCLIArgs [] args musicTests
```

> Runs the
> composed
> list of tests

If you've used a test framework such as NUnit or XUnit before, this will look quite different. But that's because Expecto is different: instead of relying on the magic of reflection and declarative attributes to discover tests, with Expecto, you simply compose tests together as lists and run your tests as a standard console application.

If you examine the previous code in a little more detail, you'll see that each test is actually just a call to a function called test, which takes an argument of the name of the test (e.g., "My guitar gently weeps") and then a body, which is the test code to run. These tests are composed together into a testList, which also has a name ("Music tests"). At the very end, you supply that test list to the runTestsWithCLIArgs function, which runs each test. When you run the console application, you'll see the following output:

```
[09:38:50 INF] EXPECTO? Running tests...
[09:38:50 ERR] Music tests.Drums go bang failed in 00:00:00.0420000.
Drums are wrong. String does not match at position 6.
➥ Expected char: ' ', but got 'm'.
expected: Ba dumm tss
  actual. Ba dum tss
    at Program.musicTests@23-1.Invoke(Unit unitVar) in Program.fs:line 25
[09:38:50 INF] EXPECTO! 2 tests run in 00:00:00.1015621 for
➥ Music tests - 1 passed, 0 ignored, 1 failed, 0 errored.
```

I've omitted some code, such as the stack trace (printed to guide you to the exact line of code that the test failed), but there's enough here to see what's going on. Of particular interest is:

- The test is shown in its fully qualified form; that is, the list it is part of (Music tests) and the name of the test (Drums go bang). This makes it easier to identify. It's also human readable because tests are just strings; you can call them whatever you want without worrying about naming conventions or class/method restrictions.
- The error is easy to understand. It uses the error message from the actual test as the header ("Drums are wrong") and then provides details about what failed.
- The expected and actual values are shown aligned one above another; the nonmatching text characters are highlighted in red to make it easier for you to pinpoint the failure.
- A summary is displayed showing that one test passed and one test failed.

Expecto and dotnet tests

The dotnet command-line interface tool also comes with a test runner, `dotnet test`. You don't really need it for Expecto since your tests are just standard console applications (it is needed for other test frameworks as we'll see shortly). You can get Expecto to work with dotnet test if you really want to; you'll need to add both the `Microsoft.NET.Test.Sdk` and `YoloDev.Expecto.TestSdk` packages and decorate your test list with the `[<Tests>]` attribute.

14.2.4 *Advantages of Expecto*

One of the key features of Expecto is that its tests are highly composable: the `testList` function itself returns a value of the same type as individual tests, `Test`. This means that you can nest an unlimited number of groups of tests into hierarchies as you see fit, such as, for example:

```
let databaseTests =
    testList "DB Tests" [ … ]            ◁┐
let businessLogicTests =                    ├ Makes lists of tests
    testList "Business Logic Tests" [ … ] ◁┘
▷ let allTests =
    testList "All tests" [ databaseTests; businessLogicTests ]
```

**Composes two lists of tests
into a parent list of tests**

This approach is not so different from Giraffe's HTTP Handler—a single abstraction that can be composed together easily in a flexible way. With Expecto, we have the notion of a Test—which may be a single test but could also be a list of tests. Or a list of list of tests! You can run one of them in isolation, or not. You can create lists of the same tests built up in different ways. It's just values, simply data, built together in lists and passed around your test code. There's no need for classes, inheritance, or attributes.

Another benefit that this "list of lists" approach gives is that you can build up the list of tests programmatically. One thing that I don't like about test frameworks like NUnit and XUnit is that you have an overarching test runner that discovers tests (typically using Attributes) and calls them on your behalf. You must work within its framework for all sorts of things. For example, what if you want to disable a test locally but have it run on the continuous integration (CI) server based on the existence of an environment variable? Or if you want to run a test 10 times, each with a line of data from a test input file. You can do both, but it involves learning more about that specific test framework using abstract features such as "Theories". Expecto doesn't need any of that; tests are just functions and can be built up as required using all the existing techniques you already know. Listing 14.4 shows how to achieve both scenarios I've just outlined using nothing but standard F#.

Listing 14.4 Programmatically creating tests in Expecto

Our production code, a simple addition function

```
let add a b = a + b
```

Programmatically decides whether to yield back a test based on the existence of an environment variable

```
let myTests = testList "My Tests" [
    if System.Environment.GetEnvironmentVariable
 ➥ "CI_SERVER" <> null then
        test "CI Only Test" { Expect.equal (add 1 2)
 ➥ 3 "Something is very wrong!" }
```

For each line in the file, yields back a new test whose name is based on the line in the file

Reads data from a file using basic .NET code

```
    for line in System.IO.File.ReadAllLines "testData.txt" do
        test $"Addition test: {line}" {
            match line.Split ',' with
            | [| inputA; inputB; expected |] ->
                let actual = add (int inputA) (int inputB)
                Expect.equal actual (int expected) "Calculator is broken"
            | _ ->
                failwith $"Invalid test data format: {line}"
        }
]
```

Create a test file, `testData.txt` that looks something like the following:

```
1,1,2
2,2,4
4,4,8
0,8,16
```

Run the application passing in the `--debug` switch and amend the call to `runTestsWith-CLIArgs` to supply the new `myTests` value. You'll receive a test result output as follows:

```
[10:06:27 INF] EXPECTO? Running tests...
[10:06:27 DBG] My Tests.Addition test: 4,4,8 starting...
[10:06:27 DBG] My Tests.Addition test: 2,2,4 starting...
[10:06:27 DBG] My Tests.Addition test: 1,1,2 starting...
[10:06:27 DBG] My Tests.Addition test: 8,8,16 starting...
[10:06:27 DBG] My Tests.Addition test: 4,4,8 passed in 00:00:00.0040000.
[10:06:27 DBG] My Tests.Addition test: 1,1,2 passed in 00:00:00.0040000.
[10:06:27 DBG] My Tests.Addition test: 8,8,16 passed in 00:00:00.0040000.
[10:06:27 DBG] My Tests.Addition test: 2,2,4 passed in 00:00:00.0040000.
[10:06:27 INF] EXPECTO! 4 tests run in 00:00:00.0574421 for My Tests - 4
    passed, 0 ignored, 0 failed, 0 errored. Success!
```

The code in listing 14.4 contains no magic features or new language techniques. It's the exact same as we've seen in previous chapters—building lists, yielding values based on conditionals, reading from the file system, or checking environment variables. Yet, once again, we can use them here for creating tests quickly and easily.

14.3 Making testable code

This section covers some tips for making F# code that is simple to test. It's by no means exhaustive, and again, you'll find books that dive into this in great depth, but whether you're new to testing or coming from a non-FP background, this list will help you as you get started.

14.3.1 Preferring pure functions where possible

Probably the most fundamental trick to writing tests that are simple to reason about is to write code that has no side effects. This means essentially no mutation or modification of external state. It won't always be possible or desirable (especially with integration tests, which may, for example, hit a database), but for testing standard functions, always aim for something that behaves like a function should. It should take all of its inputs as arguments, not some hidden global state or encapsulated private fields in a class, and returns the output as a standard return value of the function and not as a side effect of, for example, modifying the internal state of a class. There are many benefits to opting for pure functions in this way when thinking about testing:

- Pure functions are easier to write. All tests follow the same pattern: create some data for the input arguments, call the function, and assert against the output of the function.
- Pure functions are easier to read and comprehend. You don't have any hidden side effects as you might see with tests in OO designs such as "call this method and then test that this class property has been modified" or, even worse, "call this method and then check that some other method behaves in a certain way." Instead, you simply have input data, a function (or a set of functions) that you call, and a result value.
- Pure functions are inherently consistent and repeatable. You can call a pure function a million times with the same input, and you will always get the same output. That can't be said for functions that mutate state in the background because the effect of one method call may affect the behavior of subsequent calls.

14.3.2 Preferring smaller functions

This sounds obvious, but it really does make sense. Prefer smaller functions that have a fairly well-defined contract in terms of what they do. Larger functions will naturally lead to tests that have a more complex setup, will be harder to reason about, and will be more likely to break in the future when refactoring.

14.3.3 Unit testing small function hierarchies

Prefer testing functions that don't have large call hierarchies—that is, testing some function A, which calls function B, which calls function Z. There's nothing wrong with testing functions that call other functions, but I tend to prefer more of a bottom–up approach to testing: test smaller functions (or groups of functions) at lower levels. They're generally easier to test and will usually be where more of your algorithmic logic sits.

14.3.4   Integration testing higher-level composed functions

Conversely, at the higher levels of your application, it's more likely that your code will be focused on orchestrating calls and chaining functions together rather than complex, low-level business logic. These are relatively safe to do in F# with pattern matching and discriminated unions. For such high-level code paths, you may prefer to run end-to-end integration tests that focus on higher-level business scenarios, using, for example, an actual database.

14.3.5   Pushing side effects to the boundaries of your code

Where possible, try to write code that has any I/O at the edges of your application. In the core of the application, look to focus on pure functions that carry out any business logic as needed. There are names for this kind of approach, such as Ports and Adapters, Hexagonal and Onion architectures. It's not always easy to achieve, but if you can, you'll find that your code will generally be easier to test.

14.3.6   Using higher-order functions to replace side effects

When pushing side effects out isn't possible, there's still a way out. Higher-order functions can be extremely effective as an escape hatch if you want to test code that has a side effect in the middle of it. Consider the following code, which creates an invoice (as shown in figure 14.1):

```
let createInvoice customer order = result {
    do! validateCustomer customer
    saveToSql customer order              ◄─── Impure I/O within the
    return calculatePrice customer order       middle of a function
}
```

This code has some business logic, then a side effect (a call to save the order to the database), and then some more business logic. We want to test out all the business logic but don't want to extract both bits of business logic just for the sake of testing. There are ways to refactor parts of this into a pure function, but the simplest option is to replace the side effect with an argument:

```
let createInvoiceTestable save customer order = result {    ◄───── Supplies the save
    do! validateCustomer customer                                  function as an
    save customer order              ◄─────                        argument to
    return calculatePrice customer order                           createInvoice
}
                          Calls it in place of the
                          direct call to saveToSql
```

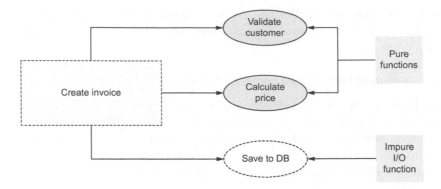

Figure 14.1   A high-level function, `Create Invoice`, which orchestrates calls to multiple child functions. `Validate Customer` and `Calculate Price` in isolation might be good candidates for unit testing as they are pure functions, whereas `Save to DB` involves I/O and probably wouldn't be a good candidate. This also has a knock-on effect of making `Create Invoice` impure and I/O-bound; you might instead elect to write an integration test that runs end-to-end, including writing to the database.

At runtime in your production system, you'll supply the "real" function that calls SQL, but in your test code, you can create a fake function that behaves however you need it to:

```
let invoiceTest = test "Create Invoice" {
    let customer = "Bob"
    let order = "Guitar"
    let fakeSave customer order = ()

    let price = createInvoiceTestable fakeSave customer order

    Expect.equal (Ok 100M) price "Invoice is wrong"
}
```

The arrange phase of the test also includes creating a fake save function.

The fake save function supplied as an argument to the now testable create invoice function

Again, F#'s type inference comes to the rescue here: you don't have to worry about type signatures or the like. Simply replace the real code with an argument; 9 times out of 10, F# will automatically figure out the type signature. Also, since we're just dealing with function arguments, there's no need for mocking libraries or the like; just create a lambda function that does whatever you need.

14.3.7 *Don't worry about encapsulation*

Lots of developers coming from the OO world get hung up on encapsulation and data hiding. There are times when this is also appropriate in F#, but it doesn't happen very often. Data is nearly always immutable, with modifications being applied to copies of source data—there is no risk of exposing data to callers for fear of them modifying it.

Leaving data public means testing what's happening when calling functions is much easier. Avoid being in situations when the only way to assert the behavior of a function call works as expected is by implication.

14.4 Working with NUnit-style test frameworks

Even though I prefer the simplicity of the way Expecto works and how well it fits with F#, it would be remiss of me not to illustrate how to use other testing libraries with F#. The two most popular at the time of writing are NUnit and XUnit. Both are more or less the same in terms of approach, so I will focus on just XUnit here.

Unlike Expecto, tests in XUnit typically live in a class library project and can't be run on their own as a program. Instead, you need a "test runner" that can discover all the tests in the project. To enable discovery, tests typically need to be decorated with an attribute such as [<Test>] or [<Fact>]. Similarly, if you want to have some shared setup for a group of tests, you create a function with a [<TestSetup>] attribute—you get the idea.

Let's port our Expecto tests into XUnit:

1. Create a new directory, `MyTestsXunit`.
2. In the directory, create a new XUnit project: `dotnet new xunit -lang F#`. This is one of the templates built into dotnet (there's a third-party Expecto template that you can download). It creates a class library project and adds a set of NuGet packages required for XUnit to work—there's nothing magical happening here.
3. Copy the production code and music tests from the Expecto application into the new XUnit class library's `Tests.fs` file.
4. Remove the enclosing test list and turn each test into a function, replacing calls to the `Expect` module with those in XUnit's `Assert` module as you go, as shown in the following code sample:

```
[<Fact>]
let ``My guitar gently weeps`` () =
    let input = Guitar
    let output = play input
    Assert.Equal("Wah wah", output)

[<Fact>]
let ``Drums go bang`` () =
    let input = Drums
    let output = play input
    Assert.Equal ("Ba dumm tss", output)
```

5. You can now run the tests by calling `dotnet test` from the command line.

On the one hand, there's less boilerplate in this sample compared to the Expecto one. You don't have to manually compose the tests together into a list or explicitly pass them into Expecto. You can still get nice naming with these frameworks, thanks to F#'s backtick (``` `` ```) methods. However, the flip side is that we're now bound to XUnit's test runner framework for doing everything, including discovery of tests via the `[<Fact>]` attribute. It might look quite appealing for a simple example like this, but once you need more tests with more flexibility and need to go "outside the box", I'd personally opt for Expecto. But the choice is yours!

14.5   *Other forms of testing*

This final section will briefly summarize a couple of other forms of testing that exist and give you some ideas of what to look at on the .NET platform for those.

14.5.1   *Performance testing*

Another form of correctness of code can sometimes be considered how quickly it performs. For example, a routine or API may need to respond within a certain amount of time to be considered fit for purpose. Often, we simply don't think about it upfront, which, in my opinion, isn't always necessarily a bad thing; I've seen colleagues (and myself) spend too much time prematurely optimizing some code when it really wasn't needed. Nonetheless, you may sometimes want to analyze how quickly some code runs—perhaps because of a specific customer requirement or because you've written a new implementation of a routine and want to compare its performance against the old one. There are several tools and libraries for this.

For starters, Expecto has a simple set of performance-based functions, such as `Performance.isFasterThan`. This allows you to supply two functions and run them both for an increasing number of iterations until there's confidence that either they're both as fast (or slow!) as each other or one is faster than the other.

However, if you need to do some serious benchmarking, the only real choice is Benchmark.NET. This open source tool takes benchmarking extremely seriously. It's even used by the .NET team themselves to test new versions of .NET. The only issue from an F# point of view is that it's very OO-ish: your benchmarks must be methods that live in a class, and any state that your benchmarks rely on must live inside that class—otherwise, you'll receive a null reference exception at run time because Benchmark.NET strips out nonessential code from your project to benchmark only what it thinks is required. Benchmark.NET can do more than just time your code; it can also measure memory usage, garbage collections, etc. and is definitely worth checking out.

14.5.2   *Property-based testing*

Another form of testing you would do well to learn a little about is called Property Based Testing (PBT). This is more about conventional unit testing of code for correctness, except instead of providing a known good result for a test (e.g., calling `add 1 1` should return 2), you instead provide properties or behaviors about the function. The PBT library then generates randomly distributed inputs of increasing complexity to ensure that the property always holds true. A popular library on .NET for this is FsCheck. Property-based tests take more effort to write than standard tests, but for situations where standard unit tests perhaps don't give you enough confidence, PBTs are great. If you invest the effort in them, they will generally have much greater value than standard unit tests because they test thousands of different inputs rather than just the one or two you've thought of yourself.

Let's take an example of a set of property-based tests. Let's say you have some code that flips the case of a string, and you want to test it—let's call it `flipCase`. You might elect to use a single test case for the word `Hello`, for example (figure 14.2).

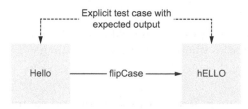

Figure 14.2   Testing a function with an explicit input and expected resultant output

However, you could also prove that `flipCase` does what it's supposed to without ever knowing either the input or output. Instead, you can supply properties that explain the *relationship* between the input and output (figure 14.3).

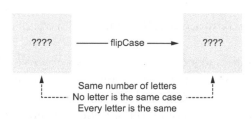

Figure 14.3   Testing a function by proving that for any given input, it exhibits a set of rules or properties that govern the relationship between the input and output

Each property shown in figure 14.3 on its own doesn't prove the `flipCase` does the right thing, but combined, all three of them do. The beauty of this approach is that FsCheck will supply strings to your code starting with a simple string such as a single letter `a`. It will then progressively provide more complex strings both in terms of length as well as the different characters it uses. Doing so provides you with a high level of confidence that your code is doing the right thing.

There are many good use cases for PBTs, and lots of free videos online for how they can be used in real-world scenarios where explicit one-off tests simply wouldn't provide that same level of confidence. This includes situations where the set of inputs is so potentially so large and varied that you couldn't conceivably hand-write unit tests for all the cases. One good example is if you have an API that exposed a number of different methods to update your customer database and want to prove that given any combination of those API calls, the database is still left in a valid state at the end. This is the sort of thing that might be very difficult to do manually—you'd have to think up different permutations by hand and still might not catch all the combinations. This is something that PBTs do very well.

However, there's no such thing as a free lunch, and PBTs do have costs associated with them:

- It is not always easy to identify suitable properties for your production code without falling into the trap of duplicating your production code in your test code.
- You may need to invest time in building custom generators—that is, code that tells FsCheck how to distribute your input data (in our case, to only use alphabetic characters and non-nulls).

I wouldn't say that PBTs are a replacement for conventional unit tests. Think of them more as a companion for specific scenarios where unit tests aren't suitable.

Summary

- Unit tests are a way of writing code to test your production code automatically and repeatably.
- While F# does benefit from unit testing, there are cases where the compiler itself can catch many potential bugs so that you simply don't need to bother with unit tests.
- You can write assertions for your tests and a runner yourself, but this is best left to dedicated unit test frameworks.
- The Expecto library is a high-quality, composable unit test library that is especially well suited to F#.
- Expecto allows you to compose tests together into nested lists of tests and build tests however you want. This is extremely useful if you need to control when and how tests are run.
- There are some basic best practices you should follow to help ensure your code is easy to test, such as preferring pure functions where possible, writing smaller functions, and using higher-order functions when you can't remove a side effect embedded in the middle of your function.
- There are other popular test frameworks on .NET, such as NUnit and XUnit. Both also work just fine from F#, although they are quite restrictive in terms of orchestration and composition of your tests compared to Expecto.
- Benchmark.NET is a high-quality, mature library for .NET that enables you to measure the performance of your code, both in terms of timing and memory consumption.
- FsCheck is a Property Based Test (PBT) library. PBTs allow you to write tests to prove certain rules or behaviors about your code when it would be too complex to do with standard unit tests.

Pure functional
programming

This chapter covers

- Functional architecture patterns
- Composing functions
- Bootstrappers and inverting dependencies
- Working with effects

So far, we've looked at specific language features and integration, but aside from the web application portion, much of the book so far has looked at each area in isolation. That's been intentional so that we can focus on one thing at a time and not lose context. However, it's also important to have an awareness of how things plug together effectively. That's what this chapter is about: we're going to look at different challenges you might face when writing applications that adhere to a functional programming (FP) architecture and different strategies for composing code together into larger applications.

15.1   *A functional architecture pattern*

While you've now seen how to create and work with expressions and immutable data, what probably won't be immediately apparent is that you can (and will) create entire applications as expressions. There are even architectural patterns for this style of development, such as the onion architecture and the hexagonal (also known as the ports-and-adapters) architecture.

15.1.1   *External and internal boundaries*

One way you can think of your application is as being divided into two areas:

- *The outside world*—The world of input and output: console input/output (I/O), databases, file systems, HTTP, etc., typically working with side effects
- *The known world*—Your application domain logic, ideally free from any direct interactions with the outside world

Typically, interactions with the outside world occur at the boundary of your application; in the known world, your code will usually be functions that take in some data, manipulate and transform it, and call other functions in a linear fashion with some data that repeat that same pattern. Eventually, everything bubbles back up to the start, which returns a value to the outside world.

Figure 15.1 illustrates this architectural approach for a web application that has a database. The outside world consists of HTTP and SQL messages; the rest of the application consists of a set of expressions-oriented functions (possibly pure functions), which take in some JSON data from a web request and validates it before carrying out some business logic and transforming data through a set of functions. Finally, the result bubbles back up the stack and ends up with a SQL statement and an HTTP response being generated.

In some languages like Haskell, this separation is enforced at the type system level so that there is a strict separation between I/O and pure code, so you can't simply make a database call in the middle of a function and just carry on as though this was a regular piece of code.

Each of the functions works purely on some input data and returns some transformed data as output to its caller (which behaves in the same way), calling other functions as needed to provide any data. The code inside these functions are themselves *also* expressions; even conditional logic, as we've seen with `if/then`, can be expressions.

There's also no so-called "spaghetti code" in F# because code cannot call other code that has not yet been declared. So, you are left with a relatively simple model of creating functions; providing data to them, which performs some transformation and returns your code a result before analyzing that result; and, finally, deciding what to do next.

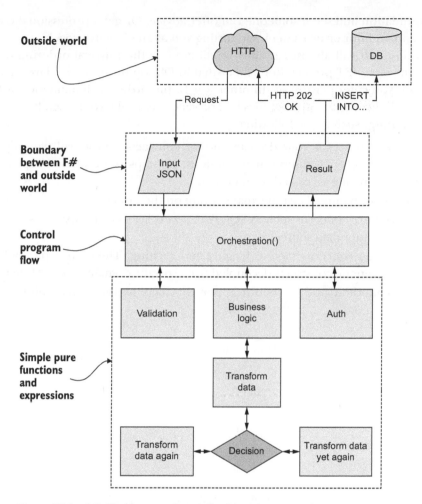

Figure 15.1   A fictional expression chain of function calls, with separation between the impure outside and (mostly) pure inner world

15.1.2 *Structuring larger functional codebases*

This final section provides some guidance on a question that I see all the time with customers and in the community about how to scale applications or at least how to structure larger applications.

The first answer is that many of the lessons you already know still apply. Whether you want to segregate your applications into horizontal tiers or vertical slices or have separate assemblies (i.e., projects) for different areas of your .NET application, that's totally fine and reasonable. Those high-level architectural best practices will mostly still be perfectly valid in the F# world. Trust your instincts: if something feels wrong, is taking a long time to do, is unreadable etc., flag it up. Speak to a colleague; see if you can run it by someone more experienced; go onto the official F# Slack group run by the F# Foundation and see if someone can offer advice. Or get a professional consultant to spend an hour or two a week supporting you as an objective coach.

One thing that will almost certainly be different is the physical ordering of files and types in your .NET project. Remember that in F#, you must first declare a type or value before you can reference it. In other words, the order of dependency of types and values will dictate the order of files in a project. A typical layout (e.g., figure 15.2) will contain things such as the following:

- Type definitions for your domain and/or contracts. These will typically be a mixture of records, discriminated unions, perhaps some aliased tuples, etc., that live in namespaces and/or modules.
- Modules containing functions that operate on the domain types.
- Infrastructure concerns such as SQL data access layers or repositories and gateways over other data sources.
- Cross-cutting concerns such as logging and caching. These are typically highly reusable, generic constructs decoupled from specific domain types or functions.
- A main method and/or bootstrapper that acts as the entry point for the application.

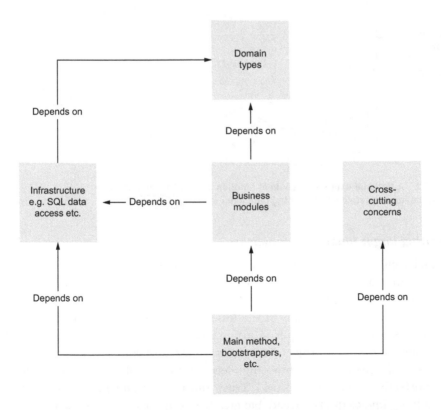

Figure 15.2   A typical dependency graph for types and modules in an F# project

This may lead to a file structure as seen in table 15.1. Remember that in F#, we don't worry too much about having a 1:1 relationship between types and files. It's not unusual to have many types declared in a single physical file, especially with a domain model made up of records and discriminated unions, each of which may only take a few lines of code.

Table 15.1   An example list of files that fit with the sample dependency design in figure 15.2

Filename	Area
Caching.fs	Cross-cutting concerns
Logging.fs	Cross-cutting concerns
Domain.fs	Types
SQL.fs	Infrastructure
PaymentGateway.fs	Infrastructure
Billing.fs	Business modules
Invoicing.fs	Business modules
App.fs	Main method/bootstrapper

15.2   *Composing functions*

This section deals with how we commonly compose functions together in F#—that is, how we combine smaller functions into larger functions. This is a core skill to learn in F# because functions are the basic component of behavior. As usual, I'm going to take an arbitrary and relatively simple problem and try to address a specific problem in several different ways. I'll highlight the pros and cons of the different approaches and try to guide you toward the appropriate scenarios. While going through this section, I highly recommend you open an F# script file and work through the exact code samples one by one, trying out each version yourself so that you get a feel for each style.

Unlike in many other languages, where it's very common to start architecting a high-level design and drilling downward, in F# I often start with something very simple at the bottom of a feature, perhaps just a simple function that performs a very basic implementation of the core functionality required. I then start to build other functions adjacent to that; then, I'll build functions that orchestrate the calling of the smaller ones together and organically work my way up to the top-level program. It's often challenging at first to do this, but I've learned to trust myself and F# that doing this generally leads to a decent solution that focuses on expressions and immutable data structures without needing to spend hours upfront pontificating about which design pattern to use.

Here's the challenge: you're working for a bank that is redesigning its ATM software and has decided to go with F#. Hurrah! As the developer responsible for ATM software, you need to write a function that takes in a Customer value and prints out a greeting to the customer before emitting a summary of their balance. If they're overdrawn, say by how much; otherwise, simply write out how much their balance is. After thinking about it a little, you end up with some code similar to listing 15.1.

> **Listing 15.1   Basic ATM logic flow**

```
type Customer = { Name : string; Balance : decimal }

let describeCustomer customer =
    printfn $"Welcome, {customer.Name}!"
    if customer.Balance < 0M then
        printfn $"You owe ${System.Math.Abs customer.Balance}."
    else
        printfn $"You have a positive balance of {customer.Balance}."
```

Defines the Customer type

A function that greets a customer by printing to the console

Unfortunately, your team lead reminds you that all code needs to be fully testable and have a number of automated tests with 100% code coverage so that the correct messages are emitted based on some different balances. Even worse, your ATM hardware supplier tells you that your code also has to support writing to the filesystem under certain diagnostic modes.

You quickly realize that the code in listing 15.1 won't suffice, as it has coupled directly to the console. How can you abstract away the dependency on printing directly to the console so that you test out the logic of the greeting strings and still plug in the printer logic for the deployed application?

There are a few ways to solve this, and while this might appear to be about how to write testable code, it's really about the challenge that I outlined at the start of this section: finding different ways of composing code together in different ways.

15.2.1 *The object-oriented approach to composition*

In this book, I've deliberately tried to avoid an OOP-versus-FP approach, but in this case, it's probably useful to outline how you might solve this using classic OO patterns. Normally, you'd use something like the strategy design pattern. This essentially would have you create an interface (or contract) called `IPrinter`, with several implementations (e.g., `Console`, `File`, and perhaps a mock version for automated testing scenarios). Your real code would then take in one of these instances and call it as required—listing 15.2 shows how it might look; I'm using legitimate F# here, as it also supports many OO constructs (required for interop with the rest of .NET).

> **Listing 15.2   Defining an interface with implementations**

```
type IPrinter =
    abstract Print : string -> unit

module IPrinters =
    let toConsole =
```

Defines an interface in F#

An implementation of IPrinter that prints to the console

```
    { new IPrinter with
        override _.Print(text) =
            printfn $"{text}" }

let toFile filename =                    ◀──  An implementation of
    { new IPrinter with                        IPrinter that writes to a file
        override _.Print(text) =
            System.IO.File.AppendAllText(filename, $"{text}") }
```

Object Initializers

One of F#'s nifty features is the ability to create implementations of interfaces without first formally declaring them as concrete types. This is such a common requirement when creating abstract factories that I'm surprised it's not in some OO languages (including C#).

I've created an interface with a single method on it, `Print`. I've also created a module with two implementations of the `IPrinter` interface: the console and the filesystem. You would then supply this interface to some class that had the `Describe` method on it. Again, OO-style code using F# is used here in the following listing.

Listing 15.3 Applying an interface to a strategy runner

```
                    ──▶  type Atm (customer:Customer) =            Defines a method on the
Creates                     member this.DescribeCustomer (printer:IPrinter) =    ◀── class, parameterized by
an ATM                          printer.Print $"Welcome, {customer.Name}!"        a kind of IPrinter
class                           if customer.Balance < 0M then
                                    printer.Print $"You owe ${System.Math.Abs customer.Balance}."
                                else
                                    printer.Print $"You have a positive balance of
         ⟹  {customer.Balance}."
```

Lightweight constructors in F#

Another neat OO feature of F# is how you create classes and constructors. As you can see in listing 15.3, the constructor is declared alongside the type definition. Even better, the value is implicitly made accessible to all members in the class. This is probably a little atypical or surprising for classical OO developers, but if you're using classes purely for holding data to be used by all methods on that class (as is typically the case in F#), it makes perfect sense.

Now, your logic for greeting a customer is decoupled from how to print those commands via an interface that gets injected in.

15.2.2 Higher-order functions

Let's now look at three techniques you can use in F# that are more functional oriented and achieve similar results. Probably the closest match to the OO approach we have just seen is *higher-order functions.* A higher-order function is a function that itself takes a function as an argument. In F#, these are very common and very easy to create. In fact, they are so easy to create that for newcomers to F# who are overly excited with this power, it's possible to overdo it without realizing and abstract your way into a dead end (more on this shortly). Look at the original code in listing 15.1—the element we wish to abstract away is the `printfn` function. In VS Code, do the following:

1 Replace all three instances of `printfn` with the word `printer`.
2 Add a new argument to the definition of `describeCustomer` (ideally before the `customer` argument) called `printer`.

That's it. You've now made `describeCustomer` a higher-order function! What's happened? You've created a new input argument called `printer`, which is the function that does the printing. In the `IPrinter` interface from listing 15.2, this is the `Print` method. You haven't specified that the `printer` argument is a function or what its signature is. However, for F#, this isn't a problem because functions are just values to F#. A function is no different than an integer or a record: you can supply them as arguments or bind them to symbols like anything else. And just like the compiler infers types based on usage for simple values or records, it can also infer that `printer` has a signature of `string -> unit` from its usage in your function, as seen in the following listing.

Listing 15.4   Passing functions as an argument to a function

```
type Customer = { Name : string; Balance : decimal }

let describeCustomer printer customer =                ←─── Supplies a printer
    printer $"Welcome, {customer.Name}!"       ←──           as an argument
    if customer.Balance < 0M then
        printer $"You owe                             Uses the printer argument in place
    ${System.Math.Abs customer.Balance}."   ←──     of printfn. We can now plug in any
    else                                            printer that conforms to the
        printer $"You have a positive               correct signature.
    balance of {customer.Balance}."    ←──
```

F# can infer basically any function as an argument. It will work with functions that require multiple arguments, functions that use generics, functions that return records or tuples, etc. Hopefully, now you're starting to see how powerful and useful type inference can be (and it gets even better, trust me!). Now you can supply any function to `describeCustomer` that fulfills this contract of `string -> unit`. Here are a couple to get you started:

```
module Printers =
    let console = printfn "%s"
    let file name text = System.IO.File.AppendAllText (name, text)
```

And you can call them with `describeCustomer` as follows:

```
customer |> describeCustomer Printers.console
customer |> describeCustomer (Printers.file "file.txt")
```

This is a good lesson to learn about working with functions if you're coming from a heavily OOP background. Interfaces that only have a single method on them are in some ways the same as functions except that functions are much more lightweight to create. If you come from a Java background, you'll probably be aware that you can essentially use lambda functions and single-method classes interchangeably. If you've done any work with C#, you'll be familiar with LINQ queries, which are effectively a functional API in C# where all functions, such as `Select`, `Where`, etc., are higher-order functions. In the previous example, I've used the pipeline for aesthetics, although it's not essential. What is especially interesting to note is the second line and how I'm able to adapt the `Printers.file` function into `describeCustomer`. Let's look at this in a little more depth:

1 We've already established that the printer argument in `describeCustomer` has a signature of `string -> unit`, so any value we pass in must have that signature.
2 The `Printers.file` function has a signature of `string -> string -> unit`. It requires a filename and the text to write to that file.
3 When we're using it in the second line, we only supply the first of those two arguments: the filename.
4 This then gives us back a new function with the remaining arguments, `string -> unit`, which matches the type of the `printer` argument exactly.

Higher-order functions are easy to get started with because you can write a function with concrete dependencies and then extract them into dependencies (function arguments) after the fact. F#'s type inference and handling of functions as first-class citizens make this a breeze to do. Compared to interfaces, they're also very easy to work with: in many statically typed OO languages, the interface needs to be explicitly applied to a type for that type to be considered compatible with it (for dynamic languages, this isn't an issue, nor is it for some hybrid languages that support duck-typing like TypeScript). When working with functions as arguments, as long as the function signature matches, it's considered compatible. So, even functions that exist in other libraries or packages can sometimes work out of the box with your code.

However, there are some drawbacks to higher-order functions that manifest as your code gets more complicated:

- If you have multiple functions as arguments, it can get complicated to reason about them, especially if those functions interact with one another. Sometimes, you'll need to "turn off" type inference by putting in explicit type annotations to figure out why things are behaving as they are.
- You can easily end up with unnatural abstractions—functions that have a type signature used purely for a specific function that makes no sense in the rest of your codebase.
- The implementation will not necessarily be composable or reusable outside of this function. For example, if you wanted to reuse the "greeting" portion of the function, using this approach would probably not be the best way of achieving that.

- Testing requires you to create a mock value somewhere. In our case, we would probably need a fake printer that recorded all the texts being printed and allowed us to read them afterward to validate the behavior.

15.2.3 Dependency rejection

One final problem with higher-order functions in F# is that F# does not enforce functional purity. If you want to write functions that are guaranteed to be pure, the simple rule is that you cannot use higher-order functions simply because the compiler can't guarantee that the supplied function isn't, for example, performing some I/O.

For many people (myself included), this is normally not a problem, and we get along just fine with higher-order functions. However, pure functions give you several nice benefits out of the box:

- All your code is inherently testable.
- You can easily cache pure functions because they only depend on data as input.
- Your code becomes easier to reason about as your functions simply operate on taking in some data and returning more data,

How could we fix the code in listing 15.4 to be guaranteed as pure and not use functions as arguments? We could split the function into two separate functions, as in listing 15.5:

- The generation of the text we want to print (the data)
- A function that accepts the text and prints it out (the external behavior)

Listing 15.5 Composing with pure functions only

```
let describeCustomer customer =                          ◁──────   A pure version
    let output = System.Text.StringBuilder ()                      of the greeting
    output.AppendLine $"Welcome, {customer.Name}!" |> ignore       function
    if customer.Balance < 0M then
        output.AppendLine $"Customer {customer.Name}
➡ owes {System.Math.Abs customer.Balance}" |> ignore
    else
        output.AppendLine $"{customer.Name} has a
➡ balance of {customer.Balance}." |> ignore
    output.ToString ()

let describeToConsole customer =     ◁─────   A function that composes
    customer                                  the greeting function with
    |> describeCustomer                       a specific printer
    |> Printers.console
```

I'm using StringBuilder here, an old .NET type that allows you to efficiently accumulate text and then generate a single string for the entire text. The only ugly part is that StringBuilder is a mutable object, so its state is not entirely clear; however, given that the scope of the StringBuilder is small, this is acceptable. The other code smell is that each call to AppendLine returns the StringBuilder itself as a result. We don't need that result, so we must call |> ignore after each call. (Remember, in F#, everything is an expression, and if you don't need the return value of a function, you need to explicitly tell the compiler to ignore it.) Note that you probably wouldn't use StringBuilder in everyday F# for something like this, but more likely a list comprehension.

The main difference compared to the higher-order function is visible from the type signature of the new `describeCustomer` function. Instead of taking in a printer function, it simply takes in the customer, as the original version of the function did. More importantly, though, it now returns a `string` rather than `unit`, since it doesn't emit anything to the console; it just returns a string of all the text that needs to be printed. It's also a pure function now that can be tested relatively easily without the need for mocks or similar—simply call the function, get the result, and test that it meets your expectations.

However, we now need extra functions to print out to the console, filesystem, etc. That's not necessarily an issue: the code for `describeToConsole` is trivial and can be easily duplicated without great cost (in fact, using the `>>` operator that I briefly mentioned earlier, the entire function could be shortened to `describeCustomer >> Printers.console`). Nonetheless, it's worth bearing in mind.

There's another limitation to this approach—while it's easy to apply in relatively simple situations like this, once you get to more complex situations with conditionals in the middle of a function where you need to call external functions only under certain circumstances, it can quickly become more difficult to work with. If you're interested, I would recommend reading Mark Seeman's excellent website (https://blog .ploeh.dk/), where he describes what he calls "Dependency Rejection" in much more depth. But beware, it's not for the faint hearted and discusses some more advanced FP concepts.

15.2.4 *Procedural composition*

This final option is a useful tool to have in your back pocket. In some ways, this is more akin to procedural code than anything else:

```
module Customer =
    let greet customer =  $"Welcome, {customer.Name}!"
    let sendMessage customer =
        if customer.Balance < 0M then $"Customer {customer.Name} owes
    {System.Math.Abs customer.Balance}"
        else $"{customer.Name} has a balance of {customer.Balance}."

let describeToConsole customer =
    Printers.console (Customer.greet customer)
    Printers.console (Customer.sendMessage customer)
```

Hard-coded dependency on Printers.console

What I've done here is split up the printing logic into a couple of simple pure functions (in the OO world, they would probably be members directly on the Customer, something you can also do with Records in F#). I've then written an untestable function, `describeToConsole`, that composes them together by hand. This code is very simple to reason about; there are no higher-order functions for a start, and we're simply chaining a few functions together. Both `greet` and `sendMessage` are testable in isolation but not when composed together with `Printers.console`.

Besides being very simple to understand and reason about, this code also breaks out individual parts of the logic into separate reusable library functions. However, the composed code is directly coupled to the console printer; if you wanted to replace that with a different printer, you'd need to replace it everywhere. Anything more than trivial logic would quickly end up in a kind of copy-and-paste hell for each different printer, but if the likelihood of that happening is low (ask yourself, how often have you needed to replace your database?) then this kind of approach may work just fine.

15.2.5 What should you use and when?

There are other options in the FP world, such as the Reader monad, a slightly more advanced topic, which, to my mind, you don't need unless you really want to push it to the max. And, if that's the direction you want to take, you should consider a language like Haskell.

The options I've provided here are normally enough to build any application you'll ever need. Each has its use and can (and should be) combined where appropriate. For example, you might want to factor out some code to share among several different locations. There may be nothing wrong with simply moving that code into some shared module to be called from multiple locations procedurally.

However, if you want some general best-practice advice to follow, I would say this: where possible, aim to keep code focused on data in, data out (i.e., that is, option 2). If they need to call shared helper functions procedurally, that's totally fine, too. If you find yourself struggling to create purely data-centric functions that are testable, introduce higher-order functions as needed for varying behaviors and so on. Be careful with them, though—add too many into the same function, and you'll quickly find yourself drowning in a sea of hard-to-understand type signatures.

15.3 Working with low-level dependencies

One example where higher-order functions don't always work so well is when you need to inject a function that's nested deep inside a call stack. This section addresses that in more detail and suggests some techniques for working around it.

15.3.1 A worked example: Working with a logging function

Let's assume we had a basic order processing function dealing with validating and dispatching orders, and we need a printer function like in the previous section for emitting log messages such as an order having been dispatched. We want to replace that static reference to the Console printer with a function argument so that we can plug in a different logger with the same signature (e.g., `string -> unit`). I've also thrown in a couple more low-level arguments: a database connection string that's required by `loadCustomer` and an authentication token that's required by `dispatchOrder`. A basic implementation will end up with code that looks something like listing 15.6.

Listing 15.6   Threading a low-level argument through several layers

```
module IO
```
A module to hold low-level I/O functions for data access, etc.

```
let dispatchOrder
    (authToken:AuthToken)
    (order:ValidatedOrder) =
    Ok
        {| DispatchDate = DateTime.Today.AddDays 2.
           Status = "Dispatched" |}
```
Low-level functions require implementation-specific connection strings, auth tokens, etc., as arguments

```
let loadCustomer
    (connectionString:SqlConnectionString)
    customerId =
    Ok { CustomerId = customerId; Name = "John Doe" }

...

module BusinessLogic

let validateOrder
    (logMsg:string -> unit)
    connectionString (order:Order) =
    logMsg "Loading customer from DB..."
    let customer =
        IO.loadCustomer
            connectionString
            order.CustomerId
    logMsg "Validated order!"
    ValidatedOrder order
```
Top-level function requires low-level implementation-specific arguments to pass through the call stack

Threads the connection string argument through several layers

```
let processOrder logMsg authToken connectionString order =
    let validatedOrder =
        validateOrder logMsg connectionString order

    match validatedOrder with
    | Ok validatedOrder ->
        IO.dispatchOrder authToken validatedOrder
    | Error e ->
        Error e
```

First, we define a few functions that handle some I/O for us—in this case, dispatching an order and loading a customer from a fictional order processing system. In this example, I've defined hard-coded responses, but you could imagine the replies here coming from a database, third-party HTTP API, etc. Next, we create a couple of functions that are going to use these I/O functions: one validates an order; as part of that, it must load the customer to ensure that the customer has sufficient funds in their account; the final function is the entry point for the whole operation and takes in all the "dependencies" required by all the child functions, calling `validateOrder` and then `dispatchOrder`.

So, what's the problem with this code? Look at `processOrder`. It takes in four arguments, but the first three are never actually required by the function itself—they're needed by functions that it calls or even worse (as in the case of `connectionString`), by a function that is required two levels down. This is not especially satisfying: the function is less readable (you can't easily see where each argument is being used since they're only used by child functions), and it makes the function appear more complicated than it is. It also introduces a degree of coupling: the high-level function is dependent on low-level implementation details (figure 15.3). If we decided to replace the SQL calls with a flat file, the connection string would need to be replaced with a file path. At this point, I should also point out that coupling isn't necessarily a terrible thing, especially if there's a very low likelihood of change (and decoupling introduces its own costs, as we'll see shortly).

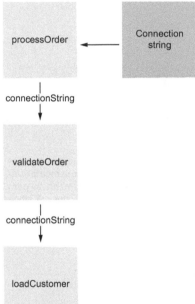

Figure 15.3   Passing a low-level implementation argument through a top-level function can cause extra coupling and complexity throughout your code.

15.3.2 *Flipping dependencies with a bootstrapper*

A way to fix this is to "flip" the "injection" of the dependency in the dependent function to the parent and thread it through. An initial implementation of this might look something like the following, where we partially apply `loadCustomer` and supply this "injected" version to `validateOrder`:

```
let validateOrder (logMsg:LogMsg) loadCustomer (order:Order) =
    logMsg "Loading customer from DB..."
    let customer = loadCustomer order.CustomerId
```

validateOrder now takes in a function as an argument instead of a connection string.

There is no coupling to the IO module any longer.

```
    logMsg "Validated order!"
    Ok (ValidatedOrder order)
```

```
let processOrder logMsg authToken connectionString order =        ┌ Partially applies
    let loadCustomer = IO.loadCustomer connectionString      ◄─┘   loadCustomer
    let validatedOrder = validateOrder logMsg (loadCustomer order)
    validatedOrder |> Result.map (IO.dispatchOrder authToken)
```
Supplies the injected version of loadCustomer

Here, we've promoted `loadCustomer` to an argument to `validateOrder`, which no longer requires a connection string as an argument. That's still not especially satisfying; the `processOrder` function still has all those arguments and now must partially apply `loadCustomer` to fit with what `validateOrder` needs. However, if you continue to "flip" the dependency for all functions all the way to the top, you can essentially invert the entire chain so that your top-level function does all the wiring and your individual functions remain free of implementation-specific arguments. We've already done this for `validateOrder`, but let's look at what `processOrder` looks like as well if we apply the same technique:

```
let processOrder validateOrder dispatchOrder order =
    let validatedOrder = validateOrder order
    match validatedOrder with
    | Ok validatedOrder ->
        // maybe more checks happen here
        dispatchOrder validatedOrder
    | Error e ->
        Error e
```

This function now does not take in any implementation-specific arguments—all usages of things like connection strings and tokens have mysteriously vanished. Instead, it just takes in and returns business data. Where have all the implementation-specific arguments gone? How have we fixed this? With a bootstrapper, or wireup, function, as seen in listing 15.7. A bootstrapper function is responsible for partially applying all the nested functions and then wiring everything together so that the real business logic functions have no knowledge of any external arguments like connection strings needed by lower-level functions.

Listing 15.7   Wiring up dependencies with a bootstrapper function

```
module Wireup

open System                                                    ┌ Extracts low-level
                                                                 configuration data from
let processOrder : Order -> Result<_, string> =                  the environment
    let authToken =                                        ◄─┐
        Environment.GetEnvironmentVariable "AUTH_TOKEN" |> AuthToken
    let connectionString =                                 ◄─┘
        Environment.GetEnvironmentVariable
    "CONNECTION_STRING" |> SqlConnectionString
```

```
let logger text = printfn $"{text}"

let validateOrder =
    let loadCustomer = IO.loadCustomer connectionString
    BusinessLogic.validateOrder logger loadCustomer

let dispatchOrder = IO.dispatchOrder authToken
```

Creates injected functions that are partially applied with configuration data

```
BusinessLogic.processOrder validateOrder dispatchOrder
```

Creates the top-level partially applied processOrder function

This wireup function knows how to get connection strings, tokens, etc., and partially applies and connects everything together so that `validateOrder` and `dispatchOrder` only require the business data as arguments (figure 15.4). To `processOrder` and `validateOrder`, all the functions that they call appear to not need anything but business values as input, even though, in reality, the implementations have already been partially applied with them. If you're struggling to see this, try it out in a code editor and look at the function signatures that the type checker infers; in effect, we're creating new functions from existing functions by providing some arguments but leaving

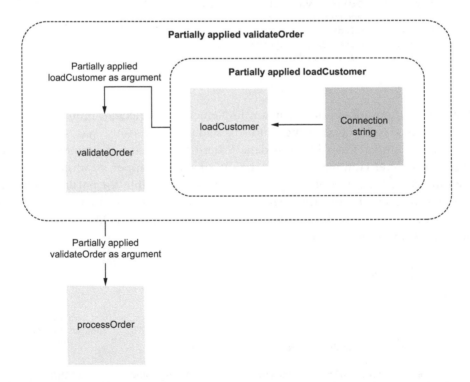

Figure 15.4   A bootstrapper function inverts dependencies and uses partial application to allow you to supply preconfigured, low-level functions to your top-level code, avoiding the challenges shown in figure 15.3.

others out so that the signatures match up. In some ways, you can think of this as conforming to an OO-style interface and injecting arguments such as a connection string in the constructor of an implementation, except we're doing this with functions.

15.3.3 Pros and cons of the wireup pattern

There are some real benefits of this approach, such as the fact that your business code looks a lot cleaner in the sense that it no longer needs to pass through arbitrary arguments just for the sake of some child function, and that code will be much easier to test (you can easily create mock functions that fulfill these simplified function signatures). But there are also some drawbacks:

- You need an extra function to wire up all the dependencies. In some ways, this isn't so bad because you clearly define where the boundaries between your IO and internal code are (and it fits with patterns like onion and hexagonal architectures), but it's extra code to write.
- The wireup function can look complicated. Even writing it here for this book took me a few minutes to think it through and determine how to create it correctly. But thankfully, it's the sort of code that you won't be touching every day.
- Be careful with higher-order functions that you artificially construct. I've already touched on this, but if you compose them together badly, you can easily end up with functions that have bizarre function signatures that are a nightmare to reason about—functions being passed around that themselves take other functions as arguments. Coupled with the type inference of F#, it can be a real pain to figure out why your code isn't compiling.

15.3.4 Applying the dependency rejection pattern

We can also apply the dependency rejection pattern we discussed earlier so that our internal functions (in this case, the validation function) only take in simple data values and no functions at all. It might look something like Listing 15.8.

Listing 15.8   Dependency rejection with computation expressions

Validation function now only takes in simple data values.

```
let validateOrderPure order (customer:Customer) =
    [
        "Checking customer balance..."
        "Validated order!"
    ], Ok (ValidatedOrder order)
let processOrder (order:Order) = result {
    let authToken =
        System.Environment.GetEnvironmentVariable "AUTH_TOKEN"
        |> AuthToken
    let connectionString =
        System.Environment.GetEnvironmentVariable "CONNECTION_STRING"
```

No side effects in the function are allowed. Log messages are returned back out.

```
      |> SqlConnectionString
let logger = printfn "%s"

logger "Loading customer from DB..."
let! customer = IO.loadCustomer connectionString order.CustomerId
let (messages, validationResult) =
    validateOrderPure order customer
for message in messages do logger message

let! validatedOrder = validationResult
return! IO.dispatchOrder authToken validatedOrder
}
```

All logging takes place in the impure boundary function.

Validation function now only takes in simple data values.

This approach is quite different to what we've had so far in this section. The process-Order function is now inherently untestable, but other code, such as the validation function, is extremely simple to reason about and pure. It only operates on data that is passed in. Even log messages are returned back out as a list of strings. These would then be logged separately by the caller. (Be aware: the list shown has a naïve implementation; if it contained millions of log messages, it would be quite inefficient from a memory/garbage collection point of view.) We've also had to split out the validation function from the loading of the customer. In the previous implementations, validate-Order was responsible for loading the customer, but now this is taken care of by the caller. I've also used the result { } computation expression here to make composing the results a little easier to see rather than piping them all together with Result.map and bind.

Using this pattern requires quite a bit of discipline to think about which functions we want to keep pure. Also, things can get complex quite quickly if there is conditional IO. In the previous example, we've essentially hidden that using the computation expression. However, imagine a situation where if validation passed, we wrote to the database, but if not, we did something else or if some low-level code deep in the call stack had some side effect that should only happen under certain circumstances. To be sure, you can work around these sorts of things, but it can require time, effort, and experience to achieve effectively.

15.4   *Working with effects*

I've touched on the idea of effects throughout the book, but I've almost deliberately glossed over them in the hope that you gleaned what they are through practical application rather than theory. This section is just a little dip into the world of effects and monads (yes, there, I've said it!) to illustrate how these things fit together. I'm also deliberately going to use these two terms quite liberally and loosely, mostly because it's not that important in the .NET world (including F#). Don't look up the official definitions of these terms and expect to see them here. Instead, I want to describe a few concepts and patterns behind them in general terms using language that I am (and, I hope, you are!) comfortable with. I'm not going to go into the hardcore functional side of things but just show you some examples of them in the .NET and F# world and draw out some learnings from them so that in the future, you can potentially identify such situations yourself and learn how to manage them effectively.

15.4.1 What are effects in F# and .NET?

From the point of view of F# and .NET, in particular, think of effects as simply a way of working consistently with some sort of wrapper type that encapsulates and abstracts some behavior. These effects are typically exposed in .NET through generic types. If you're coming from a language like C#, JavaScript, or Python, *effects* might seem an unusual way to think about this. There's no common way of working with them, but F# adopts, at least to some degree, a more generalized FP approach. The aim of working with effects in a standard, consistent way is the same as any design pattern really—to aid common understanding across a team, to help communicate with one another, and to carry out common tasks in a consistent, tried and tested manner.

> **LINQ query syntax in C# for general-purpose monadic programming**
> You can use LINQ's query syntax in C# to simulate effect management. There is even a NuGet package for this—so it is possible, but I would argue that this is an extreme use of LINQ and pushes it in directions it wasn't designed for.

15.4.2 Common effects in F#

Let's look at some examples of some typical effects that you might find in F# and .NET:

- Option
- Result
- Async and Task
- Collections (e.g., List, Array, Sequence, Map, and Set)

These might all appear distinct from one another, but from another perspective, they all have some things in common:

- They aim to simplify and generalize some kind of pattern for you.
- They can work with almost any type of data and are, hence, often generic types.
- You can typically compose two of them together to create a new, third instance of the same thing.

C# has elected to deal with each of these in very different mechanisms for each effect. For example, working with the asynchronous effect means using the `async`/`await` keyword combination. For working with nullable variables, it's the `.?` (i.e., Elvis) operator. When working with collections, it's LINQ keywords like `from … in`. But they're all doing the same thing: handling some effect for you (table 15.2).

Table 15.2   Some example effect abstractions in F#

Name	Used for working with data that . . .
Option	Might be missing
Result	Might be invalid
Task	Might not yet be available
List	May have zero or many instances of a given type

The good thing about the C# approach is that each approach is optimized for that use case. The downside is that there's no reuse or awareness of the commonalities, and each time some new effect appears in the language, you need a new set of keywords or paradigm to deal with them. Conversely, in F#, there are essentially two common ways to deal with all of them:

- Using common functions such as map, bind, and return.
- Using keywords such as let!, and!, and return within a computation expression (CE). But these CEs mostly use functions like bind and return behind the scenes; they're just syntactic sugar.

15.4.3 *Map and Bind*

The whole point of functions like map and bind is to allow us to write normal code and then have these functions do the heavy lifting of the effect check for us (table 15.3).

Table 15.3   How map appropriately behaves for each different effect

Name	Happy path	Unhappy path
Option	Data exists; apply your code to it	No data (None); return it back
Result	Data is valid; apply your code to it	Data is invalid (Error); return it back
Task	Data is available; apply your code to it	Data not yet available; keep waiting
List	List is nonempty; apply your code to all values	Empty list; return it back

Generally, map is sufficient for most use cases: it allows us to take any function that goes from 'T -> 'U, and lifts it to 'T <effect> -> 'U <effect>. Let's take a function that doubles a number and prints it as a string:

```
let timesTwo (x:int) = $"{x} * 2 is {x * 2}"          ⟵──┤ Function has signature
                                                          │ int -> string
```

Rather than making hand-rolled functions that can deal with all different effects, we can use List.map, Result.map or Option.map to lift this function to work with any of them:

```
let timesTwoOptional = Option.map timesTwo
let timesTwoResult = Result.map timesTwo
```

```
let timesTwoList = List.map timesTwo
let timesTwoTask = Task.map timesTwo
```

⊣ | **Note that Task.map is not included in the FCL.**

Because .NET and F# are open source, you can look at the implementations of each of those functions, but they will all do something to handle their specific effect in table 15.4.

Table 15.4 Illustrating the effect that `map` has across multiple effects

Effect	Input	Output
Option	`Some 1`	`Some "1 * 2 is 2"`
Result	`Ok 1`	`Ok "1 * 2 is 2"`
Task	`Task.FromResult 1`	`Task "1 * 2 is 2"`
List	`[ 1; 2 ]`	`[ "1 * 2 is 2"; "2 * 2 is 4" ]`

In other words, each version of `map` knows how to check how to handle the input effect (e.g., Is there some value? Is the value Ok? Has the Task completed? etc.) to get the real value, execute the function on that value, and then rewrap the result back inside the effect again.

The interesting parts come when you want to combine two values of an effect. Let's look at collections and the classic example of customers and orders. Each customer has many orders; you want to get a flat list of all orders in the system. For that, you can use `bind`. In F# collections, it's known as `collect`; in C# it's `SelectMany`:

```
let allOrders = customers |> List.collect (fun customer -> customer.Orders)
```

You can use the same approach for other effects as well. Let's assume we wanted to perform two division calculations one after another; to protect against a divide-by-zero, our implementation returns a result:

```
let divideBy b a = if a = 0 then Error "Divide by Zero" else Ok (a / b)
let answer = 20 |> divideBy 2 |> Result.bind (divideBy 5) // answer is Ok 2
```

You can think of `bind` as a kind of supercharged `map`, since you can implement `map` using `bind` (but not the other way around). If you're not sure about this, ask yourself: Why can you implement `Select` using `SelectMany` (or `map` using `collect` / `flatMap`) but not the other way around?

15.4.4 *Using Computation Expressions to hide bind pipelines*

There are computation expressions for most common effects (including those just highlighted). With them, you can manage everything with just `let!` and its sibling keywords `do!` (for unit values that do not need binding to a symbol), `and!` (for composing multiple values together), and `return!` (as a shortcut for `let!` + `return`). For example, the previous division code could be written as

```
result {
    let! firstCalculation = 20 |> divideBy 2
    return! firstCalculation |> divideBy 5
}
```

Summary

- It is often useful to separate code into external and internal boundaries within the world of F#; architectural patterns such as onion and hexagonal fit this approach.
- Structuring larger codebases is not complex, but you need an awareness of how types and functions in a codebase depend on one another.
- There are many ways to compose behaviors together, such as using interfaces, higher-order functions, or simple procedural code. Each has pros and cons.
- Dependency rejection is a way of writing code that focuses on only passing data to functions rather than higher-order functions that guarantee pure code in F#.
- Using a bootstrapper and the wireup pattern is a way to avoid needing to expose low-level concerns, from connection strings to high-level orchestration functions. However, it, too, needs to be used with care.
- Common effects in F# include Option, Result, List, and Task. All of them can be reasoned about in a similar fashion using `map` and `bind` and, ultimately, computation expressions.

Where next?

This chapter covers

- How to get more practical experience in F#
- Introducing F# to your team
- Engaging with the F# community
- Advanced F# language features

You've made it to the final chapter of the book. Congratulations! At this point, you have all the tools you need to start writing F# in practical applications. However, your F# journey is (unsurprisingly) not finished—after all, if you could read a medium-sized book like this and become an expert in any language, software developers wouldn't be anywhere as highly in demand as they are today.

How do you then make the leap from someone who has used F# in some small examples and seen some sample applications to someone confident enough to use F# in the real world? The answer is simple: by doing F#. If you and your colleagues want to write production-ready F#, this book should act as a guide to solving practical questions you'll face. However, you'll still need to go through the pain of trying things out in the real world (i.e., in your own business domain) until you build the muscle memory to model real-world concepts effectively in F#. This is no different from learning any other kind of skill. Think about learning to drive a car or bicycle, another spoken language, or a musical instrument: you can read all you want, but you'll need to actually do it in the real world before you really have that confidence and belief.

This final chapter gives you some suggestions and ideas for how to effectively take these next steps in that journey.

16.1   How do I start using F# in practice?

This section gives some ideas and suggestions for hands-on exercises and activities that will improve your confidence in using F# in practical situations, both in terms of your own F# skills and in terms of adoption in your organization.

16.1.1   Data analysis

Build an application that can validate and parse a dataset from one of the many free datasets online, such as Wikipedia or perhaps a data science site, and produce some analysis on it. For example, get the list of all Olympic results and calculate which country has been the most successful over all time. Or which sportsperson has the most medals. Create a web application that allows users to enter a country code and provides a textual and graphical analysis of that nation's performance over time.

These are good exercises because a wide variety of interesting datasets are available online (or perhaps at work). You can start very quickly with a single script, add NuGet package references as required, and then bring in a full-blown application for, for example, a web frontend. It's also potentially an opportunity to see how to model a domain effectively. Your source data may be in a simple flat CSV structure, but it might have all sorts of interesting elements that can be modeled and enriched through discriminated unions, Options, Results, etc.

16.1.2   Hobby projects

If you're the sort of developer who likes to write projects for fun in your spare time, the next time you get the urge to do it, write it in F#! As with anything new, you'll struggle at first as you build up your muscle memory and apply the techniques in this book to your project, but you'll quickly ramp up speed the more you do it. Yes, the first time you do this, you'll feel (rightly) that it would've been quicker to do it in whatever language you're comfortable with. But that's part of what learning something new is about. The feeling won't last forever, and soon you'll look back and realize that you're doing things more quickly than before!

16.1.3   Coding challenges

Go through an online challenge such as GitHub's Advent of Code. These kinds of challenge websites are great because they are normally designed not to be coupled to any specific language, and they will require various features of the language, such as parsing and validation, business logic, and domain modeling. You'll also be able to compare and try different approaches to the same problem, and the problems are often small enough to be solved within an hour or less.

16.1.4 *Before-and-after proof of concept*

Take an existing project or module you've written in whatever language you are comfortable with and rewrite it in F#. You'll already know the domain, so this is a great way to reimagine it using functional programming (FP) techniques in F#. Resist the temptation to simply do a like-for-like port in terms of design—for example, avoid mutable variables and statements wherever you can, preferring immutable values and expressions.

This can also be a useful way to compare F# with whatever language you're currently using, so much so that I know of at least one company that made the decision to move over to F# full-time, having ported one vertical slice of their application. The code was so much easier and clearer on the F# side that it was obvious that moving to F# was the right choice for them.

16.1.5 *Operational scripts*

Another way to start using F# is for scripts (or utility programs) that are used within the context of your application. Perhaps you need a build script to compile, test, and bundle up your application before deploying to a cloud provider. Or perhaps you need a program that can empty the local developer database, read a set of CSV files with some static data, and then reseed the database with it. These sorts of utility applications and tools are a good way of gently building up confidence in F# in small, low-risk ways.

16.2 *How do I introduce F# to my team?*

If you've been trying F# and are excited by it, you'll naturally want to share it with your colleagues. But how do you maximize the chance of success? I get asked this so much that I wrote a lengthy three-post series on my company's blog (https://www.compositional-it.com/news-blog/tag/adopting-f-series/). There's no doubt, though: it can be challenging. I've introduced F# in many teams with varying degrees of success, and those blog posts (summarized here) will help avoid the common pitfalls:

- Have a plan at the start and get it agreed to by others (and, ideally, whoever is funding your team). Have a clear understanding of what you'll be doing, what level of support you'll have (or how much time you have, for example, for proof of concept), and what you'll be using to measure success.
- Don't introduce F# on your own in a team; instead, have at least one or two other colleagues alongside you on the journey. Otherwise, you risk becoming known as "the F# dev" on the team, instead of its use spreading through the team.
- Engage with other, more experienced F# developers if this is the first time you've used F# in a commercial environment. This could involve someone acting as a mentor or coach, perhaps just an hour or two a week, or maybe someone able to act as a consultant to embed in your team for a few weeks.

- Empathize with your colleagues, especially those who are skeptical. Try to avoid an "F# is better than <insert language of choice>" argument. It can make people defensive and steer the conversation off topic. Instead, focus on highlighting the positive reasons why F# is going to be a great fit for your team. Similarly, don't be afraid of saying what the costs of F# may be; for example, time will be required to invest in upskilling; it has a smaller community than languages such as Java or C#; refactoring tooling may be different or inferior to other languages, etc.

16.3   The F# community

The F# community is small but active and welcoming. This section outlines a few elements and resources you may wish to engage with as part of your journey into F#.

16.3.1   Social media

There are the usual social media channels through which you can engage with the F# community (in addition to the official F# Slack site mentioned previously). This includes the usual X (#fsharp), Reddit, Discord groups, etc., plus free weekly newsletters on the language. That doesn't include the large number of non-F#-specific sites and social media such as FP and .NET in general.

16.3.2   Conferences and user groups

At the time of writing, the tech industry is still finding its feet post-COVID, but in-person conferences and user groups are making a comeback, while online-only (or hybrid) events are also perfectly acceptable nowadays. There are a few F# conferences and plenty of user groups across the world, while larger conferences (again, in the FP and .NET in general spaces) will usually have an F# presence as well. I've spoken at many such conferences, and people are always welcoming and interested to learn about what the "FP on .NET" story is like.

16.3.3   Open source

Open source has always been a part of the F# story, years before Microsoft finally officially decided that it was a good thing. Indeed, when I first started getting into F# in the early 2010s, I had no clue what Git or GitHub was or what a pull request was. I learned a great deal from the F# community at that time to get into the idea of open source; indeed, you'll find many great libraries that are considered de facto parts of the core F# ecosystem that are managed completely independently of Microsoft. If you want to gain exposure to some real-world (albeit from a library rather than application perspective) F# as well as open source in general and make some great contacts in the community, you could do much worse than contributing to some popular F# open source projects!

16.4 Advanced F# language features

This section briefly outlines a set of features that sit at the edge of your use with F#. You won't use these features every day, but it's useful to know about them, especially the first couple. When you do need them, they'll save you lots of time!

16.4.1 Units of Measure

This small but very nice feature of F# allows you to create generic numbers. For example, you can specify that a distance field on a record isn't just an `int`, but an `int` of meter, while another field on the same record could be a time in seconds. The compiler will then prevent you from accidentally mixing the two up:

```
let distance : int<meter> = 20<meter>        Defines two integer
let time : int<second> = 2<second>           values of different types

let x = distance + time // error: The unit of measure 'second'
⇨ does not match the unit of measure 'meter'
```

Even better, the compiler will allow you to perform actions such as dividing one unit by another:

**Dividing a meter value by a seconds value
gives a result in meters per second.**

```
let velocity : int<meter/second> = distance / time      ⟵
```

Units of measure are erased at run time; in other words, they are entirely a compile-only feature. This means that you can't use reflection on them, but also means that using them incurs no run-time cost. Units of Measure are a great example of a light-weight feature that provides a very useful aid for documentation and some extra compile-time safety with very little cost.

16.4.2 Active Patterns

Active Patterns are an extremely powerful feature of F# that can be used in multiple situations relating to Pattern Matching. The primary use cases I've seen for them include

- Enabling reusable logic across multiple pattern match expressions
- Improving readability
- Reducing/removing the need for wildcards

A simple scenario is that you're writing a system to review a school pupil's progress throughout the course of the year, which is a function of

- Their last exam result (< 50, < 75, $>= 75$)
- The number of days that they were late (0, < 5, $>= 5$)
- The number of disciplinaries they received during the year (0, < 5, $>= 5$)

This categorization may be used in multiple places—for example, generating their report card, displaying on screen, sending an email notification to the principal for students falling behind, etc. Imagine just one case that is about generating their year-end report card with some arbitrary rules for whether to score them between an A and D grade:

```
let scoreStudent (student: Student) =
    match student with
    | { Lates = 0; Disciplinaries = 0 } when student.Score >= 75 -> "A"
    | { Lates = 0; Disciplinaries = 0 } when student.Score > 50 -> "B"
    | _ when student.Score >= 75 && student.Lates < 5 &&
      student.Disciplinaries < 5 -> "B"
    | _ when student.Score > 50 && student.Lates < 5 &&
      student.Disciplinaries < 5 -> "C"
    | _ -> "D"
```

As you can see, complex Pattern Matching logic can quickly get out of hand and become difficult to read. Active Patterns can help here by making patterns that can be used seamlessly with real values without the need to first wrap them in discriminated unions:

```
let scoreStudentAp (student: Student) =
    match student.Lates, student.Disciplinaries, student.LastExamScore with
    | Punctual, WellBehaved, TopScore -> "A"
    | MostlyPunctual, Misbehaves, TopScore
    | Punctual, WellBehaved, PassingGrade -> "B"
    | MostlyPunctual, Misbehaves, PassingGrade -> "C"
    | _ -> "D"
```

This is much more readable than before, and importantly, we haven't had to explicitly create types for this. Instead, we simply apply an active pattern where required and then carry on. The code for active patterns is a function with a strange-looking definition: instead of a name, the cases of the pattern define it!

```
let (|Punctual|OccasionallyLate|AlwaysLate|) (v:int) =
    if v = 0 then Punctual
    elif v < 5 then MostlyPunctual
    else AlwaysLate
```

Returns different cases depending on some arbitrary logic

An active pattern is defined by the different cases it can return plus an input value to match on.

The compiler is smart enough to transparently replace the number of times late with the appropriate case based on usage—you don't need to explicitly do anything.

Active Patterns have many use cases, and this simple example only touches the surface—you can even pass parameters into active patterns when matching, for example. They're not required for everyday use in F#. However, if you ever find yourself struggling to make a readable pattern match and commenting them up or you're performing the same pattern match logic in several places, those are great indicators that an active pattern could be of use.

16.4.3 Type Extensions

Types Extensions allow you to simulate creating new functionality on top of existing types—even types that you don't "own". Of course, there are limitations to this; you can't access private data on that type. However, unlike C#, F# goes a little further and lets you define extensions of any member type, not just methods, so extension properties are perfectly legal in F#.

16.4.4 Implicit Conversions

For years, F# has been very strict about implicit conversions in the sense that they have never really been allowed. In F#6, this changed a little in that F# now allows you to provide your own bespoke implicit conversion members on types that you own. For example, if for some reason you wanted to implicitly convert a single integer value into a Student record that was previously defined, you could do so by defining the following member on the Student type:

```
static member op_Implicit(x: int) = {        ◁──┐   Defines a static member
    LastExamScore = x                              │   directly on the Student type
    Lates = 0
    Disciplinaries = 0                          ┌── An implicit conversion is
}                                               │   now possible between
                                                │   integers and Students.
let student : Student = 100      ◁─────────────┘
```

The compiler will, by default, warn you in nearly all the situations that this takes place unless you explicitly disable the appropriate warnings. A few are instances that built into .NET now, such as `Nullable<'T>` (e.g., you can now implicit "lift" an integer into a Nullable integer), but please don't start thinking about using this everywhere. I'm only showing you this because in certain interoperability scenarios, it can be extremely useful to aid readability. If overused or used in place of standard F# conventions and practices, they will result in code that is hard to follow and reason about.

16.4.5 Statically Resolved Type Parameters

Here's a function that looks like it shouldn't be possible (remember, `let`-bound functions in F# do not support overloading):

```
printNameAndAge {| Age = 21; Name = "Sara"; Town = "New York City" |}
printNameAndAge {| Name = "Fred"; Age = 34; FavouriteColor = "White" |}
```

The same function takes in two different types, yet there is no overloading; it's a single function. How is this possible? This is where Statically Resolved Type Parameters (SRTPs) come in. They allow you to define a function that can take in any value as long as it contains certain members, such as a method with the name `Foo` that has a signature `unit -> int` or (as in this case) a member named `Age` that returns an `int` and another named `Name` that returns a `string`. It's kind of like interfaces but without needing to specify the contract upfront on the type.

SRTPs can be used to simulate a feature known as type classes, an approach for reusability and abstraction that is more common in the "hardcore" FP world. But I would again caution you not to try to implement "Haskell in F#": the language, framework, ecosystem, and runtime are simply not designed for that kind of hardcore FP.

SRTPs are another "use with extreme care" feature. They have a mixed reputation in F# for good reason: while you can do some truly impressive things with them, they're definitely not for the faint of heart. The syntax to declare them is cumbersome (in some ways, this is by design), the compiler error messages they generate can be truly baffling, and if you go too far, the compiler will grind to a halt. To show you what I mean, here's the implementation of the `printNameAndAge` function:

The inline keyword is required for the compiler to generate a new instance of this function for each type of person.

```
let inline printName person =
    let name = (^a : (member get_Name: unit -> string) person)
    let age = (^a : (member get_Age: unit -> int) person)
    $"{name} is {age} years old"
```

Defines a set of constraints that the person value must adhere to

> **NOTE** F#7 has introduced a slightly more readable syntax for SRTP constraints. However, my advice on "use with caution" remains!

16.4.6 *Metaprogramming*

Reflection and Quotations are two mechanisms in F# to perform some kind of metaprogramming—that is, treating code as data to "write code" against code. Reflection is part of .NET and has been there since the very beginning. It's relatively slow—don't ever use it in a tight loop—but it allows you, in effect, to "turn off" the type system and write truly generic code that can operate on any type. But I've probably used it just a handful of times when working with F#. If you need to use it, you're either doing something truly dynamic, like a plugin system, or you're just doing it wrong. Sorry, but F# is designed as a statically typed language, and something is amiss if you're constantly going through reflection.

Code quotations, on the other hand, are an F#-only feature. Again, I've seen them used very rarely, but they can be used for some interesting use cases, such as transpiling code from F# into another language. The following code snippet shows how we can create a code quotation by embedding any F# code within `<@ @>`; this then gives us an expression tree of that code, which we can then interrogate by pattern matching over:

```
open Microsoft.FSharp.Quotations

let expr = <@ 1 + 1 @>

match expr with
| Patterns.Call(_, func, args) ->
```

Creates a quoted expression

```
$"Calling {func.Name} with {args}"
| _ -> "Not a call"
```

◁── **Returns "Calling op_Addition with [Value (1); Value (1)]"**

Summary

- It's important to understand that your journey to writing production-ready F# is an ongoing one; the lessons in this book need to be applied to your own real-world challenges to sustain those learnings.

- You should focus on practical, hands-on experience with F#. There are many different strategies, such as proof-of-concepts, coding challenges and hobby projects that you can use to reinforce your knowledge of F#.

- Introducing F# to your colleagues in a commercial environment, like the adoption of any technology, needs to be done in a planned manner in which you can evaluate the pros and cons and decide whether it's the right decision for you.

- F# has a number of more advanced and less everyday features that you should be aware of and investigate as you see fit. This includes Units of Measure, Active Patterns, and metaprogramming capabilities such as Quotations.

index

RELATED MANNING TITLES

Functional Programming in C#,
Second Edition
by Enrico Buonanno

ISBN 9781617299827
448 pages, $59.99
December 2021

Functional Programming in Scala,
Second Edition
by Michael Pilquist, Rúnar Bjarnason, and Paul Chiusano
Forewords by Martin Odersky and Daniel Spiewak

ISBN 9781617299582
488 pages, $59.99
May 2023

Grokking Functional Programming
by Michał Płachta

ISBN 9781617291838
520 pages, $59.99
September 2022

Grokking Simplicity
by Eric Normand
Forewords by Guy Steele and Jessica Kerr

ISBN 9781617296208
592 pages, $49.99
April 2021

For ordering information, go to www.manning.com

A new online reading experience

liveBook, our online reading platform, adds a new dimension to your Manning books, with features that make reading, learning, and sharing easier than ever. A liveBook version of your book is included FREE with every Manning book.

This next generation book platform is more than an online reader. It's packed with unique features to upgrade and enhance your learning experience.

- Add your own notes and bookmarks
- One-click code copy
- Learn from other readers in the discussion forum
- Audio recordings and interactive exercises
- Read all your purchased Manning content in any browser, anytime, anywhere

As an added bonus, you can search every Manning book and video in liveBook—even ones you don't yet own. Open any liveBook, and you'll be able to browse the content and read anything you like.*

Find out more at www.manning.com/livebook-program.

Open reading is limited to 10 minutes per book daily

MANNING

The Manning Early Access Program

Don't wait to start learning! In MEAP, the Manning Early Access Program, you can read books as they're being created and long before they're available in stores.

Here's how MEAP works.

- **Start now.** Buy a MEAP and you'll get all available chapters in PDF, ePub, Kindle, and liveBook formats.

- **Regular updates.** New chapters are released as soon as they're written. We'll let you know when fresh content is available.

- **Finish faster.** MEAP customers are the first to get final versions of all books! Pre-order the print book, and it'll ship as soon as it's off the press.

- **Contribute to the process.** The feedback you share with authors makes the end product better.

- **No risk.** You get a full refund or exchange if we ever have to cancel a MEAP.

Explore dozens of titles in MEAP at www.manning.com.

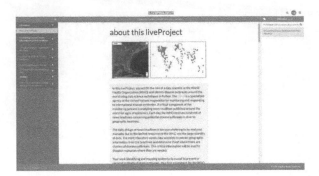

Hands-on projects for learning your way

liveProjects are an exciting way to develop your skills that's just like learning on-the-job.

In a Manning liveProject you tackle a real-world IT challenge and work out your own solutions. To make sure you succeed, you'll get 90 days full and unlimited access to a hand-picked list of Manning book and video resources.

Here's how liveProject works:

- **Achievable milestones.** Each project is broken down into steps and sections so you can keep track of your progress.

- **Collaboration and advice.** Work with other liveProject participants through chat, working groups, and peer project reviews.

- **Compare your results.** See how your work shapes up against an expert implementation by the liveProject's creator.

- **Everything you need to succeed.** Datasets and carefully selected learning resources come bundled with every liveProject.

- **Build your portfolio.** All liveProjects teach skills that are in-demand from industry. When you're finished, you'll have the satisfaction that comes with success and a real project to add to your portfolio.

Explore dozens of data, development, and cloud engineering liveProjects at www.manning.com!